# IAN BOTHAM

## The Power and the Glory

## SIMON WILDE

SIMON &
SCHUSTER

London · New York · Sydney · Toronto · New Delhi

A CBS COMPANY

First published in Great Britain by Simon & Schuster UK Ltd, 2011
This edition published in Great Britain by Simon & Schuster UK Ltd, 2012
A CBS COMPANY

1 3 5 7 9 10 8 6 4 2

Simon & Schuster UK Ltd
1st Floor
222 Gray's Inn Road
London
WC1X 8HB

www.simonandschuster.co.uk

Simon & Schuster Australia, Sydney
Simon & Schuster India, New Delhi

A CIP catalogue for this book is available
from the British Library.

ISBN: 978-1-84739-798-0

Typeset by M Rules
Printed and bound by CPI Group (UK), Croydon, CR0 4YY

For Freddie, Lily and Eve

# Contents

'Those who have been once intoxicated with power, and have derived any kind of emolument from it, even though for but one year, can never willingly abandon it.'

EDMUND BURKE, 'LETTER TO A MEMBER OF THE NATIONAL ASSEMBLY', 1791

# Introduction

A very particular type of sports star rose to prominence during what might be termed the first great age of televised sport from the mid-1960s to the mid-1980s. That there was a mass unseen audience out there somewhere in the ether seemed to affect the way these sportsmen conducted themselves, and how they viewed themselves. They became public performers in a way sportsmen had not been before. The mere presence of cameras enhanced the stature of all sportsmen regardless of how they performed, but the very best acquired a greater aura, wielded greater power, and ultimately accumulated greater wealth. With the help of television they could achieve heroic status even in a contest attended by only a few thousand, even a few hundred, people. This is of course precisely what happened with the Headingley Test match of 1981, the defining event of Ian Botham's career.

Not all sportsmen were comfortable with this shift. Some who thought little of playing in front of large crowds felt intimidated by television's faceless but all-seeing eye. For a special few, though, a heightened sense of theatre was all they could have wished for. Television guaranteed them an audience of unquantifiable magnitude and, on the basis that recordings might be repeated any number of times, it literally offered immortality – provided you were good enough to produce something worth watching again and again.

Muhammad Ali exemplified this hunger for fame through a lens but Botham fell into this category too. He saw himself as an entertainer, not only emptying bars in the grounds but filling sitting-rooms in homes, and he did so through the verve, courage and lion-hearted endeavour he brought to his play. He loved a big stage and there was none bigger than the Ashes. He displayed skill, especially with his bowling, but it was the unbridled physical commitment that stood out: he seemed to bowl forever, without ever getting tired. The cameras sometimes caught him changing boots and afforded a glimpse of battered feet and bloodied toes, a sight to turn your stomach. He was one of the bravest cricketers there has ever been.

I was among those out there in the ether, who first experienced Botham's heroics on TV. In his early years with England, his talent, exuberance and eagerness for battle leaped out of the screen. How could he be so at ease when most found it so difficult? Did he not suffer from nerves, or doubt? He was obviously personable, too; he shared in his team-mates' successes; with greater regularity, they shared in his. Most strikingly, in an era when the default setting of most English cricketers was 'safety first', he was happy to take risks, and to accept that the risk-taking was not always going to pay off. This was the price of being an entertainer: he understood it, and we the public were asked to understand as well. He embraced being our champion and loved the power invested in him. It was too good to last. He was too good to last.

Even though I lived only a few miles from Headingley, I watched most of that great innings in 1981 on TV because I had, like most others, given up on England after watching them in person being outplayed for three days. Then, when he and Graham Dilley began their mayhem, I was stuck: dare I risk the 25-minute journey down to the ground or should I stay put and be sure not to miss anything? I stayed put, or rather transfixed, scarcely believing what I was seeing. I made sure I was at the ground the next day, and saw Bob Willis wreak havoc. I wanted to be a follower of the team from that day on.

The costs of being a people's champion were to run deeper, very deep. By making such a conscious decision in the mid-1980s to wear striped blazers and strange hats, and long hair and droopy moustaches, Botham showed that he regarded the limelight as being almost as important as winning. And, because relying on his instincts had carried him so far, he believed that trusting his talent and not stifling his urges – as some would have had him do – was always the right thing to do. He worked less hard on his game and still did not agonise over failures. What was important was remaining true to the gifts for which the public loved him.

The real trouble started for Botham – as it did for all the top stars – when he stopped being so outrageously successful. People who felt they knew him from having seen him on TV were not so friendly when they met him in a pub with a few beers inside them. And administrators bewildered at the power he wielded were not always minded to cut him the slack he wanted when his instincts took him into dangerous territory off the field. The innocence evaporated and was replaced by a mistrust of the outside world – the big 'out there' that he thought he had tamed – that at times slid towards paranoia. This prompted some reckless behaviour, as though he had reckoned that if others were set on destroying him, he might as well destroy himself first.

I also witnessed this second phase of his career, still mainly on TV though also quite often at closer quarters. Botham did not now seem such a pleasant man, or such a joyous one. There was an edge to him that had not been present during his youth.

He had been hurt by the world and seemed inclined to inflict hurt in return. There was more political calculation in what he did, more hunger for power and influence, and more preening. He was less open to compromise, or reason, and more defensive. There was often only one way to do something: his way. There were still brilliant performances, but increasingly they were out-numbered by bad ones. These years were harsh, disquieting and sometimes lonely. He needed more reassurance than he let on.

Botham of course was not alone in going through such loss of grace. George Best before him, and Alex Higgins and Paul

Gascoigne afterwards, had similar experiences. They too were gifted, glorious entertainers, who were champions of the people and scourges of the Establishment. They too came into the world with little, and called on the Devil's work to fill the hours between matches. They too perceived the outside world to be turning against them. Their response was to drink to excess and behave so badly that the world could not but fall out of love with them.

There was a difference though. By the late 1980s, a common fear was held by many observers, including myself, that, as Botham began to be sidelined by an England regime intent on restoring order and discipline, his career might fall off a cliff as spectacularly as Best's had and Higgins' and Gascoigne's would. But somehow it did not happen. They could not cope with fame, but he could. He teetered on the edge once or twice but pulled back. The pleasures of everyday life meant too much to someone who, while extraordinary in many ways, was down-to-earth and normal in others.

The fear had been that once he stopped playing the loss of a mass audience could have killed his spirit, like it did the others. But crucially, he found ways to remain a public performer, through marathon roadshows, pantomime and TV shows, but mainly through mighty charity walks. These walks in aid of leukaemia were the key, because they reawakened in him the generosity of spirit that had become buried during the dark days of his celebrity. He discovered that he could use his fame to the advantage of others as well as himself. The walks also gave him the chance to show off his specialist subject, the conquering of pain.

Having hung up his boots as a player, he took a seat – if not root – in the commentary box. Some suggested he was less interested in the cricket and more in the comfortable living the job provided. If it was a tame and predictable existence after the dramas of his earlier life, it may also have been that he was content, grateful even, simply to have survived.

# 1

## Lords and Lepers

'When you heard a banging of boots and studs on the floor you knew it was time to disappear because it meant the guys were bored and on their way down ... They would have already decided to target someone. Who was it going to be? You knew they would be getting hold of somebody and stripping that person naked, laying them out on the table and whitening them all over with the whitener that was used on the boots ... Ian was the guy they picked on all the time. He was big and they knew he would always fight back. And that was more fun.'

ROLAND BUTCHER, MEMBER OF THE
MCC GROUNDSTAFF 1971–72

Britain in the early 1970s was a place that was monochrome going on grey, a bleak time of harsh economic conditions and brutal social change. For many young men lacking a privileged background, it was not easy getting a decent education or a good job. State education was going through a bitter transition to a comprehensive system, and classroom violence and truancy were on the rise, as was juvenile crime. For those who had left school, work was a much prized commodity in an environment crippled by massive oil-price hikes and epic government–union confrontations. By the middle of the decade, inflation would touch 20 per cent and more people would be unemployed than at any time since the Second World War.

The national malaise was reflected in the humiliations of England's sporting teams. The football side, victors in 1966, suffered the unprecedented ignominy of twice failing to qualify for the World Cup finals. The cricket team surrendered the Ashes to a terrifying pair of Australian fast bowlers, Jeff Thomson and Dennis Lillee, and succumbed to successive home defeats to the West Indies, much to the noisy delight of a growing immigrant population from the Caribbean. Britain's performance at the 1976 Olympic Games was an embarrassment.

Sport mirrored society's turmoil and ugliness. Many of the most enduring images were ones of violence or rebellion. Football attracted *Clockwork Orange* style thugs who indulged in tribal warfare, wrecking trains and turning residential streets into battlegrounds. Spectators routinely invaded the playing areas, some of them without their clothes. Supporters of George Davis, a former cab driver serving time for robbery, dug up the pitch during a Test match at Headingley. Billy Bremner, captain of Leeds United, perhaps the best but probably also the most physical team in the country, and Liverpool's Kevin Keegan fought each other on Wembley's turf during the Charity Shield. The British Lions made some famously violent rugby tours. Harvey Smith flicked a two-fingered salute at organisers during a showjumping event. Ian Chappell's Australians introduced cricket to verbal intimidation. Boxing, the most atavistic of sports, was at the height of its popularity.

But at the same time sport was in the early stages of being rehabilitated as a public spectacle by the most powerful medium of the age – television. The transition from black-and-white television to colour served to provide armchair viewers with the best seats in the house and, ultimately, it was the vast sums broadcasters were prepared to pay to screen sporting events (ultimately charging viewers for the privilege) that would underpin a financial boom. Between 1971 and 1976, the proportion of TV sets that were colour rose in Britain from one in twelve to one in two. For many television watchers, the early 1970s were grey in more ways than one.

But the mega-riches that television would deliver were still some way off. Sportsmen were appreciated more by fans than their penny-pinching employers and few cricketers or footballers undertook a career in the hope of getting rich. An England cricketer in the home season of 1973 earned £160 for playing in a Test, and four home one-day matches against New Zealand and West Indies were played for a total prize fund of £5,000. But by 1977 change was very plainly afoot when two high-profile figures put money before national duty. Don Revie swapped the £20,000 he was receiving for managing the England football team for £60,000 tax free to run a team in the Middle East. The Football Association attempted to ban him for ten years but Revie successfully challenged its ruling in the courts. And Tony Greig, the England cricket captain, was sacked after it emerged that he was helping Kerry Packer, an Australian TV magnate, set up a series of matches involving the world's top players. The cricket authorities sought to challenge Packer's plans but had as little joy in the courts as the FA. Such betrayals caused public outcries, which suggested that the man in the street's admiration for his heroes went only so far; he too expected them to play for love rather than money. But the die was now cast.

Ian Botham, who played his first Test for England in 1977, arrived on the scene at just the right time. In an era short on glamour and personalities, he brought to people's summers an irresistible cocktail of talent, energy and swagger. After the pain inflicted by Greig's disloyalty, he made English cricket feel better about itself. With the stench of economic failure in the air, he also made the country feel good about itself again.

Here too was another reminder – following the examples of the Beatles, the rise of northern football teams such as Manchester United, Liverpool and Leeds, and Harold Wilson's ascendancy to the premiership – that Britain's working class was on the rise. And Botham was plainly a man of the people; as one team-mate put it, he was 'a bricklayer who happened to be good at something else'. Cricket was capable of producing heroes from all walks of life but no one since Fred Trueman had struck such a chord with the common man. For this Botham won himself a fund of public goodwill, a fund that years later he threatened to drain but uncannily managed to replenish.

He also perfectly caught sport's first big financial wave. He certainly needed the cash, having been regularly short since leaving state school in Yeovil at the age of fifteen. If a love of cricket, competition and country were among his chief motivations, so too was hard economic necessity. As John Parish, the musician, who also grew up in the town at this time, once said, 'Yeovil did not have a lot going for it.' Ultimately few would live more vigorously by the Thatcherite mantra of 'go out and get what you want'.

Botham's story is a great piece of British sporting history, one of the greatest. But it was a story of glamour and grit together. And the grit came from the times in which he grew up. The 1970s was a decade from which everyone was trying to escape.

If there was one period that shaped him the most it was the time he spent on the MCC groundstaff at Lord's in the early 1970s. Fresh from leaving school at the minimum legal age, it was his first serious job and his first attempt at making his way as a professional cricketer. It was a period he would later dismiss as unimportant because being a Lord's groundstaff boy was not something to be particularly proud of – too many of them were county rejects. It was certainly not the life for a future champion.

For a working-class lad who had left comprehensive school in Somerset with few qualifications or social advantages, Botham found the elaborate hierarchy of the Marylebone Cricket Club irksome. Here was cricket's archaic social order in all its glory and he was entering at the very bottom. This was a hard, undignified first taste of the ways of the outside world. Here was grit aplenty.

Wider society may have been changing rapidly and unpredictably with trades union leaders showing themselves as powerful as prime ministers, but Lord's remained loyally class-bound, an ancient regime ripe for change but resourcefully resistant to it. Its membership was largely white and totally male.

MCC, wealthy and private, had long been the most powerful cricket club in the world. It was the guardian of the laws of the game (as it is now). Its secretary acted as secretary of the International Cricket Council, the game's world governing body. And when the England team toured overseas they travelled under the MCC flag – and would continue doing so until 1977–78, when Botham first went with them.

MCC had only recently survived the biggest scandal in its history when, in 1968, it had implicitly supported a decision to exclude the non-white Basil d'Oliveira from an England tour in an apparent act of appeasement to South Africa's apartheid government. When d'Oliveira was finally included in the team, South Africa's government objected and the tour was cancelled. A return series in England in 1970 was then abandoned after anti-apartheid demonstrations ensured that even barbed wire and barricades could not guarantee the safe progress of matches. Asian cricket bodies suspected MCC of racial prejudice and there was talk of a breakaway cricket authority being formed. MCC's role as a private club governing a public game came under scrutiny and this led to the formation of the International Cricket Council. The Council was designed to meet the requirements of a modern governing body but in fact it was a mere fig-leaf – it operated out of Lord's, its principal officers were MCC officers, and its committee was packed with past, present and future MCC presidents. Similarly the Test and County Cricket Board (TCCB), created to run the English professional game, worked from offices at Lord's. Through elder statesmen such as Gubby Allen, who lived in a house adjacent to the ground and acted as the club's treasurer, MCC continued to hold sway.

The new order was barely distinguishable from the old and even though the distinction between amateur and professional had been formally scrapped a culture remained that cricketers played for love not money. The groundstaff that Botham joined were paid a pittance, while things were so bad at Middlesex that a pay dispute – a rare thing – had recently surfaced. Any professional cricketer practising on the Nursery ground had to do so in whites, never anything as proletarian as a tracksuit.

MCC still favoured the old-style amateurs educated at public school and Oxbridge, a type that had provided the majority of England captains down the years. Indeed, Brian Close – only the second working-class captain of England in modern times after Len Hutton, and later Botham's first captain at Somerset – was sacked in 1967 after upsetting the suits at Lord's with some time-wasting tactics in a county match. Close reckoned that former Tory prime minister Sir Alec Douglas-Home, MCC president at the time, was a prime mover in the affair.

Just how little had changed became evident in August 1973 when Ray Illingworth, who had won the Ashes in Australia and then retained them at home, was suddenly and mysteriously removed as England captain during a Lord's Test against West Indies, an event Illingworth put down to 'a certain VIP in the Lord's hierarchy'. When Geoff Boycott – like Close and Illingworth a Yorkshireman by birth – was then passed over as Illingworth's successor in favour of Kent's Mike Denness, northern suspicions of a cosy Home Counties carve-up were reignited. Boycott would later complain darkly that 'a bunch of southern public-school smoothies are determined that no miner's son from Yorkshire will captain England'. Whether the conspiracy theories were correct hardly mattered; the perception was real enough. It was a perception Botham would buy into.

However unpalatable the system, the young Botham had been given a great opportunity to work on his cricket at Lord's, and it was not as though he had more attractive options. His father Les had advised him that, despite earning a trial with Crystal Palace, he was not fleet-footed enough to make it as a footballer. And

Somerset were unsure they wanted him. They were not ready to give him regular cricket even in their second team and as an impoverished club could not afford to carry passengers on their staff. Even if Botham was exaggerating (as he sometimes did) when he said that had it not been for cricket he would have ended up in jail, the sport surely was his best chance of making a success of things.

Not that the young tearaway found much reason to see it this way. When he arrived at Lord's as a junior member of the groundstaff for a brief trial in September 1971, before returning for the full summers of 1972 and 1973, he soon discovered that he was to be a serf in all but name. Wages were meagre. He started 1972 on twelve pounds a week, although Andrew Wagner, who had played for Somerset under-15s with Botham and followed him onto the groundstaff, said that by 1973 the county were supplementing their wage with an extra three pounds a week in the first year, dropping to two pounds a week in the second. This was simply not enough for some. Roland Butcher, who had emigrated from Barbados and who under Botham's captaincy would become the first black West Indian to play Test cricket for England, recalled: 'The best cricketer was a fellow called Dennis Chambers, but he didn't stay long. I started on eight pounds a week – plus an extra two pounds because I lived more than twenty-five miles away – and Chambers decided he couldn't live on that.' Others relied on parents to bail them out.

Even without an apprenticeship, Botham did not find it hard to earn more when he went back to Yeovil for the winter. One of his jobs was laying floor tiles in the local hospital. It was not glamorous but he claimed with pride that he never went a week without finding work.

Many of the tasks Botham was given at Lord's were of the most menial variety – cleaning boots, washing the pavilion windows, hauling the tarpaulin covers on and off the pitch and pulling the mighty Thomas Lord roller up and down the square. These were not tasks undertaken by the older groundstaff boys, who enjoyed much greater privileges.

The seniors were housed in better quarters, in the old bowlers' room at the right-hand end of the pavilion in what is now the members' bar, while the juniors were on the floor below, in ready proximity for a summons from Bill Jones, the head boy to the staff of forty. The seniors spent five days a week in net practice while the juniors were confined to two or three days. Seniors also enjoyed the less physically strenuous task of selling scorecards on big match-days. The seniors would be picked for the groundstaff's matches against the stronger sides such as county second XIs while the B-staffers, under the nickname of MCC Nippers, played local club sides.

The A-staffers could pick and choose which MCC members they would bowl to in afternoon nets. If they didn't fancy it, they would send along the younger boys. It was a decision almost entirely dependent on the prospects of a decent tip.

'I was supposed to keep the lads in order,' said Jones, who had been there since 1967. 'I worked out the duty rosters. The more senior you were, the better jobs you got given. We would net for two hours in the morning, have lunch, then there would be fielding, and more practice finishing about 4pm. Then we had to be available to bowl to members. Roy Harrington would ring the bowlers' room and I'd answer. If it was a good payer, I'd go, if not I'd send someone else. Ian did it. There was a guy called Manningham-Butler, a big bloke, who would bat for three hours given the chance, and not give us a penny. Word would get around, we'd send over two quicks and hope he'd be gone in fifteen minutes. It was a good way of getting a few quid.'

The A-staffers may have enjoyed advantages over the youngsters but there would be times when they were reminded of their place. 'The best part of the job was bowling to Test players,' Jones added. 'We weren't paid any extra but didn't need it. You saw how easy they made it. The day before a Test, they would come down and two or three of us would get changed into whites and go along to nets while the rest helped to get the ground ready. One time, Boycott, Illingworth and David Brown were there and I bowled

Boycott first ball. It pitched middle and hit off. Illy turned and said: "We've been trying to do that for thirty minutes. Now you can fuck off." And he sent me away.' Botham bowled at the England players before the 1972 Ashes Test but that year there was simply no preparing them for the ordeal to come, Bob Massie destroying them with one of the great exhibitions of swing bowling. Botham watched the game sat on the grass around the boundary's edge. In later years when they were England team-mates, Botham would refuse to bowl to Boycott in the nets on the basis that he had done so often enough during his groundstaff days.

Naturally, the B-staffers were desperate for promotion but it took Botham until midway through his second full summer to achieve this.

If Botham hated his junior status, there was much else that he abhorred about Lord's. He loathed bowling at the members and Jones came to realise it was not always the best thing to send him, as he would start taking the mickey by bowling full tosses and bouncers. Butcher said that Botham 'would really try to hit them [the members] because he detested those guys coming out at five to six when you were ready to go home. He would just run in and try to bounce them.' One can imagine this sturdy-framed youngster, big for his age since the age of thirteen, burning with indignation if ever an MCC member got his cover drive working against him, and eager to bounce him out of his self-satisfied comfort zone.

It was not only MCC members who took advantage. Middlesex, who leased Lord's as their home ground, would often commandeer the groundstaff boys. John Emburey, a future England team-mate of Botham, was a youngster on Middlesex's books. 'We saw a lot of him [Botham] on the Nursery. Some people abused them [the groundstaff] by saying, "Come and have a bowl, come and have a bowl," but I didn't. I actually got on OK with him, which stood me in good stead later on when I played international cricket with him. It was as though we were buddies.'

Botham never found Lord's a comfortable place. He felt that MCC officials and members always talked about players – even successful England ones – as though they were labourers on their farm. He felt unwanted and would get angry as soon as he walked into the ground. He was not alone in this. The Lancastrian Michael Atherton, whose career began more than ten years after Botham's, shared his distaste of Lord's: 'The place really got up my nose. Its gatemen were rude, its officials were standoffish.'

Although Botham could have been turned off by his experiences, his time on the MCC groundstaff only convinced him that he should pursue cricket as a career, perhaps precisely because so few people took his ambition seriously. Being so fiercely competitive, he became determined to prove them wrong.

He formed friendships with those who were also outsiders from clubs like Gloucestershire and Glamorgan as well as Somerset, all counties that received little acknowledgement from the cricketing Establishment. Long after they had gone their various ways, and Botham himself had become an international celebrity, he was loyal to these old allies, taking them out for meals, visiting sick relatives in hospital, and generally keeping in touch. Although he did not always show it, he had a fundamentally kind nature. And he never hid his modest social background: although naturally sensitive to accusations that he lacked 'class', he often displayed a determinedly plebeian image.

For those like Botham who were having their first taste of life away from home, London could prove an enormous culture shock. The capital was a world away from Yeovil, which was small even in Somerset terms. But nowhere in the county could remotely compare with the bustling metropolis. Even many years later, Australian batsman Justin Langer, who spent three years with Middlesex and four with Somerset, found the contrast stark. 'It's almost like two different ends of the world,' he said. 'London and Somerset . . . you could not pick two more different places.'

Barry Lloyd, a young off-spinner from Glamorgan, had just finished his O levels in 1971 when the county asked if he fancied going onto the Lord's groundstaff. 'I was a little boy from Neath and it was a lot of responsibility. You grew up. You learned how to live. You had to wash your kit and feed yourself and get yourself to out-matches. You'd be given a letter telling you where you'd be playing. Once I went to the Isle of Wight. I had to get a 5.30am boat train to Portsmouth and a ferry across. We were there for the love of cricket and happy to play. My father had been a miner. I told my work experience teacher at school that I wanted to play cricket in the summer and ski in the winter. He said good luck. If it hadn't been for cricket I'd have worked in a factory. It would have been the same for Ian.' After ten years with Glamorgan, Lloyd became a school teacher in South Wales.

Shortly before Botham arrived, Arthur Francis, a batsman who was genuinely ambidextrous, was sent up to London by Glamorgan to join Lloyd. 'I had left school at sixteen and gone to nets with Glamorgan,' Francis recalled. 'They asked me if I wanted to go to Lord's. I had never been away from home before. London was a big eye-opener.' Francis, too, lasted ten years with Glamorgan, during which he scored just one century, before becoming a carpenter and groundsman in Pontarddulais.

The Glamorgan and Somerset players in particular stuck together – Lloyd, Francis, Botham and Keith Jennings, also from Somerset, along with Rodney Ontong, who had been thwarted in his original ambition in coming over from South Africa to pursue a career as a footballer with Chelsea. Ontong became Botham's closest friend during this period. 'Our friendship was instantaneous,' Ontong recalled. 'We were similar types. He was a great mate, my greatest friend ... I was impressed at how he was prepared to do things his own way.' At first they stayed in a hostel run by MCC at High Elm, in West Hampstead, but later moved into their own flat near the ground before being thrown out after falling behind with the rent, after which they dossed down in the dressing-room at the Nursery end. Francis recalled Botham living in a flat in Broadhurst Gardens, two minutes from Finchley Road tube. 'We got on well and were pretty close,' he remembered. 'We played together and hung out together. We would meet for a few beers in the evening. We had no cars or luxuries and went everywhere by tube.'

The Londoners among the groundstaff looked upon this group with curiosity and amusement. 'We had a few from Somerset,' recalled Jones. 'They came across as lads from the sticks. Keith Jennings had a yokel accent.' Ian Gould, who played for Middlesex second XI at the age of fifteen and also represented Arsenal youth teams in goal, and would later play one-day internationals alongside Botham, said of him: 'He was a wild boy. They stuck together the Wales and Somerset boys and it was hard to break in with them. You either had to be a good player, or a good drinker, or have money, because they never had any. It was OK for me. I was only twenty miles away and could go home. But those lads . . . it made him streetwise. We were sent all over the place [to matches]. You would turn up at 8.30am and be told you were needed at Brighton or Eastbourne College and off you'd go. There was no pampering. He [Ian] probably wouldn't admit it but he was a naive lad when he came. Lord's was the best thing that ever happened to him.'

Another in their group was Roland Butcher, who like Jones commuted from Stevenage. Two years older than Botham, Butcher had already played for Gloucestershire's second team, sometimes travelling down to Bristol and living in the dressing-room at the County Ground with some other youngsters. The wife of the coach Graham Wiltshire would cook them breakfast. 'The first year [1971], I travelled in from Hertfordshire,' Butcher recalled. 'It was a train into King's Cross, then tube and bus. It was OK when I was heading for Lord's but when we were playing away the guys would go home to the hostel and I was getting the milk train back to Stevenage. Then I moved to Surrey near relatives and rented a room, so I didn't have to travel so far.

'Francis and Lloyd were my two best mates and Botham was in there, and the four of us got on really well. "Both" was a social lad. He liked a drink. He liked to play hard and enjoy his life.' Butcher felt that even when he was on the B staff the main benefit of being at Lord's was that he was able to practise on a daily basis. 'It was cheaper for the counties to send us there but it was also the only place where you could get that sort of specialist treatment and training,' he said.

Botham was full of life – and full of himself. 'He had great self-confidence,' said Gould. 'He didn't think anyone was better than him, whether it was playing darts or cribbage.' Bill Jones said it was Botham's swagger that led to him being picked out for what was described by some as an initiation ritual which any ground-staff boy might be forced to endure, but which Butcher – at the time a fellow B-staffer – said was an ordeal that Botham was singled out for more than anyone.

'The A staff would be upstairs and we'd be on the bottom floor straight below them,' Butcher recalled. 'When you heard a banging of boots and studs on the floor you knew it was time to disappear because it meant the A-staff guys were bored and on their way down. They would have already decided to target someone. Who was it going to be? You knew they would be getting hold of somebody and stripping that person naked, laying them out on the table and whitening them all over with the whitener that was used on the boots … Ian was the guy they picked on all the time. He was big and they knew he would always fight back. And that was more fun. As soon as you heard them coming, you would just rush out of the room. The sound of the boots was the sign. They'd come in and get hold of Botham and he would fight and struggle. They'd hold these trials too, picking out people for some minor offence or other. Again Botham was the chief target.'

Jones said that not every boy was put through these ordeals, 'just any kid that came in who was a bit lively and stroppy, anyone who was a bit arrogant or a jack-the-lad. And Beefy was a bit like that.' He claimed that attempts to whitewash Botham failed, though Butcher's testimony, and that of Botham himself, contradict that. Wagner said Botham was often the target simply because he was so rowdy. 'One or two things [items of clothing] got ripped off,' Jones said. 'It was a fairly lively encounter. He was a big strong lad and it wasn't a task to be undertaken lightly. But it was all done in good fun, although I'd admit that if you did it now you'd probably be arrested. Ninety-nine times out of a hundred these things happened when it was raining and we were hanging around waiting to go home.' The ritual stuck in Botham's mind sufficiently for him to inflict similar punishment on an England team-mate in Australia in 1979.

Butcher saw in Botham's determination to resist humiliation the seeds of his future greatness. 'Botham didn't care whether you were bigger than him, or more experienced, he would take you on. If he played you at tiddlywinks, he had to win. That was his secret. Regardless of the situation, he was a fighter. You could see that from the way he used to fight the fellas.'

These battles were also an early instance of Botham's refusal to acknowledge any kind of pain, whether emotional or physical. Whatever was meted out, he could take it.

Quite a few people, though, thought Botham was full of bluster and empty bravado. He talked himself up something rotten and imagined himself as the next great scare-'em fast bowler. His game lacked subtlety and most saw straight through his look-at-me exploits in the nets.

Botham got cross because neither Len Muncer, the head coach, nor his assistant Harry Sharp seemed to rate him. In fact, he should not have let their judgements greatly bother him. Lord's was not a school; he was not there to pass an exam but to learn what he could about the game. But he did not seem to want to learn; that only came later, under better coaches and when he had grown desperate. He later claimed that Muncer wrote an unfavourable report about him to Somerset describing him as talented but wayward, but Andy Wagner, who returned to Lord's as assistant coach from 1978 to 1984, said this story was certainly apocryphal. 'I never heard of a report being written about me back to Somerset and in six years as coach I never saw one. If there were any assessments of players it would have been word-of-mouth.'

In any case, Somerset were in a position to judge Botham for themselves because in 1973, although he was nowhere near top of their list, they called on him for several second XI matches in which he did OK with the bat, scoring 309 runs in ten innings, but was not much needed with the ball, sending down only 73 overs.

Botham's time at Lord's was ultimately a disappointment because of his own inability to make the most of it, although this failure itself would eventually spur him on. 'As long as you were prepared to listen, you would benefit,' Gould said. Botham was not prepared to. He once conceded as much, saying that he had been so stubborn that the MCC coaches had given up trying to teach him. He said he had never tried to master technique or play perfectly. Nor had he ever read a coaching manual.

That said, Muncer's ways would have tested even less-impatient pupils. Len Muncer and Harry Sharp were man-and-boy professionals who had been working in the game for decades; Muncer had first represented Middlesex in 1933 and Sharp in 1946. They weren't inclined to be impressed by cocky youngsters and their praise was hard won. Muncer was the stricter, less tolerant one; with his smartly pressed flannels and spotless shoes, he would have had no time for Botham's jack-the-laddery. 'Len was the old-school disciplinarian but Harry Sharp was a jack-the-lad himself,' Butcher said. 'You could get away with things with Harry.' Mike Brearley, who later got to know Sharp well when he acted as Middlesex scorer while Brearley was county captain, said that Sharp's theory was that players should not need to be told when they had done well. But his views, when sometimes given over a pint with the boys, were highly regarded. Botham got on well with Sharp, who liked his sunny nature and the fact that he saw the funny side of everything. He would stand behind the net when Botham was batting and say: 'Pisshole shot that, Botham, pisshole shot – but as long as it keeps working, keep playing it.'

Botham's waywardness was plain during his second full year. 'If you were in authority, he would be hard to control, though not in a malicious way,' Wagner said. 'If you were a friend, you were a friend. He was a great competitor who always had a smile on his face. He loved life. There was one time when he hadn't got any boots and Somerset sent him a pair. The spikes were too long and we spent a day trying to wear them down on the concrete. Another time he lost a week's wages for playing cards. He was his own man, as he is now. I remember him scoring a hundred against the City of London School [in 1972] and being roasted by Len for spoiling the game.' Jones said that the opposition were so weak that the coach had wanted to share around the batting: 'Muncer had told him to get out at fifty. He slogged his way to a hundred and then gave his wicket away.' Muncer would have been furious at such arrogance and insubordination.

Sharp – who thought Gould the most talented of this group – once told Botham that he should stick to football, a game to which he applied himself fiercely when the boys played games among themselves after nets. Botham would later delight in reminding Sharp of this remark and the story gained wide enough currency that years later Middlesex players would tease Sharp whenever he purred over Botham's latest exploits. 'He would say, "You watch this boy, he's good,"' Brearley said. 'We'd say, "Oh, he can't play, you're getting old, you've lost your judgement, Harry … He [Botham] is a slogger. He is an off-side slogger."' In truth, Sharp was astonished at what Botham achieved, as Barry Lloyd testified: 'Years later I bumped into Harry. He was scorer at Middlesex. The first thing he said to me was, "What do you think of Botham?!"'

By crossing Muncer, Botham found himself routinely over-looked for selection for the better matches. These games were not only good opportunities to show what you could do as a player, they were also useful earners. Lunch and tea would be free and travel expenses were also provided. But Muncer controlled the list and Botham struggled to get selected. Confined instead to yet more practice, a lifelong aversion to net sessions was born.

The overall quality of the cricketers who went through Muncer's hands was not high. He generally turned out run-of-the-mill county pros; very few came close to international recognition. Future England player Derek Pringle remembers being unimpressed by the quality of the opposition when he played against the Lord's groundstaff while at Cambridge in the late 1970s. 'MCC groundstaff boys were looked on as second-class citizens,' he said. 'Their counties didn't quite want to get rid of them but they didn't want to keep them either.' David Graveney, who knew Botham throughout his younger days, said: 'Those people [MCC groundstaff] were on the margin as to whether they were going to make it or not.'

Indeed, many groundstaff boys ended up working as coaches in independent schools. Bill Jones left to teach at UCS Hampstead, while Wagner eventually ended up as cricket master at Radley, where his charges included future England captain Andrew Strauss. Botham's parents only agreed to him joining the groundstaff when it was explained to them that should he not make it as a player there would be the option of him becoming a schools coach, a point that probably established in his own mind the idea that coaching was a job for failed cricketers, and therefore one to be avoided at all costs.

Botham's peers shared Muncer and Sharp's reservations about his capabilities. 'He wasn't the best cricketer among us by a long way,' said Butcher. 'He was a big lad who just liked to hit the ball. His bowling was really done in the nets ... Harry Sharp used to say Botham just couldn't bowl.' Wagner and Francis agreed that Botham was rarely seen bowling outside practice sessions. 'He played mainly as a batter,' Wagner said. 'He hit very straight and hard and loved hitting you out of the nets ... With the ball, he would run in off eighteen paces and bowl bouncers. His style just didn't suit Len. He just wanted to whack it out of the park. I remember Len saying to me once, "How does he get people out?" To be honest, many people shared the same view.' Francis said he remembered Botham as 'a middle-order batsman who played shots and hit the ball a long way ... he did not want to bowl medium-pace, but fast'.

Emburey agreed. 'He was just a swashbuckling cricketer. In the nets he tried to spank it around [with the bat] and bowl all sorts. You could not envisage that he was going to develop into the cricketer he did. I remember Harry Sharp saying, "Bloody hell, he's indisciplined, he doesn't do this, he doesn't do that." And yet this guy became the best all-rounder England has produced. The thing was that he played with freedom. He wasn't fearful of anything. If he failed, he failed. The thing he was thinking about was his success – and winning.'

Botham may not have learned much from Muncer or Sharp but from Jones he first learned how to swing the ball. 'I was a similar bowler to him but he would never bowl in front of me [in matches],' said Jones. 'I was often captain, of course, so I could bowl myself if I wanted to but I was also older and more experienced. I bowled outswing. He could bowl outswing but he didn't know where to pitch it or what pace to bowl, things that depended on the weather and the state of the pitch. I wouldn't say he stood out especially for his ability. He was a big strong lad who could throw the ball a long way, hit it miles and tried to bowl a hundred miles per hour. He hit the ball well and I thought he would play county cricket but he was still very head-strong when he left us.' Lloyd agreed that Botham did not stand out for his ability. 'We were all of a certain standard and if you'd asked me if I'd thought he would be one of the greats I'd have said no.'

One area in which Botham clearly was outstanding was his fielding. Jones said he was the best at that age he had ever seen. 'He had brilliant hands and could take effortless one-handed catches.' Butcher said that he and Botham were always in competition in the field. 'I regarded myself as a very decent fielder but he was always trying to outdo me,' he said. 'He wanted to be the best slip fielder, the best outfielder, and have the best arm.'

*

Even if there were humiliations to be endured, Botham's time at Lord's gained him entry into the community of cricketers and it was a world that he loved. For a people-person such as himself, the playing, drinking and general mate-ship that a cricket dressing-room provided could not be bettered. One of the few incidents from his Lord's days that he recalled with real pride was him downing a yard of ale to save the face of the MCC Nippers during a post-match drinking session with a team from St Mary's Hospital. That would have been every bit as important to him as winning a game.

Cricket gave him an identity and access to a 'club' with a diverse membership that, if it did not actually knock down class barriers, at least challenged them. On the field of play, the lad from an ordinary social background could get the better of someone with the most privileged of upbringings. As with so many aspects of his life, Botham's response to this environment was contradictory: he desperately wanted to be respected for his cricket but despised the authority which could grant approval.

He did find though that through cricket he could, if he wished, form friendships with people from all walks of life. This would become another central feature of his personality. He might have been suspicious of anyone in authority, or who was very clever or highly educated, but in some instances this could be overcome. He was to acquire an extraordinarily wide range of friends and acquaintances. John Barclay, who was educated at Eton and started out with Sussex at around this time, said that he and Botham got on unexpectedly well. 'I think he was faintly amused by me because I was a blocker,' Barclay mused. 'Here I was, with a typical public school background, and yet I "blocked" it. He thought I should be a flamboyant stroke-player. He respected ordinary county professionals – good players with no great pretensions. He had no delusions of grandeur about himself.' Even after he had become an established star, Botham was not above deliberately playing out a maiden over from a county stalwart whom he respected.

If he liked someone, no matter whether they were lord or leper, he would treat them the same. It was one of his most admirable traits. 'Ian has gone through life finding bonds with other people,' said Barry Lloyd.

Apart from leaving Lord's with an aversion to net practice, he also departed with a burning desire to confound those who did not recognise his talent. He wanted to prove that Muncer and Sharp were wrong, and the egg-and-bacon-tied MCC members who no doubt thought that the best cricketers in the country had to come from the grandest schools and the finest cities. He never forgot that no one at this time spotted his potential as an all-rounder, and would still complain about it long after he had joined Somerset. 'What really annoyed him when he was on the Lord's groundstaff was that he felt he could bowl,' said Vic Marks, a Somerset contemporary. 'And if he wasn't bowling he was not at his most potent as an all-rounder. Bowling made him free as a batsman, allowing him to play with abandon. Although he probably didn't quite rationalise it like this at that time, if he wasn't regarded as a bowler he wasn't half the cricketer, even a quarter of the cricketer, he could have been.'

It was no coincidence that when he later returned to Lord's as a Somerset and England player, he did some striking things with bat and ball.

Working at Lord's also taught him where the power lay, and ultimately that he should pursue that power for himself, outsider or not. Whichever team he was later playing for, leadership would be an issue. If Botham was not actually captain – and a recurring theme in his career was that he often wanted to be captain – he posed challenges for those who were. They either thrived or died.

Botham's last days at Lord's brought him into close proximity with the company he would eventually seek to keep. He was on crowd-control duty at the Benson and Hedges Cup final in July 1973 when a fine all-round performance from Asif Iqbal won the day for Kent. The following month, the last Test of the summer – a game remembered for a hoax IRA bombscare – witnessed a graceful century from Gary Sobers, the world's finest all-rounder; unbeknown to the public, it was made on the back of a night of much drinking and little sleep. And the weekend after that, the Gillette Cup final was contested between counties who each boasted a world-class all-rounder. Both of them happened to be from southern Africa: the powerfully built Mike Procter could have been designed to satisfy Botham's dreams, bowling very fast (off the wrong foot) and hitting the ball miles, and his ninety-four runs and two wickets were central to Gloucestershire's victory over a Sussex side defined by the charismatic presence of their towering blond captain Tony Greig. Raised in South Africa to an Edinburgh father, Greig had recently established himself as England's best all-rounder. His duck had killed off Sussex's chances.

Botham was on groundstaff duty during that match too but afterwards he began an urgent search for junior members of the Sussex squad who might be able to give him a lift down to Hove. He had just received a summons from Somerset to present himself there for a John Player League match the next day. They had injury problems and their interest in the competition was over. Botham was to be given his first-team debut.

As he went out of the Lord's gates that night, Botham would probably have reckoned that, at seventeen years of age, he was ready for life as a fully fledged county cricketer and that the time was ripe for him to go out and shake a few trees. But even a man who would become famous for writing his own scripts could not make it all happen straight away. At Hove, he scored just two runs, bowled three expensive overs and Somerset were beaten easily. The following Sunday, against Surrey at the Oval, he again scored two, bowled only four overs for the wicket of New Zealand batsman Geoff Howarth (taken with a full toss), and Somerset lost again.

In one special moment at Hove, though, he did take a fine running, diving catch. The victim was Greig, England's star all-rounder. Only Botham could have seen the moment as significant.

# 2

## Northern Families

'"Both" was having a fantastic time. There was "his" Stand
and there was "his" mate playing out there. He got Elton
to stop and sing "Happy Birthday" to Marie. The amazing thing was she loved it and went out onto the balcony
and almost like the Queen Mum gave a regal wave. It was
sweet. Against the odds, it was a good moment.'

VIC MARKS, SOMERSET TEAM-MATE,
ON BOTHAM GETTING ELTON JOHN TO SING
'HAPPY BIRTHDAY' TO HIS MOTHER AT TAUNTON

Botham's ancestry provided few clues that the family would produce someone so hungry for fame. The lives of earlier generations
of Bothams had passed largely unnoticed in working-class toil.
They were not leaders but the led. Unlike Ian, whose every move
and every utterance would be publicly scrutinised, they anony-
mously travelled life's road, not even going to the bother or
expense of recording their births, marriages or deaths in newspapers. It was a shortfall in publicity he would more than make up
for.

The only predecessors Botham mentions in his books are his
parents, although this should not be taken as a lack of pride in his
background. He was always loyal to the area around the Humber

in which his father's side of the family had lived for generations. He married a girl who came from the same area and there they together bought their first property, a small farm-worker's cottage in Epworth, North Lincolnshire. They later bought their main family homes in North Yorkshire.

So, although Somerset was home for much of his early life, in adulthood his links with the North were steadily to be re-established, even though he remained a Somerset cricketer until he was thirty. As a player, his relationship with the Somerset public was equivocal. Some Taunton folk saw him as too flash, brash and brilliant to be one of their own, and part of him did not regard himself as one of them. As Brian Close used to do, after he had finished a match and faced a few days off, Botham would promptly drive back up North to be with his family and go shooting with his friends. And his cricket may have been with Somerset but he played his football for Scunthorpe United (and briefly Hull City reserves). He was passionate in his support for 'the Mighty Iron'.

During the nineteenth century, Botham was a common name in the area around Beverley and Driffield, due north of Kingston upon Hull, and Hornsea, on the coast to the northeast. Hull was flourishing on the back of a boom in shipbuilding and commerce and rose to the position of England's third-largest port, attaining city status in 1897. On the back of Hull's success, neighbouring areas benefited greatly. Beverley developed significant trades in iron, coal and leather, shipbuilding and agricultural implements, while Hornsea became a fashionable seaside resort where wealthy Hull businessmen set up palatial villas.

It took time for this localised industrial revolution to make itself felt upon the Botham family. In 1861, a John Botham, the son of a shepherd and husband to Sarah Taylor, was running the White Horse Inn on the Beverley–Driffield road (Ian's thirst was clearly hereditary) and in 1871 his only child, George Chappell Botham, was working as a book-keeper in Driffield. What a delicious irony that one of Botham's ancestors should carry the name of one of his fiercest enemies in cricket! But George's life was to change significantly after his wife Rebecca Ann Hutty, the daughter of a relatively affluent Beverley draper, with whom he had had five children, died of tuberculosis at the age of thirty-four. George moved to Hull, where he spent more than twenty years as a managing clerk to an engineering firm. At first he employed a housekeeper who home-tutored the children but George soon remarried, to Emily, with whom he had five more children.

The path of the first of George's four sons, Herbert Botham, did not run smooth. He would only live to thirty-two and when he was about twenty he met Hannah Cherry, the daughter of John Cherry, a successful manager of an engineering and brickworks company in Hornsea. Cherry worked for Joseph Armytage Wade, one of the leading entrepreneurs in the region, who had established various railway links from Hull, including one to Hornsea. A few years earlier, Cherry's name had gone on the patent for a helical centrifugal pump alongside Wade's, and Cherry had seemingly benefited financially because shortly after that he bought property and land in Beverley (Cherry went down in family folklore as an 'inventor', but Wade would probably have been the prime mover behind the development of the pump). How pleased Cherry was with his daughter's liaison is unclear but the answer may be 'Not very'. Young Herbert was at this time in modest employment building and repairing mill machinery – his job description was 'millwright' in the 1891 and 1901 censuses – and very soon Hannah fell pregnant with his child.

With Hannah seven months pregnant, she and Herbert married at the Zion Independent Chapel in Bridlington a fortnight before Christmas 1890, and two months later, on 14 February 1891, Herbert Valentine Cyril Botham – Ian's grandfather – was born. The 1891 census has them living at 179 Brickyard Cottages in Hornsea, which sounds very like a modest home close by John Cherry's brick and tiles works. Their immediate neighbours were an engine driver and an engine fitter. Three years later, their daughter Rebecca Annie died in infancy. By early 1901, they were living in better quarters in Priory Road, Beverley, near Hannah's father.

But by June that year Herbert himself was dead and when John Cherry died in 1902, Hannah was bringing up three young children, Herbert Valentine, Helga and Arthur, who was only seventeen months old. How she managed is unclear but she was probably supported by the Cherry family, who maintained the hydraulic engineering business into the 1930s, when it was sold on.

It appears that in the years leading up to and during the First World War, Herbert Valentine was employed in engineering, and was thus spared the call to arms. According to his marriage certificate of Christmas Eve 1919, he was a 'patternmaker', a job that entailed making wooden or iron moulds for use in a foundry, and as his address was given as Dunston on Tyne in Gateshead – some hundred miles north of Hull – it is possible that he was working there as a shipfitter on the Dunston Staiths, the largest coal-shipping point in the region.

Perhaps it was through his work that Herbert met his future wife, Emily Halliwell, whose father was an engine fitter. The couple were married in Scarborough at St Mary's Church, a short walk from the cricket ground where his grandson would play his first match for England nearly sixty years later. Herbert was apparently still working in Gateshead in 1923 because their first child Leslie – Ian's father – was born there that year. However, five years after that Herbert, Emily and young Leslie had moved to the old Botham stamping ground of Beverley where Emily, like Herbert's mother Hannah, lost a child shortly after giving birth, this time a boy, Clifford.

At some point, Herbert and Emily moved to her native Sheffield, possibly because Hull's industries became a major target for Luftwaffe bombing during the Second World War. Sheffield itself was not spared attack but Hull was bombed more heavily than any other British city outside London and 1,200 civilians were killed. Herbert died in Sheffield in 1946, aged fifty-five.

With Leslie, we get the first detailed picture of one of Ian's predecessors. By all accounts, in general build Les bore little
resemblance to his eldest child and many who saw them together
in subsequent years would be struck by the contrast between the
father's slender build and quiet manner, and his physically imposing son, confident to the point of brashness and in every way a
man of mighty appetite. Some pointed to the incongruity as
reason why Botham apparently responded well to father-figure
types such as Brian Close and Mike Brearley who captained him
with such success. There may be some truth in this; Botham
plainly worked well under those who gave firm and unequivocal
leadership – as Close and Brearley did – but that did not necessarily mean he always toed the line even with them. It took time
for him to come to respect Brearley, for example. Surely the fact
was that whatever the father was like, he was going to be overshadowed by a son with such an extraordinarily forceful
personality.

Botham himself described his father as tall but whippet thin,
someone who could eat anything he liked and never put on
weight; he always had energy to burn. He was an old-fashioned,
honourable man, quite fixed in his opinions and quietly determined. Les would support his son at some crucial early moments
in his career.

Others noted that Les was very much a man of his generation,
someone who had entered adulthood during a time of war and
national crisis. Peter Robinson, a Somerset player and coach during
Botham's early involvement with the club, remembered Les as
being among the better sort of fathers who accompanied the early
efforts of their sons: 'He was very supportive. He didn't interfere.
It wasn't, "My boy this, my boy that." You can have a lot of pushy
parents. I've met a few. He wasn't like that.' David English, who
became a close friend of Botham's in the 1980s, said of Les: 'He
was a gentle, lovely man. Very kind and such a gentleman. Almost
a distinguished chap.' But Graham Morris, a photographer who at
around the same time gained Botham's trust in a way few reporters

could, thought Les a slightly cold fish. 'You met the parents and could tell that Beefy took after his mother. It was the build ... his dad was quite slim and angular. I wouldn't say he was particularly well educated but he gave the impression of being slightly aloof, whereas his mum was much more fun and gregarious.'

As Ian would do later on, and previous Bothams had done before, Les left school at the earliest opportunity. He joined the Fleet Air Arm, effectively the navy's air force, as a petty officer and stayed there twenty years. It was a technical job, fitting up planes as his father had once fitted ships. Don Shepherd, the great Glamorgan bowler, did his national service near Malvern as an air mechanic in the Fleet Air Arm just after the war in what must have been a similar role. 'We looked after a number of aircraft,' Shepherd recalled. 'I started out on old Tiger Moths, learning how to sew wings. We never went to sea.' Les, though, moved locations and at the time of Ian's birth was stationed near Londonderry, Northern Ireland, while his wife kept the family home in Heswall, Cheshire.

Les had met Marie Collett at HMS *Ariel* in Lancashire. She was three years younger than him and her father Albert, originally a farmer, had died before she was born. Dudley Doust, an American-born sports journalist on the *Sunday Times*, who wrote an early book on Botham of forensic detail, traced Ian's maternal antecedants to Cumberland, where a great-great-grandfather, a mid-Victorian sea captain named Henderson, put out from Whitehaven in the schooner *Huntress*. A great-grandfather, Joseph Higgins, was harbourmaster at Maryport and also a water-diviner. Ian's mother remembered her old grandfather walking over her father's farm in Cumberland, twig in hand.

Marie's family moved to Bradford, where she grew up. She had trained as a nurse and during the war had served in the voluntary aid detachment as a dental nurse. She and Les were married in Scotland and she suffered four miscarriages before successfully delivering Ian – at a hefty 10lb 1oz – on 24 November 1955. Dale, the second of their four children, arrived two years later and Les quit the Fleet Air Arm in order that the family could settle in one place, taking a job as a type-test engineer at Westland Helicopters in Yeovil, a small engineering town on the Somerset–Dorset border. Within a few years Westland had become a significantly bigger company and Yeovil's major employer. Les would stay with Westland for the rest of his working life.

In terms of personality, Ian was far more his mother's son than his father's. If anyone made Ian a 'people person', it was her. David Graveney, who knew the family from early on, said: 'The old man was a little in the background . . . his Mum was the more outgoing one.' David English said that in terms of character, Ian was 'the spitting image' of his mother. Botham himself said that his father was a disciplinarian but his mother more steely. David Foot, an astute West Country sportswriter throughout Botham's career, remembered Marie as a key figure in her son's development. 'She was quite dominant and protective. The father was more subordinate. I didn't see them often at matches. I'm not sure how close Ian was to them. He occasionally played golf with his father. They lived in a semi in Yeovil and he went to the secondary school, not the grammar school. They weren't particularly well off.' But Botham remembers a family holiday to Lloret de Mar in Spain when he was about nine years old.

Vic Marks remembered Les and Marie occasionally making the journey from Yeovil to watch their son play at Taunton, but the visit he recalled most vividly was the octogenarian Marie accompanying her son to an Elton John concert at the county ground in 2006, several years after the club had built an Ian Botham Stand in his honour. 'There were twenty thousand in the ground and it was a great success,' Marks recalled. '"Both" was having a fantastic time. There was "his" stand and there was "his" mate playing out there. It was Marie's birthday and he got Elton to stop and sing "Happy Birthday" to her. The amazing thing was she loved it and went out onto the balcony and, almost like the Queen Mum, gave a regal wave. It was sweet. Against the odds, it was a good moment.'

Between them, Botham's parents passed down to him some deep-seated, old-fashioned beliefs in Queen and country, a legacy no doubt of their wartime service. 'He definitely sees the weakness in gratuitous traditionalism but loves the traditionalism of his country,' said Rod Bransgrove, the chairman of Hampshire who became a close friend of Botham's after Botham had retired from playing. 'He sings the national anthem with his hand on his heart. He is incredibly, unbelievably, patriotic. He celebrates St George's Day and he's a huge monarchist. If there was a war tomorrow, he'd sign up to defend his country. Not that he'd necessarily think much of some of the others in the trenches with him.'

Les and Marie also gave him an intense love of sport and competition. With his lithe build, Les was built for speed and he proved to be both a good footballer and runner. He ran for East Yorkshire and had a trial for Hull City, and at one point thought of taking up football professionally, but the pay was poor and he considered the risks too great. He also played cricket to a reasonable standard, though it was said that Ian got his cricketing ability from his mother, who represented a Royal Nursing Corps team.

David Gower, who spent as much time with Botham as anyone as cricketer, commentator and friend, reflected on the origins of Botham's sporting talent: 'They were a good family. I suppose by the time I knew Les and Marie they were already getting on, not aged but middle-aged, and I've no idea what they were like as twenty-year-olds, no idea whether Les was a similarly stubborn sportsman at the age of twenty-two, whether Marie was a they-shalt-not-pass type hockey player. But there must be something in the genes. I don't think it is necessarily the way you're brought up. Something like that [sporting ability] has to be innate.'

The sporting genes did not however find their way to Botham's siblings – sisters Dale and Wendy, and the youngest of the four, brother Graeme.

Family formed a central pillar of Botham's life. Throughout his playing career, when he was often under enormous strain and frequently apart from his family for long periods, it was they who appeared to provide a stable source of emotional strength without which he would never have survived as well as he did. His reliance on family was not a manufactured thing but a genuine feeling that this was how life operated: relatives were people you kept close whenever you could. Not that this was always possible. His name would be linked to sex scandals, and he admitted to being unfaithful to his wife Kathryn, but the idea of divorce would have gone against the grain with him – and her. There were occasions when there appeared to be a serious risk of Kath leaving him: once she pulled back from an initial threat to do so; another time, she told him he needed to change his behaviour and he seemingly did so; on a third occasion, when he admitted to a two-year affair, she decided to stay, in Botham's words, 'for the sake of the children'. If he considered leaving her, it did not come to anything.

It was striking that no sooner had Botham reached adulthood, and become a professional county cricketer, than he went about setting up a family of his own. Equally revealing was his choice of wife-to-be. Kathryn Waller was the goddaughter of Brian Close, Ian's captain at Somerset, and her family came from Thorne, twenty miles southwest of Hull. Gerry and Jan Waller were friends of Close from his days at Yorkshire and had provided him with a refuge when he was being hounded by the media about the loss of the England captaincy in 1967; after he joined Somerset, they would occasionally come down to Taunton to watch him play, bringing daughters Kath and Lindsay with them.

That was how Ian met Kath in 1974 and – after claiming the unlikely satisfaction of seeing off a rival suitor from Cambridge University – by September that year he had proposed. He was eighteen, she was nineteen. Kath was taking a business studies course at Lanchester Polytechnic in Coventry and between times working for her father's drum-kit firm. Ian's father and Close both had their doubts – Les worried if Ian could afford it while Close, who had himself not married until thirty-four, questioned whether it was a good idea when Ian would be travelling so much – but each gave his blessing. Whatever doubts Kath's father might have had were softened by Ian's efforts in tracking him down to ask permission for his daughter's hand. The wedding took place sixteen months later, in January 1976, and the following year the first of their three children, Liam, was born. Worries about money were eased that winter when Ian lived with the Waller family while Gerry employed him as one of his sales representatives. Gerry later gave the couple the deposit on their cottage in Epworth, eight miles from Thorne.

The choice of home was significant. If Epworth was where Kath had grown up, it was also where Ian wanted to live – in an essentially rural, village atmosphere, where life was defined by family and friends, domesticated animals and rolling acres. Whatever happened to him in later life, Botham never lost his love of the countryside, and of the rod and the gun, and whenever he had free time from cricket, he would eagerly return to this existence. At the 1979 general election, he voted for the party of traditional rural interest, Margaret Thatcher's Conservatives, rather than James Callaghan's Labour Party. Botham was as excited by stalking a deer as he ever was setting a trap for an opening batsman. The Bothams took holidays in places like the Lake District and Scotland; city dwellers they were not. Generally, Botham was to find peace in the countryside and trouble in cities.

Crucially, the family provided a framework within which Botham could operate. It reminded him that there were things he should not do, and limits beyond which he should not go, as firmly as any captain ever did – which is not to say that he did not sometimes put the framework under severe strain. Going away and playing his cricket and returning to a stable, supportive environment was essential to him. His long absences put a huge strain on his wife, who sometimes objected to the demands being made of her, but the fact she remained loyal was fundamental to his success. Theirs was a marriage built on traditional lines, with Kath very much the home-builder.

Botham's attitude never changed. 'I'm not a "new man",' he said in 2010. 'I was able to keep my mind firmly on my cricket after [my children] were born. I respect the feelings of the "new man" but I'm an "old man". If I was playing now, I still wouldn't be flying home for the birth ... I'm afraid I would be at the game. And my wife would be telling me to be there too.'

Sarah, the second of their three children, confirmed to the *Sunday Times* in 2010 that it was Kath who was responsible for their upbringing: 'I find it funny when Dad tells people he was a disciplinarian when Liam, Becky and I were small: I can't remember him being strict at all. He was away on tour so much that Mum was the one who would discipline us. I'd feel sorry for her when he came home. Suddenly it would be, "Who wants to play with Daddy?" and she'd be left on her own. Seeing Dad was a treat ... when Dad came home it was holiday time.'

Botham's commandeering of the Waller family through Brian Close provided an early example of him abiding by the principle that 'a friend of yours is a friend of mine'. As a photographer who regularly followed Botham's England matches, Graham Morris saw how this worked. 'It was a very close-knit family. He and Kath were always in touch. If she was not around then they'd be on the phone, always talking to each other. And his parents and her parents were all big friends, and any time there was a Test match [in England] both families would turn up ... both sets of parents, Kath, Kath's sister Lindsay and her husband Paul. So he had more of a family life when he was playing for England than for Somerset, because when he played for Somerset Kath was up the other end of the country. There was always lots of relatives around. Ian was a big family man. Northern families are like that.'

This of course made Botham's infamous joke in 1984 about Pakistan not being a place where he would send even his mother-in-law highly misleading. Anyone drawing the conclusion that he had no time for Kath's mother could not have been further from the truth. Botham said in a sincerer moment: 'My mother-in-law is delightful.' He also had a great fondness for Gerry Waller, with whom he played golf and whom he treated as one of the lads.

Gerry would join him on trips to watch rugby internationals and occasionally come out on tour.

Ian's father died in Taunton in December 2005 at the age of eighty-two. He had been suffering from Alzheimer's and had apparently not recognised members of his family for some time. Had Les lived another eighteen months, he would have seen his son become by some distance the first Botham to receive a knighthood.

Academic education had almost no impact on Botham. Various accounts (including his own) of his time at Milford Junior School and Buckler's Mead Secondary in Yeovil make clear that he had little interest in conventional learning. The stories that survive relate to his indiscipline, general mischief-making and prowess at athletic pursuits, not of him preferring one area of study over another. Once he had discovered an aptitude for sport, this earned all his energies and enthusiasm. Otherwise schooling shaped his personality only in so far as it convinced him that the way to find out about a thing was to experience it rather than read about it. He had about as much time for putting his head in a book as most of his forebears.

Botham claimed that when he left school – at the legal minimum age of fifteen and with an unknown number of qualifications – he did not even look back as he walked out of the gates for the last time. If that was said to imply that he had no regrets about his lack of erudition, it may not be quite accurate. The issue of intelligence would become a sensitive one with Botham and, not unnaturally, he took quick exception to anyone who suggested he was dense or uncultivated.

Not that he hid his failed school career; he would make occasional reference to it. He admitted to having been a member of a gang that went around terrorising other pupils. 'At school I was aggressive and wanted to do things now not tomorrow,' he said in *It Sort of Clicks*, published in 1986 and ghostwritten by his erudite Somerset team-mate Peter Roebuck, who took a First in Law at

Cambridge. 'I was in trouble all the time.' And Botham more than once alluded to his nickname at school being Bungalow because 'there was nothing upstairs'.

But he did dabble in a little rewriting of history. He once said that he had deliberately failed his eleven-plus exam because he wanted to go to Buckler's Mead, where they played football, rather than the grammar school where it was rugby only (rugby was a sport he never got on with). But he did not repeat this claim elsewhere, admitting only that he had failed the exam 'by some distance', adding: 'If the eleven-plus had been a quick single, I'd have been stranded halfway down the wicket.' He wasn't unintelligent. He simply had no interest in anything that would not further the aim he had set himself of becoming a professional sportsman.

But Botham could be prickly on the issue of his 'learning'. He would seek to impose himself on others through means other than words – his sheer physical superiority was usually a powerful starting point – and his response to journalists who wrote scathingly of him would be to sever relations (and instruct team-mates to do likewise). This unimaginative tactic merely prompted some to interpret his behaviour as bullying or boorish, and attracted even crueller jibes. 'I have always been physically frightened of people whose bodyweight in kilos is numerically higher than their IQ,' wrote Frances Edmonds – wife of Cambridge University-educated England spin bowler Phil Edmonds and herself multilingual – of Botham.

It was perhaps because the advantages of size and strength were less effective against those with an agile mind and quick tongue that Botham was initially wary of those with lofty academic educations – of whom cricket still attracted a fair few in the 1970s and 1980s.

That athleticism came first and books second was not a great surprise given Botham's extraordinary build. The heavy baby soon turned into a sturdy boy, then an imposing man-child, who had reached six feet in height by the age of fifteen. This sheer size gave him a distinct advantage over his contemporaries, as did a November birth date that put him among the older children in his school year. Modern research shows that in sport children born nearer the start of the academic year are far likelier to prosper, as they are more likely to be selected for sports teams, leaving younger rivals to fall by the wayside through want of opportunity. This certainly seemed to be the case with Botham, although he was so precocious in build and ability that he forged to the head not only of his own year group but the one above as well. At the age of nine he was playing cricket with eleven-year-olds and at thirteen was playing alongside, and in some instances captaining, boys of fifteen. Stories abound of his ability to hit and throw a cricket ball huge distances. The first trophy he ever won was for a throw of 207 feet in an under-13 competition in London. His parents recalled that he also had fantastic eyesight and reactions, and were not surprised at his ability years later to pick them out in even the biggest crowds.

Botham also shone at football, at which he captained the school team despite an early tendency to get sent off, and badminton, a sport his mother had played well. Even at this age, though, his approach to sport involved a strong 'social' element, as George Rendell, a French teacher who ran the Buckler's Mead badminton team, discovered when in Botham's last year he took a team to play at Wells Cathedral School. When the teams came to have their meal, Rendell found that the sandwiches for six had disappeared. It transpired that Botham had eaten the lot and when Rendell found him he was smoking a cigarette in the dressing-room. 'He was always full of life and zest, yet there always seemed to be an ulterior motive . . . like nipping off to the Green Dragon for a pint,' Rendell recalled. Chastised for frequenting pubs at so young an age, Botham invited masters to join him. 'There were times when I found myself almost agreeing to do it,' Rendell added.

Botham admitted that he did not endear himself to everyone. 'The parents of my contemporaries probably had me down as an arrogant little so-and-so ... but that self-belief was also what made me a fierce and successful competitor. People at school sometimes called me a bighead but I used to think, "No, I'm not. I'm just very good at this, a lot better than you."' Botham's mother said he was never malicious, just a good-natured rascal.

An apparently granite-hard self-belief would be a feature of Botham's cricket but he later conceded that his displays of bravado hid 'genuine fears and insecurities'. He had a number of problems that perhaps in themselves were unimportant but taken together may well have promoted a general sense of anxiety. He suffered from claustrophobia (a contributory factor to his aversion to net practice) and a fear of heights, while it emerged at primary school – when the skies in the pictures he painted were rarely blue – that he was colour-blind. Nor can his lack of academic success have done much for his self-esteem. He said that from an early age he found it impossible to admit to a mistake, a trait very much apparent throughout his playing days when he would always have a ready excuse for why he had dropped a catch, bowled a bad ball, or got out to a silly stroke.

Someone of weaker disposition might have been beaten by these problems but Botham shook them off, as he did a nasty skin condition shortly after leaving school. 'It wasn't acne, it was worse than that,' remembered Peter Roebuck. 'I think it was eczema, which was exceptionally upsetting to most youngsters, but he simply brushed it off, disregarded it. His ability to do that was remarkable. He just went marching along into life. That showed a rare power. He was unstoppable in so many ways. It took people a while to work that out.'

Botham may have been an outdoor type but one thing he did like staying indoors for was to watch films. Indeed, probably more of his childhood heroes were drawn from the screen than from sport. Peter Hayter, the ghostwriter of Botham's first autobiography, felt this played a big part in forming his outlook. 'He was a man who lived other men's dreams, but they were his dreams as well,' Hayter said. 'When he told me about John Wayne being his favourite actor and Westerns being his favourite type of movie, he was expressing his feeling that a man could be a hero in real life as well as in the movies. Wayne was the strong, silent hero, always trying to defy the odds. That was the way Botham played his cricket and lived his life. For most it would have been a hollow cliché, but for him it was real. He would often act first and consider the consequences later. Whatever he did he did without fear or use of the brakes. And of course a by-product of that is that you sometimes crash.'

If English cricket did not have much money in the early 1970s, Somerset cricket had far less. This was a club that regretted the passing of the amateur in 1963 more than most. The club found it difficult to pay a full squad of professionals and tended to appoint captains who had strings other than cricket to their bows so they might have means of supplementing Somerset's meagre wages. Even the introduction of three one-day competitions between 1963 and 1972 had not enabled them to win a trophy for the first time in their near hundred-year history and in 1969 they sat deservedly at the foot of the county championship. Such a shoestring operation deserved little better. Somerset's facilities were as embarrassing as their youth policy. No county was closer to bankruptcy.

The club's response to the crisis of 1969 – a season, *Wisden* recorded, clouded by 'administrative differences of opinion' – was blatantly expedient. Over the next four years it imported more than half a team's worth of players from other counties, older cricketers of skill and experience who were willing to play the autumn of their careers more for love than lucre. Perhaps this was why even in dark times the team retained a sense of bucolic fun. Part of Somerset's particular charm was that they took games to out-grounds such as Clarence Park in Weston-super-Mare and the Recreation Ground at Bath, where the dressing-rooms held the questionable promise of icy showers and splintered benches but local knowledge of pitches helped the home team.

Some of the new acquisitions were to play significant parts in Somerset's future glory. In 1970, along with fast bowler Allan Jones from Sussex and talented wicketkeeper-batsman Derek Taylor from Surrey, Tom Cartwright arrived from Warwickshire. One of the finest of all English medium-pace bowlers and unlucky not to have played more than five Tests, Cartwright could have earned more by staying put at Warwickshire or accepting an offer from Leicestershire, but Somerset put together a job-share scheme that suited him perfectly – to play in the summer and coach in the winter at Millfield School, where Colin Atkinson, a former Somerset captain, was about to become headmaster. Cartwright wanted to coach and in his particular way would prove very good at it; with the help of broad-minded committee-men such as Atkinson and Roy Kerslake, a solicitor who ran the cricket committee and second XI, he would eventually revitalise the club's grassroots development.

Cartwright, who died in 2007, explained in *The Flame Still Burns*, a biography of him by Stephen Chalke, why he gave up life in the West Midlands, where he had spent his winters working on the car production lines, for a slow-moving market town where he had to wait three months for his first wage. 'At Taunton the walls used to stream with water; you couldn't hang your clothes up in the dressing-room and leave them overnight,' he said. '[But] there was still a real connection between the spectators and the players. Somerset people are fairly down to earth. They're not over-impressed by flannel ... For me, moving to Somerset was like being reborn.'

The following year, Brian Close followed from Yorkshire along with Hallam Moseley, a Barbadian. Close was the most contro-versial of all the signings. He was thirty-nine years old, there were doubts about his fitness and – three years after England removed him as skipper – Yorkshire had sacked him as player and captain for among other things publicly disparaging one-day cricket. It was also thought that his abrasiveness aggravated young players. With typical belligerence, Close rejected all charges. 'They said I didn't like one-day cricket but I played it and we won two Gillette Cups at Yorkshire and in 1974 I hit more sixes in a John Player League season than anyone ever had before. And as for not helping youngsters, by the time I'd finished playing I'd made more youngsters into top-class cricketers than anybody. After one season at Somerset, Brian Langford [who was Somerset captain at the time] said, "I think you ought to be captain." I said I didn't want to; I'd had enough of it at Yorkshire. But I did it and under me we began to shape ourselves into some sort of side.'

Despite Somerset's repeated requests, Close refused to make his home in the county. His wife and family remained in Yorkshire and in the winter he rejoined them to work as a sales representative in the pub trade. It was essential he kept up this job. 'I had to think what would keep us going after I'd stopped playing,' he said. 'In Taunton I kept a room at a little pub behind the ground called the Crown and Sceptre which I had to pay for. I had seven lovely years at Somerset but the most I earned in a season was about £3,000 and out of that you had to pay your own travelling expenses. It was a wonderful life but you didn't make a living out of it.' Close resorted to a controversial means of supplementing his income in the winters of 1973 and 1974 when he captained two private tours of apartheid South Africa funded by businessman Derrick Robins (something which may have encouraged Botham to give serious consideration to signing up to similar enterprises years later).

Close and Cartwright formed a crucial alliance for six years. The first three were as comrades on the field, Close as impassioned leader of an XI he was determined to take to victory in every game and Cartwright as tireless spearhead of the attack; the last three with Close still captain but Cartwright, who had effectively given up playing because of injury, now in the role of full-time coach, though he rarely travelled to away matches. Cartwright's hard-headed pragmatism was the ideal counter to Close's recklessness and impatience. If things went wrong, Close would always – like Botham – have an excuse. Cartwright was usually on hand to calm him down, lighting him a cigarette and putting it into his mouth.

When Cartwright arrived, Somerset's youth system – such as it was – was still in the hands of Bill Andrews, a former fast bowler who had first played for the county in 1930 and was now in his sixties. The county had under-15 and under-19 teams, Andrews running the under-19s so chaotically that he would often summon too many players for one match and too few for another, while the team would go weeks without a fixture and then play several in short order. His judgements on players were also widely questioned, his preference for anyone hailing from his own region of Weston being a well-known weakness.

The young Botham was already known to Somerset by this stage, but he, like many other aspiring young cricketers, was scarcely benefiting from such a dysfunctional development programme. Few home-grown youngsters had come through the ranks. Two who did were left-handed batsmen Brian Rose and Peter Denning, though neither enjoyed a smooth transition into the first team. Rose, from Weston, had had the benefit of going to the local grammar school but his progress was disrupted by spending three years in further education in London. Denning, a dazzling fielder, was a butcher's son from Chewton Mendip.

Graham Burgess, who played for the county from 1963 to 1979 before becoming a coach at Monmouth School, remembers coming across Botham in the indoor school at Taunton at a time when the county's professionals were required to coach local boys for two weeks before each season. 'I should think he was nine years old,' Burgess said. 'I didn't see him again until he was in his early teens and don't know how much coaching he had had. I wouldn't say Bill Andrews wasn't a fan. He said to me, "This boy can bat a bit." He was a very natural player on the leg side. The thing that stood out was his self-confidence. Ian was not a class batsman or bowler but he had something about him. He backed himself. He was a ferocious hitter.'

By thirteen, Botham's efforts for his school team had earned

him selection for Somerset under-15s. In a match against Wiltshire – hardly the strongest of cricketing counties – he rescued his
side from a bad start to score a match-winning eighty, a performance that earned him a write-up in the local newspaper. Chris
Twort, who helped organise schools cricket in the area, remembered the game. 'The first couple of wickets had fallen cheaply and
he was told to play himself in but he was out about twenty minutes before lunch for eighty. He just whacked it. He was only
thirteen, which was a bit unusual, but he was still one of the bigger
lads and did not look out of place among fourteen- and fifteen-
year-olds. He played for the under-15s for three years before
moving on to Bill Andrews' youth team. He rarely bowled. His
bowling was considered a bit of a joke and it contributed to him
never being made captain. Phil Slocombe was captain.'

A year later, Botham was chosen to play for the West in a
regional festival in Liverpool, the precursor of the highly regarded
Bunbury national under-15 tournament run by David English.
There, in a match against the North, he rather confounded his
reputation as a joke bowler by taking a clutch of wickets in circumstances that varied according to who was giving the account.
Botham claimed he took seven wickets bowling to carefully laid
plans, others said his haul was five wickets and owed much to luck
and a dodgy pitch. His father's memory was that he took six wickets. Botham's view was certainly coloured by the fact that even
after this effort he was not chosen for a combined English Schools
Cricket Association team – effectively a state schools team – to
take on a Public Schools XI in the festival's grand finale.

Ironically, ESCA had been set up in part to provide working-
class talent with greater opportunities and Botham and his father,
who had accompanied him to Liverpool, sought out the festival
organisers to ask why Ian had not made the XI. Botham said they
were told that he was considered a batsman rather than bowler,
and asked if he would act as 'thirteenth man'; his father promptly
declined and took his son off home. Botham suspected that they
did not pick him because he was a yokel from the Southwest and

the selectors had already decided to choose someone who just happened to come from the Home Counties. His suspicions were reinforced when he learned that Graham Stevenson, from Yorkshire, and Paul Romaines, who hailed from the Northeast, had also failed to make the combined team.

As with his mates on the Lord's groundstaff, Botham was to develop a lasting kinship with Stevenson and Romaines through this shared disappointment. Years later, he was to play a big part in Romaines reviving his career with Gloucestershire by putting in a word with David Graveney.

To add to Botham's sense of grievance, two other young Somerset cricketers, Vic Marks and Peter Roebuck, were chosen for the public schools team and posted a big stand for the first wicket. At the time, Roebuck knew more of Botham than Marks did. 'He was a handful,' Roebuck said. 'He had something different, if not necessarily special. It was a surprise that he wasn't picked for ESCA, particularly when we heard he'd got wickets in a warm-up game. Then we gathered he had got them luckily, bowling all over the place. That was a familiar tale.' Marks said he couldn't remember having coming across Botham at this point – he was playing most of his cricket at Blundell's – and was only later made aware that, as he put it, '"Both" had packed his bags in disgust, leaving Pete and I free to play our cover drives without him.'

Botham did not give up and nor did his father. The following spring, Botham was back for more pre-season coaching from the Somerset professionals, this time at Millfield. According to Cartwright, it was during this session that he first noticed Botham – not that he then knew his name – among a group being instructed how to drive tennis balls. Cartwright was impressed by how well this big lad's arms worked together and he asked Andrews who he was. Andrews dismissed Botham as an unimportant lad 'from the sticks' and encouraged Cartwright instead to take a look at Slocombe – who was very much a 'coached' player – from Weston. A few weeks after that, Somerset for the first time played at Yeovil – on the Westland Sports Ground no less – and Les Botham took the opportunity to take Ian along and seek out Jimmy James, the Somerset secretary, to whom he announced: 'This is my son Ian and he wants to play cricket for Somerset and England.' Les Botham may have been a mild-mannered man but in this instance he displayed the kind of belligerence for which his son would become famous.

Their perseverance paid dividends. With Botham leaving school that summer, Roy Kerslake suggested to the Bothams that Ian be sent up to the MCC groundstaff. In the circumstances, it was all the county could offer an enthusiastic youngster who was not yet ready for county cricket, if indeed he ever would be. Despite his blunt words to Jimmy James, Les Botham was actually far from convinced that his son's dreams of playing for Somerset, let alone England, could be realised, and he needed some persuading to agree to Kerslake's plan. Perhaps he remembered how he himself had decided against pursuing football as a career. 'Les was insisting that Ian had to go into an apprenticeship,' recalled Tom Cartwright. 'So I joined in and said that he possibly had a brilliant future. I often wonder, had Roy not been so insistent, if Ian would have finished up as a plumber or an electrician.'

A crucial thing happened while Botham was at Lord's. In 1972, Somerset decided to abandon its recruitment policy and opted to develop its own talent. Buying in players, even on Somerset's hard-bitten terms, was proving too expensive. 'We were operating on a shoestring and it was a struggle to balance the books,' Kerslake said. 'So we tried to recruit our own. Rightly or wrongly, it was cheaper than bringing people in from outside.' In April of that year, Jimmy James met Cartwright at the Star hotel in Wells and offered him the post of player-coach. Bill Andrews was removed and Cartwright spent the winter overhauling the dilapidated youth system.

It was at this point that Cartwright first helped Botham with his bowling, the start of a process that ultimately led to Botham becoming the world's most dangerous swing bowler. Cartwright,

who understood the mechanics of bowling as well as anyone, got
Botham to shorten his run-up and use his body more than his
arms in delivery. Not that Cartwright's methods, built on relent-
less accuracy, were ever really replicated by Botham, who drew
batsmen into mistakes with balls of varying lines and lengths. But
a talent they did share was making the ball swing, a knack
Cartwright had not discovered himself until he was twenty-four.
Of his coaching sessions with Botham, Cartwright said: 'He might
not be the brightest in some ways but I found him not only a willing pupil but an ideal one, and he learned to swing the ball both
ways as quickly as anyone.' In this instance, Botham's desire to
learn overrode his dislike of practice.

Although Botham was of more Conservative bent, his anti-
Establishment tendencies may have been encouraged by
Cartwright, who came from a staunchly Labour family and was
not afraid to speak out in demand of better pay and conditions,
even though he came to learn that fellow players who grumbled
about their treatment were rarely bold enough to back him up. He
finished his days at both Warwickshire and Somerset wrangling
with the committees. He was a fierce supporter of the anti-
apartheid movement and it was his withdrawal from the 1968
tour of South Africa that led to Basil d'Oliveira's incendiary call-
up. Cartwright insisted that he was genuinely unfit to tour but
admitted he was disturbed when he heard news of cheering in the
South African parliament when d'Oliveira was omitted from the
original tour squad. Nor did MCC's eagerness for him to declare
himself fit to tour (and thereby prevent the need for d'Oliveira to
take his place) make him any less uncomfortable.

Like Botham, Cartwright was inspired to play well at the cricket
Establishment's home of Lord's, but he was more mindful than
Botham of its traditions. Once, he attended a lunch at Lord's
during Botham's time as England captain and was shocked to see
Botham not wearing a tie. 'No one said anything but I couldn't
stand it,' Cartwright recalled. 'I really gave him hell.'

Peter Roebuck, who entered the Somerset first team in the same season as Botham, said that the special chemistry created by Cartwright and Close was vital. 'Botham was very lucky, we all were, in having the combination of Close and Cartwright – the technical analyst in Cartwright and the determined never-say-die character of Close. You wouldn't have wanted a hundred per cent of one, and none of the other, for they had failings, Close with his reckless gambles on the field, and Tom with the fact that everything was rational and he wasn't a warm-hearted person.'

At the end of 1973, Somerset, prompted by the stick of financial constraints and the carrot of the young talent they found at their disposal, took the plunge. They set aside £6,000 to pay for six youngsters. Five were locals. There was Botham from Yeovil, a big off-spinner from Weston called John Hook of whom little more would be heard and three young men from private schools, Peter Roebuck and Phil Slocombe from Millfield and Vic Marks from Blundell's. The sixth player was a shy, poor and withdrawn young West Indian batsman called Vivian Richards, who had been playing club cricket in Bath.

This was a bold investment that would have far-reaching consequences. It created the base for several years of success in one-day cricket but also sowed the seeds of grave trouble beyond that.

Given their diverse backgrounds, the dynamics among this group were tricky. Botham naturally gravitated towards Richards as one who had also not gone to public school, although he was to be quite close to Roebuck for several years before a spectacular falling-out. The person he took strongest exception to was Slocombe, who he felt had under-bowled him when they had played together in youth matches. He also felt that Slocombe had acquired a superiority complex after switching from Weston Grammar School to Millfield. It was a view shared by others. 'He [Botham] didn't like Slocombe,' Marks recalled. 'He thought he was "up" himself. Slocombe was a good-looking batsman and good fielder. We all called him "Sir Leonard". He wasn't that obnoxious, but "Both" didn't like him, Tom Cartwright didn't like him and Pete [Roebuck] couldn't stand him.'

Botham's relationship with Slocombe took a decisive turn for the worse at an early stage. One day, in front of team-mates, Slocombe upbraided Botham as 'ignorant'. Roebuck, who was present, described the incident as the start of Botham's 'most bitter, most lasting argument at Somerset' (Roebuck was writing shortly before his own relations with Botham nose-dived). In Roebuck's view, the fault was all Slocombe's. 'When we first joined Somerset, we used to change in the back room of the old pavilion at Taunton. It was a little store-room really. Ian was making some rough and ready jocular remarks, telling some tall story or other. His language may have been a bit colourful. Slocombe called him ignorant and I knew it was a mistake. It touched a sensitive point in Ian's character. It was the fear of rejection by the Establishment, the fear of being cast as an ignoramus. Slocombe crossed a line. There was a vulnerability about Ian, and some of us felt protective of him, and Slocombe didn't seem to sense that. Moving to Millfield had affected him. He began to have airs and graces, which Botham didn't appreciate. There was a tension between them. I thought Slocombe was insensitive.'

The Slocombe incident may explain a curious claim by Botham that he deliberately acted 'as the dumb country yokel' after joining Somerset's first team. He said he reckoned that by presenting himself as 'a thick hick from the sticks', he would be no threat to anyone and could get on with working on his game without attracting attention. 'While everyone else was deep in discussion and argument, I could just concentrate on playing cricket and having a beer or two afterwards,' he said.

Cartwright felt that the educational privileges enjoyed by Roebuck, Slocombe and Marks made it difficult for Botham to mix socially. 'It wasn't as easy for Ian as people think . . . He didn't make a fuss about it, didn't let it show, but I have always felt that people didn't really understand how somebody from his background had to push and struggle against the others from different backgrounds,' Cartwright said. 'His [background] was a very ordinary one compared with some of the people he was competing with.'

Not that Roebuck, Slocombe and Marks played much for Somerset at first. Roebuck and Marks were on their way to Cambridge and Oxford respectively and spent much of the 1974 season helping out on the groundstaff. Roebuck played twice while Marks and Slocombe did not make their championship debuts until 1975. Roebuck said that Marks and himself were paid £15 per week, and thought Botham might have been on £20 and Richards on £25. Marks remembered the low wages, but did not particularly care. 'It never crossed our minds not to do it. For Pete and me, it was a nice gap-year thing to do. Money was not a particular consideration. "Both" wouldn't have had any other option but sport; he was always going to try that. So there was really no debate. I know there were those who fretted about their next contract but I don't remember us worrying much. Cricket was in our blood.'

# 3

## Life-force

'He was very vociferous, Ian. He was only a kid and Closey were captain and Close is setting the field and changing the bowling and he were at him, Botham – "What you doing that for? Why you doing this?" At him all the time. Closey was bowling and we were knocking the ball around easy, and Botham's throwing his hands up and he said to Closey: "What you bowling for?"'

DAVID LLOYD, OF LANCASHIRE, ON PLAYING
AGAINST BOTHAM IN 1976

Against all expectations except his own, Botham was playing for England within three years of his county debut. During much of that time he continued to be underestimated by good judges, but what they did not know, what they could not know, was the depths to which his determination ran and the talent that lay within. Whether or not his indignation was justified after his treatment at Liverpool and Lord's, he expected no favours and thrust himself into competition and confrontation with opponents and team-mates alike. They may have been more experienced men, even better cricketers, but he was not satisfied until he had got the better of them.

Ruthlessly ambitious though he was, even Botham would not

have dared view himself as a future rival to the best all-rounders of the day such as Gary Sobers, who was knighted in 1975, Mike Procter and Tony Greig. Indeed, there were setbacks that made him doubt he would ever get anywhere in the game. While out on a training run in the winter of 1974, he was overcome by a tightening of the chest; it transpired he was afflicted with asthma and subsequently needed an inhaler to deal with it. An early concern was looking better in comparison to Somerset team-mates such as Phil Slocombe, whom he didn't rate, and Viv Richards, whom he did. He was furious when Slocombe was chosen ahead of him for MCC against the Australians in 1975 – it was Slocombe's first full season in county cricket and Botham's second – and for MCC versus the champion county the following summer. Even Botham had to admit that Richards, with whom he immediately became firm friends (and rivals), was the best new player in the Somerset team, and clearly intent on going places himself.

And then there was Brian Close and Tom Cartwright, neither of whom had played as often for England as they ought to have done. Botham intended to bat as bravely as Close and bowl as tirelessly as Cartwright – but for country first and county second.

As he was made to wait for recognition, Botham's impatience grew. He hated hearing that he was too young and inexperienced. As far as he was concerned, if he was good enough he was old enough. He was convinced that he was better than some players who he saw preferred to him. He suspected, too, that his background counted against him. Few cricketers travelled so far on a sense of indignation.

Not everyone saw things as he did. Graham Burgess, one of the elders in the Somerset team, liked the young Botham but feared that he might not be going about things the best way. He saw a lot of drinking and horseplay. One day Burgess tried to tell him as much. 'One of our watering holes was the Gardener's Arms in Taunton, past the station,' Burgess recalled. 'Ian could drink and smoke quite well. He was the first at the bar and would be there on the card table. I remember saying to him once, it was probably his first season on the staff, "You don't think you'll make the grade, then, carrying on the way you do?" "Yes I will," he said. "And I'll do well." And he wasn't talking about Somerset but England. When I said "make the grade", I had meant county cricket, not international cricket. He was cocky, never down in the dumps. And that is half the battle. Some of the older pros thought: "Who is this bloke?" No one realised how good he was, not until he played Test cricket. He kept working.'

Jim Laws, a friend of Botham's who ran a betting shop, confirmed Botham's capacity for drink and late nights. Often they ended up in the 88400 Club in Taunton. 'I'd hear someone say, "I see Big Head's in,"' Laws said. 'Ian would ignore it but after a while go and sort them out. If he hadn't got married when he did, I reckon he would have been inside.'

Vic Marks, who once described Botham as 'a hooligan in the nicest sense of the word', agreed that there was a disparity between Botham's view of himself and how team-mates saw him. 'I suspect that without us recognising it, we regarded him as a lovable buffoon who was clearly talented, and larger than life, but not a potential world-beater. Now whether "Both" ever thought that I don't know. It's quite possible that he would say that the foolery was a bit of an act, and he was more aware of how good he could be than he let on. If we were on twelfth-man duties, we always watched him. You'd peek out and see what he was going to do next. If it was his day, he could hit it miles ... But no one had any perception that "Both" would be something special, though he was mischievous and brave.'

Nor were opponents convinced. David Lloyd, who would later work alongside Botham as a TV commentator, remembered the Lancashire players discussing the relative merits of Somerset's young all-rounder and their own Bob Ratcliffe. Lloyd played in Botham's first-class debut at Taunton in 1974 in which Botham hit three boundaries before gifting his wicket and then bowling three unproductive overs. 'I always remember us comparing our Bob Ratcliffe to this lad from Somerset. They were both about the same sort of standard. Who's the better one? Bob had a sort of hop, skip and a jump bowling action, hit the seam on green pitches, and this other lad were a tear-arse, he just run in, and come in and give it a bit of a whack. We were debating that Bob was probably the better cricketer.'

When Lancashire and Somerset met two years later in 1976 – the year both Botham and Ratcliffe were awarded their county caps – their verdict hardly looked awry. Over four days at Weston-super-Mare, Ratcliffe's bowling was instrumental in Lancashire winning both the John Player League match and championship game, in which he took 7–67. He dismissed Botham each time.

And yet this championship match also provided evidence as to why Botham and not Ratcliffe was picked for England two weeks later in a one-day series against West Indies. Botham did not do much with bat or ball but Lloyd, in scoring a second-innings century that set up Lancashire's victory, saw at close quarters this bumptious youngster constantly demanding of Close to be 'in' the game. 'He was very vociferous, Ian,' Lloyd recalled. 'He was only a kid and Closey were captain and Close is setting the field and changing the bowling and he were at him, Botham – "What you doing that for? Why you doing this?" At him all the time. Closey was bowling and we were knocking the ball around easy, and Botham's throwing his hands up and he said to Closey: "What you bowling for?" "Because". That were it ... "Because". He wasn't short of a word.'

This was extraordinary behaviour because in the Somerset team Close's word was invariably final: most young players obeyed Close's instructions without question, and lived in constant fear of a dressing-down. In the field, they would tear a mark in the turf with their studs as insurance against Close, who forever tinkered with his field settings, accusing them of standing in the wrong place. 'We got moved every time we looked up,' said Peter Roebuck, 'so we kept our heads down and made a scratch in the ground so we could say to Closey, "Well, you wanted me here and this is the scratch." It was self-protection. We would never have dared challenge him.' Yet even at twenty, Botham was demanding explanations from his captain. There was no forelock-tugging from him. 'Botham wouldn't bother with any of that,' Roebuck added. 'He stood up to Closey.'

But Botham knew there was a line with Close which he could not cross. Even in his mid-forties, Close was an imposing figure, barrel-chested and utterly fearless. He was not physically intimidated by Botham's size and Tom Cartwright reckoned that this played its part in keeping Botham in check. Close naturally concurred. 'He [Botham] used to answer back and was a bit cocky, but I always had the last word. I just told him to bloody well shut his mouth.' It was from Close that Botham acquired the belief that a match was not over until the last ball had been bowled.

For all his pent-up fury at those he imagined were blocking his path, Botham played one-day international cricket for England by the age of twenty and Test cricket at twenty-one. He was fortunate that England were a struggling team, and desperate to unearth new players, but it was a striking achievement. Few had appeared for England at a younger age, although one who had was Close himself, which in itself carried a warning. First picked at eighteen, Close was chosen only once more before his twenty-fourth birthday.

Remarkably given his early experiences, it was Botham's bowling that was to prove his stronger suit at this time. His batting took longer to develop on pitches that were in those days still uncovered, and would be in county cricket until 1980. Although capable of cultured strokeplay, he could have been mistaken in his first two seasons for an entertaining tail-end hitter, failing far more often than he succeeded and making basic errors of judgement. Close started him out in the Somerset first team batting at seven, but as Botham's workload with the ball grew he more often found himself at eight, a position he still occupied at the start of 1976, his breakthrough summer with the bat. That year, pushed up the order on a regular basis to provide quick runs, his championship return rose above 900 and his average, which had hovered around seventeen in the previous two seasons, almost doubled. With sixty wickets as well, he was finally shaping as the all-rounder he had wanted to be.

His most celebrated innings before appearing for England, which came against Hampshire in a Benson and Hedges Cup quarterfinal in 1974, has to be seen in this context. Only selected because of a last-minute injury to fast bowler Allan Jones, Botham went in at number nine with Somerset 113–7 – soon 113–8 when Tom Cartwright was out – chasing 183 to win. Seventy were needed from fifteen overs. With the sun going down, it was a near-hopeless situation that gave Botham licence to chance his arm. No one was going to blame him if he got out. It was significant, too, that his batting partner was Hallam Moseley, a have-a-go hitter himself who in a similar situation against the same opponents the previous year had almost carried Somerset to victory.

Initially, the pair matched each other blow for blow, although against the hostile fast bowling of Andy Roberts – like his friend Viv Richards an Antiguan, and the fastest and most feared bowler in the world – both were largely content with straight-batted defence. It was only when they had raised the total beyond 150 – a process that took nine overs – that, in the words of Henry Blofeld in the *Guardian*, 'the realisation dawned all round the ground that it might just be more than a final despairing flourish.'

It was then that Roberts, striving for the knockout blow, bowled Botham a ferocious bouncer. Botham threw up a hand to protect his head and the ball deflected into his mouth, causing him to spit out blood and two broken teeth. After taking a glass of water, he waved away further help. As he was playing for a captain who never acknowledged physical pain – Close had himself once scored a century after losing four teeth – it was unsurprising that Botham opted to carry on. Close would have expected nothing else.

From this moment, Botham was emboldened to take the lead. Despite later suggestions that he took toll of Roberts, it was in fact the lesser bowlers he now targeted. In the next over, he swung

Mike Taylor over backward square leg for six and straight-drove him for four. Two overs after that, he hit Bob Herman over square leg and out of the ground. Moseley then fell lbw to Roberts, which brought in Bob Clapp with seven runs needed from sixteen balls. A scrambled three gave Botham the strike for the penultimate over from Herman and the chance to win the game before Roberts could take the last over. He played and missed three times before unfurling off the last ball a crisp cover drive to the boundary.

Mobbed as he left the field, the eighteen-year-old savoured the exhilaration of confounding the odds for the first time. For all the help he had received from the other tail-enders, it was he who had done it. Of the thirty-two runs that were scored after he had been hit by Roberts, Botham had contributed twenty-six of them. It was a revelatory moment for player, public and press – a glimpse for all of them of his future as a match-winner. County cup matches then aroused tremendous interest – there were 6,500 in the ground at Taunton that day – and Botham's youthful bravery against Roberts provided a compelling storyline, the first of many he would deliver. 'He lifted the game from a state of conventional excitement to one of unbelievable suspense and drama and finally into the realms of romantic fiction,' wrote Blofeld. Sought out by journalists afterwards, the teenager dragged on a small cigar and answered questions wearily but patiently.

Peter Roebuck, who was operating the scoreboard rather badly with Vic Marks, recalled the feverish mood. 'Those were the days before helmets, and there was Botham, a buccaneeringly brave character, just brushing off his blow. The others down the order . . . were a bit worried but there was no sign of that from Ian. He hooked and cut Roberts and played exceptionally well. Vic and I and plenty of others enjoyed his dare-devilry and broad humour. There was a life-force about him. He dared to do things others would not.' Graham Burgess concurred: 'He never turned his back on fast bowling.'

Botham may have been named man of the match for his two wickets and unbeaten forty-five but Somerset were still not sure they wanted him in their championship side. He played in their next three-day game against Yorkshire because Cartwright was injured but when Cartwright recovered Botham was left out once more.

Three weeks later, though, he scored an aggressive maiden fifty against Middlesex. 'He was quite an iffy batsman then,' said Middlesex's captain Mike Brearley, with whom Botham would later work so compellingly for England. 'He played very free off-side shots. I didn't realise how good a player he was because he always gave the bowler a chance. He was talented but loose.' Brearley's own development as a batsman had been hindered by him spending several years as a lecturer in Newcastle after leaving Cambridge but since becoming Middlesex captain in 1971 he had started to push himself towards England selection. Brearley was not the only older player taken aback at Botham's gung-ho approach with the bat. Norman Gifford, the Worcestershire and England left-arm spinner, walked down the pitch at New Road after Botham had slogged his first ball for four and said: 'You know you can't hit every ball for four, laddie.' Botham grinned back: 'I know, but I can bloody well try.'

Perhaps it was significant that another important innings in his development came against Tony Greig. Botham's eagerness to do well against England's star all-rounder had perhaps contributed to a string of failures against Greig's bowling but at Hove in May 1976, with Greig now England captain, Botham played his most mature innings to date – mature at least until he was out for 97 trying for the boundary that would have given him his first century. He took particular toll of Greig's bowling and his runs ensured Somerset escaped with a draw. Derek Randall, who played alongside Greig and Botham for England, said that they developed a definite rivalry: 'They were both very competitive. It was all-on between them.'

This performance earned Botham promotion and for much of the second half of 1976 he batted at five and sometimes even at four in the championship. Whereas when he had occasionally batted at six the previous year he had failed, he now showed better discipline in building an innings, even if many of his efforts eventually subsided in overambition. These did not go down well with Close. After Botham had lost his wicket at a delicate juncture of a home defeat to Yorkshire there was a ferocious row between them, even though Close was not actually playing in the game. Roebuck recalled: 'Ian got out in a stupid way but he had made runs and couldn't understand why Close was blaming him. "How many did the rest of them score?" he asked. That was a typical Botham response. But afterwards they probably had a whisky and a beer together. There wasn't animosity between them, but there were explosions.'

As Close may have suspected, Botham was on the cusp of very good things if only he could retain control. In the next match against Hampshire he returned career-best figures of six wickets for sixteen runs and in the game after that at Trent Bridge not only achieved his maiden century but carried Somerset home in a stiff chase against the clock. The pitch was a beauty for batting, Nottinghamshire's Clive Rice was unfit to bowl, and Botham was dropped early on, but his batting touched new heights as he saw the job through with an unbeaten 167, having scored a sparkling 80 in the first innings. Close spent the tea break on the final day imploring Botham not to mess up. 'I kept telling him to keep his mind on what he was doing.'

Randall, who himself scored a double-century for Nottinghamshire in this game, described it as a 'fantastic' innings, while Rice said: 'I told everyone there and then that he should play for England that summer. It was a phenomenal innings from one so young.'

Full of promise it may have been, but such an innings would be a rarity for Botham, who would only once again score so many in a championship innings. Brian Rose, who had started playing regularly for Somerset the previous year and would take over from Brian Close as captain in 1978, felt that Botham's style of batting was defined by his workload as an all-rounder. 'He had this fantastic ability with the bat,' he said. 'He had a good technique, playing forward for example, and always took on bowlers if they bowled short, but opening the bowling for Somerset and the amount of overs he bowled for England had a detrimental effect. But he enjoyed being asked to make a quick eighty rather than bat for six hours and, to be honest, Somerset usually wanted him to play shots. There was myself, Dasher [Denning], Roebuck and Viv [Richards] in front of him, so we usually got quite a lot of runs. We didn't need a stoic player blocking it at number six.'

Botham's bowling was, then, his stronger suit. By the time of his first one-day games for England, he had taken more than 150 first-class wickets, including twelve hauls of four wickets or more. He was raw and prone to over-aggression but finished as Somerset's leading championship wicket-taker in 1975 and 1976, in the second year as Hallam Moseley's regular new-ball partner. He no doubt delighted at what Len Muncer and those 'Home Counties' schools selectors would have made of it as they surveyed the county scoreboards in their morning newspapers. He probably didn't stop to consider, as they might have done, how many of his victims had succumbed through not taking his bowling seriously enough.

It had taken time for Brian Close to take Botham's bowling seriously. At first, Close was prepared to give him plenty of overs in one-day cricket but used him only sparingly in the championship. Botham was often expected to bowl in the style of Tom Cartwright, the man he was understudying, and it was a style he would occasionally adopt in later years when containment was required. 'My little Tom Cartwrights,' he would call his medium-pacers. Nor did they do badly for him in one-day cricket, although the sight of wicketkeeper Derek Taylor standing up to the stumps – as he did for Cartwright – rather than fifteen yards back probably offended Botham's pride.

Botham's first chance to bowl a decent number of overs in first-class cricket came against the Pakistanis at Bath ten days after his batting heroics in the Benson and Hedges Cup quarter-final in

1974. Promoted to open the attack with the uncomplaining, hard-working Moseley, he took the wicket of Shafiq Ahmed with his very first ball – the sort of dramatic notice-me moment for which he would become famous. He had a very decent game as he also took an exceptional catch to dismiss Asif Iqbal, a diving effort in the deep, and batted pugnaciously for 32, nearly taking Somerset home as they chased 320. They fell just five runs short. However, two days later his costly bowling contributed to a heavy defeat to Leicestershire in the Benson and Hedges Cup semi-final, a sting-ing defeat for Close at the hands of his friend and rival Ray Illingworth.

Graham Gooch, who would play Roundhead to Botham's Cavalier towards the end of their careers, was struck by the gen-tility of Botham's bowling when he took the field against him for the first time just after this. 'He swung the ball at old-fashioned English military-medium pace,' Gooch recalled.

By the time Botham was into his ninth first-class game, he had the grand total of two wickets to his name, but things now started to turn in his favour. With Cartwright sidelined for two months, his work increased, and two late wickets helped seal an innings win over Glamorgan at Swansea. In the next game against Notts he claimed three wickets for the first time, though his efforts went largely unnoticed amid an accomplished all-rounder performance from Gary Sobers.

A week later, Botham claimed his first five-for as the Benson and Hedges Cup defeat by Leicestershire was avenged in the championship on a damp green seamer at Weston-super-Mare where he got through more than fifty overs in the game. It was just the sort of match for which Weston was – and Botham would become – famous. 'Weston was just a public park,' Peter Robinson recalled. 'Somerset thought the council were looking after it, the council thought the club were looking after it. The grass had to be cut with a scythe. But no one minded. The bowlers liked it. It got them away from the flat wickets at Taunton. You never knew what sort of wicket to expect. Some were horrendous.' Botham was Somerset's leading wicket-taker in the game but also their most expensive as the wilier Moseley, Burgess and Brian Langford gave away nothing. It was perhaps their miserliness that encouraged the batsmen to go after Botham with results that would become all too familiar.

Crucially, by 1975 Botham was stronger than he had ever been, partly as a result of him spending the winter working as a labourer. He had never been reluctant to bowl fast but the difference now was that Close was ready to let him. Close had noticed that even in his first season Botham had possessed the ability to bowl the occasional quick ball and this was even more the case now. 'As his strength grew – and he was a strong lad in any case – he gained a fair bit of pace,' Close said. 'He could bowl within himself and keep pulling out a quick one as something different. And he was strong enough to bowl a bouncer, which helped a lot because it stopped people going onto the front foot. Almost every game he played he improved.' It was Close rather than Cartwright who was the prime mover in Botham lengthening his run and bowling faster, even if it was Cartwright and Burgess who helped him master an inswinger to go with his natural outswinger. And the change worked: Botham became a regular wicket-taker and Close sometimes even gave him the new ball, with which he dismissed two of the best opening batsmen in the country, Yorkshire's Geoff Boycott and Alan Jones of Glamorgan.

Having rarely played alongside Botham before 1975, Brian Rose was struck by the speed of his bowling this year. 'He [Botham] made an instant impact with me with his bowling. People forget that apart from swinging the ball he was quite quick and could be quite nasty. He made batsmen jump. I don't think he ever got much lighter but he got stronger – strong in the legs, strong in the chest – and once Tom Cartwright had got him to get his shoulder round more in his action he started really swinging the ball – and bowling quicker.' Botham's pace and blatantly aggressive demeanour began to take batsmen aback; some froze, others played untypically reckless strokes.

He continued to be an effective bowler for much of 1976 even as his batting blossomed. With Somerset having parted ways with Allan Jones, a flighty, temperamental but gifted fast bowler who tested Close's patience to destruction, Botham to his relish started to open the bowling on a regular basis. He got through more than fifty overs in three of his first five championship games – gathering eight wickets against Glamorgan and eleven against Gloucestershire – but was sometimes irrationally keen on banging the ball in short. *Wisden* voiced its disapproval by stating that 'his bowling gathered in accuracy and experience perhaps a little more slowly than might have been hoped'. But Botham was unfazed. 'He had never been the most accurate bowler but once he got quicker accuracy didn't matter so much,' Burgess said. 'If he bowled a bad ball, it didn't worry him.'

The workload took its toll in this heatwave summer and, as his batting came to the fore, he was sometimes spared the job of opening the bowling. But he was no less of a force for it: coming on first change at Bournemouth in late July, he tore out six Hampshire wickets for ten runs in nine overs. His swinging pace was not only too much for the batsmen but also one of his fielders, Vic Marks, who put down three catches in the slips in only his second game since arriving from Oxford. One of the drops occurred in an over in which Botham claimed four wickets, including that of Barry Richards. Brian Rose described it as one of the finest overs he ever saw. 'Every ball was different ... three outswingers, one short and sharp into the ribs, and two inswingers.'

Before he played for England, some of the most intense games Botham played in were those between Somerset and near-neighbours Gloucestershire. These local derbies were usually played over Bank Holiday weekends in front of capacity crowds, and with plenty of friendly – and sometimes not-so-friendly – rivalry they were right up Botham's street. These matches tended to go emphatically one way or the other but in the mid-70s the dominant player was often Gloucestershire's star all-rounder Mike

Procter, a whirligig fast bowler and destroyer with the bat of anything other than very quick bowling.

David Graveney played for Gloucestershire against Botham many times before becoming the first cricketer to represent both counties, a switch of allegiance that did not go down well in some quarters, with Bristol gatemen still giving him a frosty reception long after he had stopped playing and become chairman of England selectors. 'There was always an undercurrent between Gloucestershire and Somerset,' Graveney recalled. 'A lot of it centred on Bristol – with Bristol Rovers, Gloucestershire and Bristol rugby club all north of the river and aligned together, and Bristol City, Somerset and Bath rugby club all south of the river. Somerset even used to play some home games in Bristol. There was never really love lost between different parts of the city. "Both" spent quite a lot of time in Bristol. He had friends there and he and I had quite a lot of common friends. Bristol and the surrounding area isn't that big. "Both" and "Procky" became good friends too, and "Both" liked to take on friends on the field. They had similar lifestyles. They enjoyed a beer after the game.'

Gloucestershire matches were guaranteed to bring out Botham's competitive spirit and his terrific effort with the ball in the May Bank Holiday match of 1976 at Taunton gave another early indication of his heroic potential. Operating in favourable bowling conditions, he wrecked Gloucestershire's first innings with a return of 6–25 spread over the first evening and second morning. Holding a lead of 254, Close opted to enforce the follow-on but with Bob Clapp and Graham Burgess both injured Somerset's remaining bowlers found life hard. Botham carried the attack for the rest of the second day, sending down a staggering thirty-seven overs by stumps and eventually finishing with five more wickets. But Gloucestershire had got themselves 118 in front and it was a lead they managed to defend by eight runs thanks to Procter taking six wickets with off-breaks bowled at express pace. Procter remembers bouncing out Derek Taylor with one and Botham, much to his mortification, was bowled by another for three.

Amazingly, when Procter began his carnage Somerset had needed only twenty-two more to win.

He had provided Botham with object lessons in two things: the old Close mantra of never giving up until the last ball was bowled, and never being afraid to try something different with the ball. Botham took good notice on both counts.

Botham's overall development was helped by him playing for a county that was finally going places. Under Close's fierce, slightly unhinged leadership, a team of seasoned pros and gifted young-sters was melding into a mercurial force, one that provided direction to Botham's competitiveness and talent. No game was to be wasted, and few were.

Botham's striking progress was a feather in the cap of Close, who gained a reputation at Somerset, as he had at Yorkshire, of being severe in his handling of young players. When Botham and the other new boys arrived in 1974 they were initially made to change in the Taunton pavilion in what Marks described as 'a poky little shit-hole' at the back of the old dressing-room, but evidence of this kind of divide between capped and uncapped players was not confined to Somerset; it was standard around all the counties.

Close occasionally handed out rollickings – Botham received one in his first season for nearly messing up a routine run-out in a Gillette Cup quarterfinal – but he quickly moved on. His habit of wondering aloud whether a young player's mistakes had cost the team the match – a fate Viv Richards endured – may have had more of a detrimental effect. But Allan Jones's departure for Middlesex, where he would find the more rational guidance from Brearley, was not an example others followed. 'He does chase the young pros but it is right that he should,' Peter Denning once said of Close. 'Brian is very much part of the team, socially after the game. He has a real sense of humour and we have a good atmos-phere in the dressing room.'

Close often drove Botham and Richards to and from Somerset's away matches – invariably at impatient speed – and the conversa-tion formed a vital part of their education. 'We talked about what had happened in that particular match, how things had worked, things you'd done wrong, things you did right, how players played,' Close said. 'That's half the battle when you're trying to win matches, knowing how the other side play. And he [Botham] caught on very quickly. He was a good listener. We got on like a house on fire. I was pleased with the positiveness of his play. He was always trying things. I don't know if we were similar characters but we both went onto the field to try to win.'

Vic Marks dismissed the suggestion that Close was something of a tartar. 'There was a perception that he was hard on the youngsters but I'm not sure it was true. It was a bit of a myth. He was not a bully. Talk to "Both" or Viv now and they just think the world of him. I remember a sweet story about how in 1976, when Viv was playing for West Indies and Close for England, and Close was getting a battering from Andy Roberts and Michael Holding at Old Trafford, Viv was fielding close in and whispering to him, "You all right, captain?! You all right?!" Close just growled. Viv was quite concerned about him. I reckon it was actually the old lags at Somerset, those set in their ways, who found the advent of Close more difficult. Close was actually harder on them than he was on the youngsters. Not that the likes of Merv [Kitchen] and Budgie [Burgess] were obstructive but Close and Cartwright couldn't have given a toss about protecting them because they were quite excited by the youngsters, Viv especially.'

Towards the end of his reign, friction undoubtedly grew between Close and the Somerset committee, but his dynamic captaincy laid the foundations for the club's later success under Rose. Although he failed to lead them to a first trophy, Close took them near on several occasions – frequently enough, in fact, that it was suspected that his demands might have been adding unnecessarily to the pressure. In the championship the county performed respectably enough – 1975 aside, when they went two months without a win – without ever being in serious contention for the title, but in all three one-day competitions they looked like potential winners at one time or another, an ironic situation given

Close's sniffiness towards a brand of the game that he thought too formulaic. Somerset were losing semi-finalists in the Benson and Hedges Cup in 1974 and the Gillette Cup in 1974 and 1977, but their most agonising failures came in the John Player League. Had they won a game with Leicestershire that was ruined by bad weather they would have been champions in 1974 and two years later, amid high drama in Cardiff, they were beaten in their final fixture by one run when a tie would have been enough to give them the title.

The team's support grew, further galvanising the players and boosting the club's faltering finances. 'We built up a good following,' Roy Kerslake recalled. 'We started to have coach-loads going everywhere. We were lucky. There was no other professional sport in or around Taunton. Yeovil football club was thirty miles away. Money started to come in that would help us build the main pavilion that is there today. It was a direct result of the success on the field.'

Vic Marks thought that the mutterings about Close's dictatorial style also reflected concerns among senior committee-men that the captain had become too powerful and was getting in the way of the future development of the side. This was a problem that would confront them again several years later when Botham was in charge. That was when they would really find out what player-power looked like.

If playing under such a restless force as Brian Close was one thing that lent focus to Botham's cricket, another was playing alongside Viv Richards. Richards was not only more gifted than Botham, he was also three years older and further along in his development. Within eighteen months of their first meeting, he was playing Test cricket for West Indies and scoring a century in his second game. By the time Botham himself was playing Test cricket, Richards was an established star on the world stage.

Their early friendship, forged in days before the wider public knew who they were, was deep and kept them close for many

years, but there should be no mistaking who was the senior partner. When they opposed each other on the field, Botham was
always striving to get the better of Richards, but rarely managed it.
Botham might have dismissed him in the occasional Test match or
one-day international, but Richards was simply too good to be
dominated by him or any other bowler. Their personal fortunes in
Tests between England and West Indies, and the results of those
matches, pointed to only one winner. Vic Marks believed Richards
always knew he held the upper hand. 'In their heart of hearts they
both knew that if there was a contest between them then Viv had
the advantage. Certainly deep down Viv knew that.' It was no
coincidence that Botham's first really good all-round season with
Somerset occurred in 1976 when Richards was absent with West
Indies.

In this sense, Botham's relationship with Richards was unique.
Botham set himself up in particular competition with friends and
rivals, and Richards was very much both of those, and yet in no
other instance did Botham come off second-best to quite the
extent he did with Richards, not even later with Imran Khan.

A significant element in the relationship was that Richards, like
Close, was not physically cowed by Botham. Richards was shorter
than him but powerfully built and armed with a short fuse and
pugilistic temperament. Tom Cartwright thought that Botham
needed someone he respected to occasionally grab him by the
collar and say, 'Look, stop', and Richards could and did do that.
He would say, 'Well then, big fellow. You want to fight?' And
Botham would think better of it. Botham said this was why they
never had a serious row. One of the fundamental reasons why
Botham's career hit trouble later was that few people were able to
stand up to him.

Richards himself felt that Botham turned himself into a force
through sheer guts as much as anything, plus a willingness to
ignore conventional thinking. 'He made himself into a great
player,' Richards said. 'What I saw back then [in their early days
at Somerset] was his determination. I saw it in that match against

Hampshire, in the way he stood up to Andy Roberts. Everyone was fearful of Andy Roberts then. I could see that here was a special character. Many county pros played as if they expected to fail. They were taught how to play, and were full of technical jargon, but no one wanted to watch them. Ian was different. He'd heard all the mumbo-jumbo and pleased himself what he wanted to do about it.'

Richards was inspired by Botham's confidence, just as he was inspired by Close's bravery. But neither Botham nor Close could outdo Richards for guts. Richards never wore a box protector until he came to England and never a helmet, even after protective headgear became commonplace. Botham could be recklessly brave but he wore a helmet against the West Indies pace attack. Richards was always an inspiration to Botham – especially when things were going wrong. 'He fills me with fresh courage,' Botham would say.

Richards was grateful to Botham for making him welcome in England at a time when others were not prepared to show him such warmth. The son of a prison warder from Antigua, then a little-known island at the eastern end of the Caribbean that had no history of producing cricketers, Richards was brought over by Somerset in the spring of 1973. It was a gamble. He had played two seasons of island cricket with modest results but it was rumoured that he was something out of the ordinary. Joining a first-team net session, he excited Tom Cartwright with how still he kept his head while batting. Cartwright wanted an overseas player who could grow with the team and Richards seemed to fit the bill.

'It would be good for him and good for us,' Cartwright said. 'I thought he'd stay around a long time and be loyal ... People say Viv was arrogant but it wasn't arrogance. He was seeking to impose his will on the people out on the field. That's what cricket is about ... Viv was the least arrogant person I've ever worked with. He was a smashing kid.'

Richards spent the summer of 1973 playing for the Lansdown club in Bath with a view to him joining Somerset the following year. It was a tough time in an alien environment but Botham extended the hand of friendship. Botham may have seen in Richards a fellow 'outsider'. Certainly, over the years they would share a mistrust of the Establishment, Richards for his part being made to wait by the West Indies board to inherit the captaincy from Clive Lloyd. For a time, Botham copied Richards' habit of wearing Rastafarian wristbands as a show of support for the 'underdog'.

They had played several county under-25 matches together in 1973, in the first of which Richards was out for nought and took five wickets with unknown off-breaks. After the game Botham, who had scored ninety-one, joked, 'From now on, I'll do the batting and you do the bowling.' Richards recalled: 'I was new in the country and he was the most receptive [person] I met. That is how we became friends.' Botham's naturally warm-hearted nature and experience of multicultural life on the Lord's groundstaff had made him as colour-blind in the racial sense as he was already visually.

By the time they had joined the Somerset staff in 1974, they were billeted together in a club flat in Greenway Road, Taunton, along with Dennis Breakwell, a nervous 25-year-old left-arm spinner who had joined the county from Northants following the breakdown of his marriage. Enjoying a second bachelorhood, and hardly being overworked by Close, Breakwell kept late hours. Life in the flat was chaotic and order was restored only by mercy missions to Botham's parents in Yeovil. 'We never paid the electricity and would play cards by candlelight,' said Breakwell, who now acts as groundsman at King's College, Taunton. 'Allan Jones lived in the flat upstairs. It was a bit of a dive. It had two bedrooms, lounge and kitchen, bathroom and toilet. Beefy had one bedroom. I shared the other with Viv. I was usually the first one up and the last one in. The first car Beefy ever drove was a Ford Granada, a great big tank of a thing. He reckoned he could drive from Taunton to Yeovil [about twenty-five miles] in nineteen minutes by the back lanes. God knows what would have happened if he'd met anything coming the other way.'

Richards remembered the trips to Yeovil as opportunities to drop off their laundry with 'Mama B' before Ian would take him out for the evening to meet his mates. 'He was like the local boy made good,' Richards said. 'He was like a great person . . . He was very outgoing.'

Richards soon realised that life with Botham and Breakwell was not necessarily conducive to playing good cricket and he said that before the end of that first season, 'alarm bells did begin to ring.' Asked if Botham ever did the cooking, Richards replied: 'Well, he brought in the liquid stuff . . .' Botham confessed later that it was after turning eighteen, which he did in November 1973, that he first tried marijuana at a party.

Richards had begun the 1974 season brilliantly, scoring a match-winning eighty-one not out in the opening Benson and Hedges Cup match at Swansea before taking seventy-four runs off Sussex in his second championship appearance and a breath-taking century off Gloucestershire in his third, taking the attack to Mike Procter in a manner few managed. Soon after that he contributed to championship wins over Kent, Yorkshire and Glamorgan. This was all before Botham had made any sort of mark in three-day cricket. 'Within a few weeks of the start of the season, Viv had people aghast,' Vic Marks recalled. '"What have we got here?" they were thinking . . . No one took "Both" as seriously as they did Viv and there was nowhere near the same expectation.'

The awarding of Richards' county cap was a formality but in the second half of the season his championship form fell away. 'Irregular sleep, I hate to admit, was gradually catching up on me,' he said. When he returned for the 1975 season, he tactfully pulled out of sharing home again with Botham and Breakwell and took lodgings with Hallam Moseley. He later rented a room from Roy Stevens, the Somerset secretary, before buying a flat on Galveston Hill in Taunton where Botham would later sometimes stay. Not that Richards became a paragon of virtue away from the Botham–Breakwell axis; later that year in Australia he took a rare direct hit on the head in a match against New South Wales after his reflexes had been dulled by a late night.

Botham and Breakwell, meanwhile, took a flat in St James's Street, Taunton, for the 1975 and 1976 seasons before Breakwell remarried. During the intervening winter Breakwell helped Botham decorate the cottage that was to be his first home with Kath. During this time too Breakwell introduced Botham to fishing, something that would become one of his greatest passions, taking him to Loch Lubnaig near Callender to bait his first worm. Breakwell had no idea then that Botham would become one of the world's most famous sportsmen. 'He was just my mate. If you'd asked me in 1974 if he'd go on and do the things he did I would have said no. Peter Willey at sixteen was the best young cricketer I'd seen and I never thought Beefy was in that class. He improved beyond all comprehension.'

Breakwell thought Botham and Richards were cut from different cloth. 'They had great respect for each other's abilities but were different guys,' he said. 'Viv was not a big drinker. I've seen Beefy challenged to drink three pints in one minute and do it. I don't think they always saw eye to eye, but there was always mutual respect.' Vic Marks agreed that it was partly a marriage of convenience: 'They were drawn together more than anything because of their stardom.' And once their playing days were over Richards and Botham went very different ways. Richards, the fundamentally more serious character, had Caribbean politics in his mind and was probably not keen to be linked too closely to the less judicious entries on his old friend's CV. 'There are a few scars,' said one Test cricketer who had played alongside both. 'They are not that close now. Viv always had the edge.'

Peter Roebuck felt Botham and Richards were both aiming for the top and intent on getting there. 'Viv, like Ian, had that sense of destiny, that refusal to step back, and that carried him along. Some orthodox thinkers thought he played across the line too much but the younger players at Somerset never underestimated him. They did not think Botham would become a legend of the game but they thought he would keep going upwards too. One of the first things that stood out about them was their out-fielding. They were both fine fielders.'

There was rivalry mixed in with the friendship from the start. 'They weren't experienced enough to help each other much, but they wanted to outdo each other,' Close remembered. 'They spent a lot of time together because they were two bright young lads, great lads. They were great pals but there was competition. It made each of them think, "What you can do, I can do better."'

The notion that Botham and Richards spent years together at Somerset as partners in destruction would be misleading and they were certainly not mutually dependent as performers. Indeed, their captains understood that it was best if they were kept apart so that Botham did not start trying to out-hit Richards. Richards usually batted at three or four and Botham, once established, anywhere from four to seven. 'It was rare for them to be at the crease at the same time,' said Brian Rose. 'This might have been because Roebuck batted for long periods and Viv was out before Ian came in. [When I was captain] I very rarely promoted him [Botham] because I tended to think it didn't work. It rarely does. They think they have to play differently. We used to have a very stable batting order.' Rose was adamant that on the few occasions Botham and Richards did bat together it certainly didn't affect the way Richards played. 'Viv wasn't bothered at all,' he said. 'I don't think it concerned him.' This was a view shared by Marks: 'The tendency was for Viv to play like Viv and for "Both" to play outrageous shots.'

Roebuck saw it as his job to stay in long enough to keep Richards and Botham apart. Of the two, he preferred batting with Richards: 'I never batted with anyone who tried as hard as Close but Viv was next. In his younger days, when he was "hot", he turned that sense of trying into a passion. You responded to it. It was one of the reasons it was easy batting with him. Botham wasn't like that. He was a swashbuckling partner. His innings tended to be happenings.' Others who batted with them agreed that

Richards exuded intensity but many found Botham's relaxed manner and fast-scoring ways a big help as it took the pressure off them. Even so, he shared surprisingly few large partnerships, which may support Roebuck's theory that his big innings were not constructed in conventional fashion but were self-contained 'happenings', one-man *tours de force*.

Botham and Richards did not in fact both score fifties as teammates until three years after first playing together, although interestingly before that they did each make half-centuries from opposing sides when Somerset played the West Indians in the early weeks of their 1976 tour. Having dismissed Richards for 51, Botham led an audacious counterattack after Somerset's top order had succumbed to Roberts and Wayne Daniel. He hit hard for 56 during a partnership of 69 with his captain Close, whose over-my-dead-body innings of 88 had clinched his own Test recall.

This was the game in which Botham had finally been awarded his county cap, two years after Richards but (as it would prove) two years ahead of the 'cleverer' of the county's 1974 signings, Slocombe, Roebuck and Marks. It has been suggested that Botham more or less demanded his cap. Certainly, as newlyweds, he and Kath were short of money and a county cap meant a doubling of his annual salary to £1,000. 'I've had to fight for everything I've got,' Botham would say later with regard to his early money struggles. 'We had nothing when we got married and if we spent twenty pounds we would worry about it.' Later, when money stopped being a concern, he became by his own admission quite irresponsible with his spending.

Viv Richards' avalanche of runs in the baking heat of 1976 inadvertently assisted Botham's promotion to international cricket. So superior were Clive Lloyd's West Indians that the England selectors were driven to give youth its head. At first, they had countered the speed and hostility of Roberts and Holding by calling on the experience of Mike Brearley, John Edrich and the ageless Brian

Close himself. They acquitted themselves reasonably well but the Test series was still lost 3–0.

With the Ashes also in Australian hands, it was time to try new faces and for three one-day internationals in late August the selectors called up the uncapped Graham Barlow, John Lever, Derek Randall and, by five years the youngest of the quartet, Botham. Graham Gooch, given a brief run the previous year, was recalled.

That Close was a trusted ally of England captain Tony Greig was a factor in Botham's inclusion, as were memories of how Botham had coped against Roberts two years earlier. Having recommended Botham's selection to Greig, Close naturally did not think the move premature. 'No, it wasn't a surprise that they picked him when they did,' he said. 'He had the ability to swing the ball both ways and batting-wise he wasn't frightened of anybody. When he had ducked into Andy Roberts' bouncer, he had sort of shrugged his shoulders and got ready for the next one ... That showed how tough he was.'

Nor did Botham give any sign of nerves when the new-look squad gathered at the team hotel in Scarborough the night before the first one-dayer. Pat Gibson, cricket correspondent of the *Daily Express*, noticed as much. 'He was already very full of himself and very comfortable with the other players,' he said. 'He seemed to know them all. They were in the bar the night before the game and he was totally relaxed about it. He was twenty years old.'

Relaxed or not, Botham's inexperience was to be exposed. He was suckered into hooking at the seventh ball he faced, a bouncer from Holding, who had heard on the cricketing grapevine that Botham always took on the short ball. Botham also bowled three expensive overs near the end of a game West Indies won at an insolent canter thanks to an unbeaten 119 from Richards. There was a revealing exchange between them when Richards reached his hundred off Botham's bowling. 'I went up to congratulate him and he smiled at me,' Botham said. '"Man," he said, "You go back there and bowl. I'm not playing for Somerset now. I'm playing for West Indies."' By now that little bit older, wiser and more savvy,

Richards had grasped what Botham had not, and would not ever fully, that their friendship had to be put on hold when they faced each other at international level.

Botham was left out of the second one-dayer at Lord's but played in the third in Birmingham without doing much of note as England slid to a third emphatic loss. Of the four new boys, he did the least. Barlow had scored eighty in the first game, Randall a sparkling eighty-eight in the second, while Lever had dismissed the mighty Richards for a duck in the third. All three were chosen for the winter tour of India. Botham was not. Like Close, it seemed, a first taste of international cricket was to be followed by a lengthy wait for a recall.

# 4

## The Greasy Pole

'If "Both" took against someone he would be unforgiving. It might be someone who had played for England and whom he didn't think was very good, or someone whom he thought was a bit up himself, or pleased with himself. There were people he would dismiss as useless players and he would never revise his opinion – and he would convey a bit of that scorn.'

MIKE BREARLEY, BOTHAM'S FIRST TEST CAPTAIN

The period between his omission from the tour of India and Australia in 1976–77 and the point at which he established himself in the England Test team in early 1978 was a tough one for Botham. Those who later imagined that his greatness as a cricketer was always assured, or that he was never prone to self-doubt, might consider this time more closely. During those eighteen months, Botham talked a good game, as he always would, but his outward confidence hid an inward anxiety that he might continue to be overlooked by England, and that the rejection might prove permanent. His hostility towards those who had not selected him, and those he perceived had been chosen in his place, was heartfelt and only thinly disguised. He was an angry young man.

He would frequently challenge Tony Greig about why he had not taken him to India. Greig was certainly the right man to ask, and the right man to blame, because although there was a panel of selectors chaired by Alec Bedser, Greig as England captain possessed the principal voice in which players took the field with him. 'Alec was a fantastic bloke,' Greig recalled. 'He asked me to come to meetings with my team in mind, and then hear them out if they felt strongly about something, but they wanted me to have the team I wanted. That was the way it worked and I had the casting vote, although one of the first things Alec said to me was that they didn't ever intend voting. It was a very civilised approach.'

Although Botham has claimed that he got 'the distinct impression' from Greig that he had done enough to be selected for India, and even that Greig told him to 'pack his bags', Greig is adamant that he had not wanted Botham. 'He would have been hopeless in India,' he said. 'I knew a bit about India and he had no idea. I've had this discussion with him on numerous occasions. I had learned a lot from Tony Lewis in '72 [when Lewis captained England in India] and we made some smart selections. When you go to India you had better believe that it is not a matter of running down the wicket and hitting people for six. I reined in my game totally. The only time I hit over the top was to spread the field. I took players who I thought were really good players of spin. We were up against one of the great spin attacks of all time. I even left Bob Taylor behind as reserve wicketkeeper and took Roger Tolchard instead and he played as a batsman and won us a Test match. Tolchard as a batsman was a much better selection than Taylor and better than Botham. Botham hadn't earned his stripes. He was just not a good player of spin at that stage. I'm not too sure he was ever a good player of spin. It was the same with David Steele. I thought he would be lunging forward and getting caught at bat-pad.'

Botham could hardly quibble at the selections of John Lever and Derek Randall as both had good tours, but he did not forget that Graham Barlow and Chris Old were chosen ahead of him.

Old's preferment was a more direct threat as Old was himself an all-rounder and several times over the next twelve months he was chosen ahead of Botham for Tests and one-day internationals. Botham's own relationship with Old was never warm and there were to be some uncomfortable incidents during the Yorkshire player's rare England appearances under Botham's captaincy. 'I don't think he [Botham] had the greatest admiration for Old,' Brearley conceded.

Brearley also knew that Botham's opinion of Barlow – a perky character who played alongside Brearley at Middlesex – was not flattering either. Barlow's England career proved short-lived – he was dropped after the first home Test of 1977 and never toured again – and this would only have confirmed in Botham's mind that Barlow should never have gone to India in the first place. Botham made a point of taking Barlow's wicket when they first faced each other in the 1977 season. 'If "Both" took against someone he would be unforgiving,' Brearley said. 'It might be someone who had played for England and whom he [Botham] didn't think was very good, or someone whom he thought was a bit up himself, or pleased with himself. There were people he'd dismiss as useless players and he would never revise his opinion – and he would convey a bit of that scorn.' Botham admitted he sulked at his omission from the tour and that Kath told him he was 'hell to live with'.

Instead, Botham was sent as one of four up-and-coming youngsters to play club cricket in Australia under a scholarship scheme organised by the TCCB and paid for by Whitbread, the brewers. Botham said later that the trip was of limited value but that may have been because he achieved little in terms of runs and wickets, and did not want to be there in the first place. He enjoyed himself socially but on the field operated on a short fuse.

While Mike Gatting and Bill Athey, batsmen at Middlesex and Yorkshire respectively, were sent to Balmain in Sydney, Botham and Yorkshire all-rounder Graham Stevenson were dispatched to University Cricket Club in Melbourne. Botham and Stevenson had known each other since their time together at the schools festival in Liverpool, and their paths had since crossed in county cricket. Stevenson was a talented cricketer – a swing bowler, hard-hitting batsman and strong fielder in the mould of Botham himself – but he was to lack the firm guidance at his county that Botham enjoyed. Too many people were happy for Stevenson to play the fool and he was to fail to fulfil his potential, although he was another of Botham's friends who would play for England during his time as captain. In Melbourne, Stevenson lodged with Frank Tyson, the former England fast bowler, in the suburb of Kew while Botham stayed in Doncaster East with the family of Geoff Miles, University's wicketkeeper, who was a similar age to Botham.

Melbourne was Botham's first taste of life overseas and, although a far cry from the intense demands of a Test tour of India, proved a tough enough trial. Melbourne district cricket was strong, with state and Test cricketers featuring regularly, and Botham and Stevenson were not automatic selections; wet weather further restricted their opportunities. Gatting and Athey played far more games over in Sydney. In the four matches Botham played he scored 44 runs and took five wickets at 58.4 apiece. Stevenson fared slightly better but they could not prevent University finishing bottom of the table with one win.

Botham felt one of the main benefits of his time in Australia was that it further sharpened his competitiveness. He was impressed by the loyalty to flag and country shown by Australians and reckoned some of that patriotic fervour – to an extent already inculcated in him by his parents – rubbed off and worked to his advantage when he returned home to a country where cynicism was rife.

As far as some of the Australians were concerned, Botham's competitive instincts were already honed enough. Tim Harms, a University team-mate and now a teacher in Adelaide, recalled: 'He was loudly proclaiming that he was going to knock the Aussies off when they toured England. You got the feeling he was on a bit of a mission and he absolutely believed that he was good enough to play against the Australians and do well. But quite frankly a lot of the guys thought he was full of bullshit.'

Botham and Stevenson arrived shortly after Christmas. Brushing off his jet lag, Botham – unlike Stevenson, who opted to rest – threw himself into his first game against Northcote on a fiercely hot day. The match did not go well but he impressed with his commitment. 'He got smashed a bit but the fact that he was strong enough to bowl ten overs in that heat so soon after his flight suggested he had a bit of spine,' Harms said. 'I was then involved in him being run out. He played the ball towards mid-wicket and called something but I wasn't sure what it was. It sounded like "No", so I hesitated and called "Wait", and he stopped. He was wearing runners [training shoes] and slipped. He tried to make his way back but was run out. He was pretty unhappy and when he got into the dressing-room – we had this beautiful old wooden dressing-room – he apparently launched his bat across the room. He never said anything to me, but it was probably my fault.'

Unflattering though Botham's record was, his talent was evident. He amazed team-mates with his ability to throw the ball prodigious distances and take catches standing a metre and a half in front of his fellow slips. Harms recalled University's visit to the Junction Oval to face St Kilda, whose side contained two promising young Victoria bowlers, Shaun Graf and Colin Thwaites. Botham and Stevenson sometimes trained with the Victoria squad and Botham surprised team-mates by announcing that Thwaites's leg-spin would not be a threat. He then backed up his words with deeds. '"Both" came in and just took to him [Thwaites],' Harms said. 'He scored thirty-odd and hit some magnificent inside-out cover drives. Graf banged it in short outside off stump and "Both" hit him through point too. You could see that he was talented.'

John Hendry was University's captain and coach and is now director of student welfare at Geelong Grammar School. He had more to do with Botham than anyone at University and was impressed by his ability to read the game. 'He was a very confident young man and strong willed, but quick to learn,' Hendry said. 'He was a good student of the game for a boy of his age.' Hendry remembered Botham's part in University's solitary victory. Things had got tense in the field, and words were being exchanged with the opposition batsmen, and Botham was briefly diverted from the task in hand. 'Then I noticed a sense of calm came over him as he recognised he had become distracted,' Hendry said. 'All of a sudden he composed himself and in two overs of bowling he turned the game round. He took control. It was inspiring.'

Unfortunately, Hendry found – as other captains would – that consistency was not Botham's strongest point. 'There were other times when he would be completely irrational and seem not to take any notice. There was an occasion when we came up against a spinner we had faced in the nets only a few days earlier. I was batting and Ian came out to join me. I said, "Now you saw this fellow the other day, what did you think?" And he said, "Oh, I can pan him." And he was out two balls later. But he was full of life and adventure and tried things that others wouldn't have been prepared to try. The game in those days was very orthodox and change wasn't something that was looked on favourably by those who controlled it.'

Botham and Stevenson's duties included coaching youngsters and during one session at Benalla, Botham was asked by a fifteen-year-old fast bowler called Merv Hughes whether he would advise him to take up a cricket career. Botham suggested he would do better in golf or tennis. 'There's more money in it,' he explained.

Towards the end of Botham's time with University occurred one of the most infamous, and hotly disputed, incidents of his career – what is commonly referred to as a 'bar-room brawl' with Ian Chappell, the former Australia captain. Chappell was thirty-three and had retired from international and state cricket the previous year; he was now captaining North Melbourne even though he had played most of his earlier cricket in South Australia.

Nearly all the 'facts' surrounding the incident are the subject of dispute or confusion but thanks to fresh research and the testimony of witnesses as well as the two central protagonists a clearer picture emerges. The incident was linked to an acrimonious match between University and North Melbourne played over two successive Saturdays in February in which both Chappell and Botham took part. When asked about this game, Botham thought he had missed it because of a shoulder injury, but in fact he did play, although not in very distinguished fashion. On the first Saturday, University scored 273, Botham opening the batting and scoring just three. The following weekend, North Melbourne overhauled this score easily, reaching 302–3 by the time the game ended to win by 29 runs on first innings.

Botham and Chappell crossed swords in the MCG bar next door to the Hilton hotel close to the Melbourne Cricket Ground on the night before the second Saturday of the game. Botham believes the incident occurred after he had been bowling at the Victoria state players in the MCG nets, and Chappell happened to be in the bar. Chappell says the argument arose out of Botham claiming that Chappell had sledged him during a Somerset–Australians match at Taunton, a claim Chappell rejected, pointing out that he had not played against Somerset for many years. This led them onto the relative strengths of English and Australian cricket and the exchange of threats about how they might fare against each other on the pitch the next day, specifically Chappell facing Botham's bowling, as indeed happened.

John Hendry, University's captain, believed that relations between Botham and Chappell were not improved by Chappell surviving a run-out appeal during his innings of thirty-eight, which ended when Stevenson dismissed him. Hendry recalls that the University players were incensed at the decision. 'It was an aggressive game played in a juvenile way,' Hendry recalled. 'He [Chappell] was lucky. If he had not been a former captain of Australia he would have been given out.' Botham's figures – 0–86 – suggest he did not bowl well. He was easily the most expensive bowler, but he may have been trying too hard to back up his words of the previous evening, when he had (according to Chappell) vowed to all but knock Chappell's head off. Chappell said that, for all the talk, Botham did not bowl any bouncers at him.

What may be relevant to Botham's version of the 'bar-room brawl' is what happened subsequently. Less than three weeks later, Botham and Stevenson joined up with the England squad that had arrived in Melbourne to play Australia in a one-off match to mark one hundred years of Test cricket. Gatting and Athey may have enjoyed better action in Sydney, but Botham and Stevenson now had the privilege of bowling at the England players in the nets and helping out around the dressing-room during a game watched by big crowds that included an imposing gathering of former greats from Australia and England. Botham was still annoyed that he was not actually a member of the tour party that had just won an historic series victory in India, and John Lever remembers Botham saying to him during that week, 'I should have been playing in this,' meaning the Centenary Test. Bob Willis said that while Stevenson behaved like the model junior pro, Botham showed neither shyness nor humility and was telling everyone how he would soon be playing for England. Willis did not take to him at all. Lever confirmed that it was at this point that the story about Ian Chappell surfaced. It is easy to imagine what the thrust of Botham's account to the England players might have been – that while you guys were tramping around India, I was thumping the man who masterminded Australia's victories in the last two Ashes series.

Botham thumping Chappell is certainly a common portrayal of what was understood to have happened. Over the years, versions of the incident have varied – Botham's books have sometimes even claimed that it took place during the Centenary Test itself, while he was 'drinking with players from both sides' (note the implied familiarity) – but the general thrust was always the same, that he had been provoked beyond endurance by some derogatory remarks about English cricket from Chappell. He had then 'flattened' Chappell, who went 'flying over a table and crash-landed in a group of Aussie Rules footballers, spilling their drinks in the process'.

However, Botham's claim that he punched Chappell has no supporting witnesses – certainly no one from the England and Australia teams. Chappell said merely that during a heated exchange in which they both rubbished each other, Botham had pushed Chappell backwards off his chair. Graham Stevenson backed this up: 'No, Beefy did not hit him. He just pushed him a bit. He was a big man, Beefy. Chappell was reading the newspaper and saying some critical things about English cricket and Beefy challenged him. There was a bit of shoving.' The England players would only have had to listen to Stevenson's version of the story – and surely they must have asked him about it – to suspect that Botham was gilding the lily. Lever confirmed as much: 'There was a clash with Chappell but I think a lot was made of it.'

When told that no witnesses could be found to him having 'chinned' Chappell, Botham said to me that his team-mates would not have wanted to say anything publicly that might have got him into trouble. That might be a fair argument at the time, but surely thirty years later there is little point in anyone maintaining such secrecy. He admitted that he did not hit Chappell in the face but in the chest. It is hard to imagine such a blow sending a man flying over a table, but then Botham, as we all know, is an extraordinarily powerful man.

Another aspect to the story that was disputed was what happened after the 'punch/push'. Botham claimed in his first autobiography that Chappell fled the bar, throwing an insult as he went through the door, and Botham gave chase, only abandoning his pursuit when a police car happened to cruise past. Chappell said in his autobiography that Botham stopped when he was held back in the street by a team-mate, at which point Chappell decided to disappear 'because the situation threatened to deteriorate even further.'

Like Botham, Chappell appears to have moderated his account over the years. There had been suggestions that Botham had attempted to attack him with a broken bottle, something Botham vehemently denies. Although he claims Botham was holding a glass, Chappell agrees that was not the case but does not withdraw comments he once made on TV that Botham was an 'habitual liar'. When George Carman QC asked Botham about these comments during a libel trial in 1996, and questioned why he had not sued Chappell for them, Botham had replied: 'He's an Australian and I didn't take any notice.'

John Hendry, who was not present in the bar, said that had punches been thrown, let alone a 'glass' wielded, the incident would certainly have been pursued at a disciplinary level and he, as University's captain/coach, would have become involved. 'I've heard many stories about this incident – and that is what they are, stories. I don't know that it came to anything other than them prancing around. If there had been punches thrown, there would have been a lot more made of it. There has been a lot of posturing by both sides. I was not there but I wish I had been because I would not have let it happen.'

For all the fuss that has surrounded the incident, it was probably not in itself extraordinary, shoving and shouting in bars being not uncommon among this generation of sportsmen. What was unusual was the length of the stand-off that followed, which said a lot about the mulish nature of Botham and Chappell. Had they soon after agreed to shake hands and make up, the whole thing would now be forgotten. But neither of them could do that. Sharp words were still being exchanged when the pair crossed paths in the car park at the Adelaide Oval during the 2010–2011 Ashes series, though both rejected a newspaper report that there was a physical confrontation. 'There were some words exchanged but we were not at each other's throats,' Chappell said.

The night before Botham and Stevenson returned to England, the family Botham had been staying with laid on a farewell meal, with John Miles, Geoff Miles's father, inviting Frank Tyson to join them. John Miles had grown fond of Botham but he was taken aback at Botham's overarching self-confidence. 'The last night they were here, they'd had a few corks [beers], and we were talking about this and that,' Miles said. 'And "Both" and Stevo were going on about how anyone from south of the Thames was no bloody good and couldn't play. The only people who could play were Hutton from Yorkshire and anyone else from the North. The likes of Denis Compton from down South couldn't play. So I went upstairs and got a *Wisden* and said, "Look, you two bigheaded so-and-so's" – actually, poor Stevenson hadn't said very much – "the people you are criticising, here are their Test figures." And I read them out . . . Ian Chappell, Greg Chappell, Denis Compton etc. There were a lot of Australians and a lot of Poms. And I said, "You two can't even make a bloody run for University or get a wicket."'

But as would so often happen, Botham was to have the last laugh. Two years later, John Miles found himself in Perth on business while England were there playing a Test. Botham by this time had just achieved the fastest double of 1,000 runs and 100 wickets in Test history. 'I rang up the English hotel and got through to "Both",' Miles recalled, 'And I said, "Both", there's a guy here that said you couldn't even make a run or take a wicket for University . . . but is there any chance of a couple of tickets for the Test?!" . . . "Both" not only got me a couple, but they were in a prime location right next to the players' area.'

While in Australia, Botham learned that he was to become a father. He and Kath were to be young parents – he was twenty-one and she twenty-two – and they were both delighted. This was a very difficult period for Kath, though, separated for several months from her new husband and facing the prospect of this being how she would regularly spend her winters. He admitted later that he was unable to appreciate her problems and attempted to brush them off, which only led to rows between them. She would never find his long absences easy, as he belatedly came to understand. She suffered sleepless nights and, in his words, 'terrible feelings of insecurity and loneliness . . . descended on her whenever I left for an overseas tour.'

Botham returned to England in more of a hurry than ever to get into the England side. After taking the wickets of Graham Barlow and Mike Brearley in his first game, he faced Leicestershire in a Benson and Hedges Cup match at Taunton. Barry Dudleston, then a seasoned opener with Leicestershire, was taken aback at how confrontational Botham was. 'I was opening the batting and he came on as first change. He didn't look a great athlete, heavy-set and long hair. His bowling was medium pace, not naturally quick, but in his first over he bowled a bouncer which took me by surprise. I top-edged it for six. He swore at me. There was not much of that in those days, certainly not from a youngster. I swore at him and told him to go back and bowl.

'I thought, "He's so stupid he'll bowl me a bouncer." He did. I hit it so well it barely went ten feet off the ground towards the corner where the president's tent was. I hadn't noticed before but Hallam Moseley was down there and he caught it above his head. I had to walk past Botham [back to the pavilion] and the expletives were even worse than before. He was aggressive and, as we would find out later, he had a talent for taking wickets with bad balls.'

Botham's luck changed a few days later. On Sunday, 8 May 1977, the day he played in a Somerset side dismissed for fifty-eight runs in the John Player League at Chelmsford, news broke of what represented the biggest single break of his career – the secret recruitment of thirty-five of the world's leading cricketers by Kerry Packer, an Australian entrepreneur.

Packer owned Channel Nine TV and had been thwarted in his attempts to win the contract to cover internationals in Australia, the Australian Cricket Board preferring to maintain its comfortable relationship with the government-run Australian Broadcasting Corporation despite Packer putting in a larger bid. Refusing to accept defeat, Packer had calculated that he could set up his own matches in competition to the Establishment and screen them on his own channel, easily being able to trump the meagre wages

offered by cricket authorities who had for too long taken the players for granted.

The contracts Packer offered – worth the equivalent of around
£25,000 per season for the best players – thoroughly dwarfed fees
that amounted to £210 per Test for England players and £150 for
Australians. Many could not afford to say no. The cricketing
Establishment tried to block Packer's plan in the High Court in
London but suffered a shameful defeat.

At a stroke a large number of top players were set to be removed
from the international arena and their places filled in many cases
by middle-ranking cricketers who had previously had little hope of
appearing in Tests. This was especially true of Australia, who provided eighteen of Packer's original signatories. During the two
years that the game was split into two camps before the Australian
Cricket Board sued for peace by granting Packer the TV rights he
had sought, Australia's official team was unrecognisable from the
one Packer had plundered. West Indies lost four players – including Viv Richards – to Packer's first draft, as did Pakistan, while
South Africa provided five, although given the anti-apartheid ban
this was of no great consequence.

It was Packer's signing of Tony Greig as one of four England
players that held the greatest significance for Botham. This was
something that could never have been anticipated. As England's
captain and principal all-rounder, Greig had been an automatic
selection and at thirty had years more Test cricket in him. That he
could turn his back on England when he was in such an advantageous position showed just how alluring Packer's money was. That
Greig had, along with Ian Chappell, acted as one of Packer's chief
recruiters only compounded the betrayal and ensured that his dismissal as captain was swift (he was sacked within five days and
replaced by Mike Brearley) and he did not return even after peace
broke out. All of a sudden, Greig's Test career was ending and
England were on the lookout for a new all-rounder.

Botham was thus presented with two golden opportunities.
One was to fill Greig's shoes, the other was to do so in matches

against opponents themselves weakened by Packer defections. By the time of the truce, Botham had played seventeen Tests, eleven of them against seriously below-strength Australia and Pakistan teams and the other six against a New Zealand side of only modest ability. It was a wonderful way to be eased into Test cricket – and Botham took full advantage.

Greig himself believed that Botham's career might have been very different had it not been for Packer's World Series Cricket. 'But for World Series, I would have played on and Botham would have taken more of a bowling all-rounder's position in the England team,' he said.

Botham enjoyed a third benefit from the creation of Packer's World Series. In an effort to ward off further defections, the cricket authorities substantially increased their match fees, so that cricketers, whether they joined Packer or stayed within the Establishment fold, were soon being paid better than they ever had been. Even before the TCCB acted, David Evans, a self-made millionaire who ran an industrial refuse collection and cleaning business from Luton, put up funds for England players to receive £1,000 per Test, a five-fold increase on what they had been receiving. It was also inevitable that such things as advertising insignia became more commonplace. Packer was dragging cricket towards a fully professional era.

Not that some needed much encouragement. Greig not only recruited players for Packer; he also tried to persuade them to join his bat sponsors, St Peters. Despite repeated requests, Botham turned him down, staying loyal to Worcester-based Duncan Fearnley, whom he had only just joined from Stuart Surridge. Fearnley was paying Botham only £150 per year but the chief value of the contract was an unlimited supply of bats, which Fearnley tailored to his needs. Contrary to popular belief they were not especially heavy. Until 1979, Botham used a bat weighing 2lb 6oz – which was relatively light for the time – at which point he moved up to 2lb 8oz. He wanted bats he could swish around.

Packer had planned to announce his World Series during the first Ashes Test in June, thereby maximising publicity and making it harder for bans to be slapped on his recruits. In the event, journalists got wind of the story earlier than that, although by the time they did the Australians had begun their tour of England and were actually enjoying a barbecue at Greig's home in Hove. It was swiftly agreed that Packer players on both sides should be allowed to see out the Ashes, otherwise there might not have been a series at all. Thirteen of the seventeen touring Australians had committed themselves, as had Greig, Alan Knott and Derek Underwood from England.

Botham soon had the chance to put forward his case for England selection. Within three weeks he had faced Greg Chappell's Australians twice. In the first game for Somerset he shone, starring with bat and ball in a famous win for the county, but under the captaincy of Brearley for MCC – the first time he had been picked for this pseudo-Test trial fixture – he fared less well. Perhaps overeager to impress England's new captain, his gung-ho approach proved so wasteful that Brearley ticked him off and pulled him out of the attack. 'He bowled bouncers on a slow pitch and got hit for a lot of runs by Rod Marsh, who pulled, hooked and cut him,' Brearley recalled. 'It was a learning thing.' Botham was named in England's squad for the one-day series – Brearley's first official assignment in charge – but he was left on the sidelines for all three games along with his friend Mike Hendrick, while Chris Old played in every game and did well.

Hendrick, a fellow Northerner, was an important figure in Botham's early success. He was seven years older than Botham and had already tasted Test cricket, so could dispense wise counsel. His unwaveringly miserly bowling was the perfect foil for Botham's ultra-attacking methods – Botham rated him his favourite bowling partner. While Botham generally got close into the stumps and swung the ball away, Hendrick came from wide of the crease and pitched the ball on off stump and made it hold up. Not that Hendrick's advice was always heeded. In the MCC versus champion county match at the start of the season, Botham had beaten one batsman time and again with his outswinger but insisted on throwing in the occasional inswinger which would veer down the leg side. Hendrick told him to forget the inswinger but Botham refused. 'I'll get him out with it,' he said. And he did. 'That was my first experience of "Both" knowing best,' Hendrick said.

With the Ashes series beginning without him, and England going one up in the second Test, Botham could do nothing but wait – and try his all in county cricket. For about a month, he produced one hefty all-round performance after another, including scoring sixty-two and taking ten wickets against Sussex, with Greig in their ranks. Then, one evening in late July, Botham found his pint in the Gardener's Arms in Taunton being interrupted by Dennis Breakwell walking in with the news that Chris Old, who had played in the first two Tests, was injured. The next day Botham was named in England's squad for the third Test along with Hendrick and Geoffrey Boycott, returning after a self-imposed three-year absence. Botham received a letter telling him he would be paid £210 (the new rates had yet to come in) and to present himself to the captain at 3pm the afternoon before the game.

The timing of his call-up could not have been better. He was in the form of his life, having taken forty-eight wickets and scored a hundred and two fifties in his last seven championship games. He was fortunate too that morale among the Australians was close to collapse as divisions between the Packer signatories and the rest widened by the day. Even on the flight over the players had downed copious quantities of alcohol as though requiring Dutch courage to get through the trip. Gary Cosier, one of the four Australians who had not signed for Packer, described it as 'an awful tour'. He said: 'There were arguments all the time . . . You'd be on the bus and thirteen blokes would get a package from Packer while the four of us twiddled our thumbs.' David Hookes, one of the Packer players, conceded later that the thirteen should have been sent home.

Botham was naturally nervous at the prospect of his first Test and was lucky that Hendrick was alongside him. Hendrick calmed his anxiety by distracting him with talk about shooting – a sport they were both keen on – and teed up Botham's first wicket by tying down Greg Chappell and Hookes at the other end. Botham's first spell had been as erratic as his bowling for MCC; when he now returned, Chappell spied easy pickings. 'It was a great fat long-hop, wide of the off stump,' said Chappell. 'I got so excited that I lost my concentration.' He chopped the ball into his stumps. As Barry Dudleston said, Botham had a talent for taking wickets with bad balls.

Heartened by his wicket, Botham settled into his work, raising his pace and, remembering how he had disappointed Brearley for MCC, striving not to forget that wickets were the main aim. Including Chappell, he removed four batsmen in the space of 34 balls and later added tail-ender Jeff Thomson as a fifth, to end his first day of Test cricket with a return of 5–74 from 20 overs. 'There was no great fuss made of him,' Hendrick recalled. 'It was just, "Well bowled."' As if that was not enough, Botham also met the Queen this day; in the Midlands as part of her Silver Jubilee celebrations, she was introduced to the teams during the final session.

Botham's luck continued. Batting two days later, he was dropped at slip off his first delivery and beaten numerous other times but survived to contribute a useful twenty-five. He went wicketless in Australia's second innings but Hendrick, Underwood and Bob Willis ensured that England's target was kept within manageable bounds. They won by seven wickets to go 2–0 up in the series.

Such a successful debut was an enormous boost to Botham's confidence and in his next match for Somerset, against Northants at Weston-super-Mare, he experimented ambitiously with the ball, picking up three wickets bowling outswingers from wide of the crease. This became an established phenomenon: the more success Botham had, the more willing he was to try new things. He varied his pace, line and length as well as his position at the crease, prompting Brearley to say that if he had to describe Botham's bowling qualities in one word it would be 'versatility'. 'I do not think I have encountered another bowler who can call on such a range of dangerous deliveries,' he said. Botham had quickly grasped a fundamental truth that all kinds of balls can take wickets; sheer variety was in itself a kind of magic.

Old was still injured and Botham retained his place for the Leeds Test. He failed with the bat as Boycott's hundredth hundred helped England build a formidable score but just as they prepared to bowl the skies conveniently clouded over. Brought on as first change, and bowling throughout with Hendrick operating at the other end, he swung the ball extravagantly, taking wickets with late outswing and inswing – five more of them, this time at a cost of only 21 runs as Australia folded for 103. His victims again included wicketkeeper Marsh and Thomson, bowled by an unplayably late outswinger.

Botham failed to make an impact in the follow-on innings before withdrawing after turning his left ankle trying to field the ball with his foot; the ankle had been vulnerable since a football injury a few years earlier and would remain a constant concern. He was receiving a painkilling injection at the moment Hendrick claimed Marsh as his eighth wicket of the game to deliver England the Ashes. Diagnosed with a fractured metatarsal, Botham's foot was put in plaster. His season was over. Had he played in the final Test and Somerset's last three championship matches, he might have achieved a rare season double of 1,000 runs and 100 wickets.

Botham's broken foot proved a doubly traumatic experience. Sent for treatment to Musgrove Park hospital in Taunton, he encountered children who were dying from leukaemia. It was a harrowing experience – all the more so because the birth of his first child was imminent – and one that made a lasting impression. He was shocked to discover the rate at which children died of the disease: in 1977, the rate of those surviving five years after diagnosis was barely 15 per cent. Over the years, Botham was to make regular visits to leukaemia wards before embarking on his prodigious fundraising work.

With Ian in attendance, Kath gave birth to Liam about a week later on 26 August. Ian asked Viv Richards to be godfather.

Botham had certainly made a mark as a Test cricketer, but it was as a bowler, not an all-rounder. He had batted at number eight in both games, three places below Greig, who in the series took seven wickets and played important innings in the first, second and fourth matches. 'Basically, Ian arrived as a bowler,' said Greig. 'He was a very good bowler. He swung the ball out and was aggressive. I loved the aggressive way he played cricket. That was his special talent.'

Just as the Australians who had signed for Packer went through immense strain, so too did Greig. He had lost the captaincy of an England team that he had helped create. 'It was nice to stay part of the side,' he reflected, 'and I must say that Brearley made that easy for me. But it was stressful. You like to be relaxed when you play cricket. But Brearley had my team. It was my Ashes-winning side, really. An Ashes-winning victory was what we were working towards and it ended up on Brearley's CV rather than mine.

'I had taken him as my vice-captain to India because Boycott wouldn't come. Brearley was lucky to be in that situation. I had said to Boycott that he could have the vice-captaincy and then, who knows? As it turned out, he would have ended up as England captain, which might not have been in the best interests of English cricket. But the fact of the matter is that Brearley was given the vice-captaincy because Boycott said he wouldn't come.'

Had Boycott and not Brearley become England captain, Botham's story might have been very different.

*

Unlike a year earlier, Botham's selection for his first winter tour – four months in Pakistan and New Zealand – was a formality. He was one of five fast bowlers chosen along with Bob Willis, Chris Old, Mike Hendrick and John Lever, and the tour fee was an enticing £5,000. He was, though, to endure more frustration before establishing himself in the team. Even with Tony Greig out of the reckoning, Mike Brearley was not persuaded that Botham had to play. Old, if fit, was to be given priority in Pakistan, and Mike Gatting too.

Botham endured a bout of amoebic dysentery in Pakistan, as did Hendrick, but this was not the reason he took no part in the Test series. After not being chosen for the opening warm-up in Rawalpindi, he played in every other game outside the three Tests. He simply didn't shape up well. His gung-ho approach was not suited to the attritional nature of Test cricket in Pakistan, where outright results had always been notoriously difficult to achieve, and with both teams having lost players to Packer, caution was the order of the day. In an early net session against local leg-spinners, Botham tried to smash the bowling out of the ground; his efforts were, in the words of Brearley, 'hopeless'. There were not many leg-spinners in English cricket but Essex had one in Robin Hobbs and Hobbs had bamboozled Botham on their first meeting. Nor did the ball swing much in Pakistan and swing was what made Botham's bowling dangerous. Brearley gave him just twenty overs in two three-day warm-ups and he took one wicket. He was also afflicted with a no-ball problem – a rare occurrence for him – which further undermined the case for his inclusion in the team for the first Test in Lahore.

Brearley went for Old instead, batting him at number seven. Old scored two runs and took one wicket. 'With the ball not bouncing above waist height in Pakistan, I thought Old might get more runs than Botham,' explained Brearley. 'Ha-ha ... not one of my better judgements!' Botham was upset but his protestations fell on deaf ears. He gave some livelier performances in the first two one-dayers, which England won, but was still not wanted for the Tests, even once Old was left out after Lahore and Brearley broke his arm before the third match in Karachi, leaving Boycott in charge right through to the end of the tour in New Zealand.

Lever felt Botham was someone who needed to feel totally

confident of his health to perform well and in Pakistan that wasn't the case. 'He lost a lot of weight and struggled,' he said. 'During the [second] Test in Hyderabad, I was throwing up for the whole of the rest day, and we had to bowl next day. Times were different, you got on with it then. Pakistan was the sort of place you never felt 100 per cent well. I think he [Botham] needed to feel that.'

There was another factor in Botham's omission: the youngest member of the tour party had some growing up to do. Disconcertingly, he played as though taking part in a club match, and although this carefree approach would later be seen as a virtue, at this stage it caused mistrust. This was, too, his first England tour and touring life in any country required tolerance and patience; in Pakistan, where there was so little socially for Westerners to do, it was vital. These were not qualities Botham possessed in abundance and his behaviour suggested he needed time to adjust to his new life. Not that his high spirits weren't appreciated. His teasing of Boycott, whose solitary ways made him a natural target for collective humour, was among the more memorable features of the tour. Botham would appropriate by force Boycott's supplies of Dundee cake, and caught him in a headlock when he tried to leave the team room with a bottle of wine. Although fifteen years his senior and a veteran of more than sixty Tests, Boycott took the joshing in good part. Confined to his hotel room when ill, Botham fended off boredom by killing mosquitoes with a bullwhip.

The most striking example of Botham's immaturity was his behaviour towards the media. A few newspaper and radio reporters were all that the cricket-touring British media amounted to in those days and they were virtually co-opted as members of the tour party. They would travel and often dine with the team and were not treated as objects of suspicion in the way they would be later, when the financial rewards for staying in the Test team became such that all press criticism was unwelcome. 'We knew them all and grew very close to some,' Lever said of the journalists who toured in the late 1970s. 'We felt we could trust them. They weren't under the pressure to produce stories that they would be later. The integrity was still there.'

Botham's arrival rudely interrupted this agreeable calm. On the second night of the tour, players and press were invited to a High Commission function in Islamabad at which, as usual, the drink freely flowed. Afterwards they were ferried back to the hotel in Rawalpindi by High Commission drivers and Botham happened to share a car with Steve Whiting, the new cricket correspondent of the *Sun*. While Botham rode in front, Whiting took the back seat with Mike Gatting and the late Graham Roope. Accounts of the conversation that passed vary. Some suggested that Whiting, a club player himself, had told Botham he was lucky to be on tour because he was no more than a glorified club cricketer. Whiting claims that Botham had said that he did not want to turn into a bitter ex-pro as so many did and Whiting had replied that he was 'just a kid' and might view things differently when older. Whiting concedes that Roope told him afterwards that he had 'gone in a bit hard'. Botham, Whiting claimed, had brandished his fist and said, 'Outside, you get this.' Sure enough, when they got out of the car a scuffle ensued, Whiting calling it more of a wrestling match than a fight. Whiting said that Gatting had told him to 'fuck off into the hotel', which he did.

Shortly after returning to his room, Whiting was visited by another England player who asked whether he intended to write about what had happened, and he said that he did not. 'I remember the kerfuffle the incident caused,' Pat Gibson said. 'I told one or two of the senior players that there wasn't much future in players hitting press men.'

The late Don Mosey, who covered the tour for BBC radio, said that the next evening Botham created 'a scene' in the British Embassy's staff club. Mosey and Whiting, too, recalled an incident when players and journalists travelled to the Khyber Pass, stopping off to visit a bazaar in Landi Kotal. There, according to Mosey, Botham was seen haggling with a local outside a coffee shop. Climbing back onto the bus, Botham was asked if he had bought anything. 'No,' he replied. 'He had some of the local cannabis but it was poor stuff, poor quality.' Mosey saw this as the young Botham bluffing, trying to appear a man of the world.

Perhaps because of the Whiting incident, Ken Barrington, the tour manager, was assigned to take Botham under his wing, which he did initially through games of golf. This proved the start of a special relationship. Barrington, the son of a soldier, came from Reading but had a West Country burr to his voice that might have resonated with Botham. As a prolific batsman for England in the 1960s, Barrington had worked hard to achieve what he had; he was an example of what could be attained by dedication and discipline. An experienced tour manager, he had a talent for helping players unlock the secrets to their game and was to be one of the few people in cricket Botham listened to. Barrington would help him cure his no-ball problem, which was caused by him landing on the ball of his left foot, one reason why Botham had broken a bone there a few months earlier.

Marginalised, Botham spent much of his time in Pakistan at a brooding distance from Brearley, feeling ignored and unwanted, and perhaps a little intimidated by this plainly clever man. He suspected Brearley thought him a wild youth who wouldn't do as he was told – they had had an argument during a one-day international after a mix-up in the field – and feared he looked upon him with contempt. Brearley admitted that he had wondered why they had brought this reckless individual on tour. That they would eventually form a bond was unimaginable.

Conditions in New Zealand were much more akin to those in England and, even if the cricket was again attritional in nature, Botham was a logical selection for the first Test in Wellington. A week before the game, he had appeared to be playing off for a place with Mike Gatting. Then a batsman who bowled more often than he did later, Gatting had made his Test debut as Brearley's replacement in Karachi and Botham feared that even though Brearley was no longer on the tour as a player – he remained in attendance in a journalistic capacity – his influence might see to it that Gatting, a Middlesex team mate, would retain his place.

The issue was settled in the final warm-up against Canterbury when Botham scored an unbeaten 126 while Gatting was twice out cheaply. The Canterbury attack contained four who would bowl for New Zealand in the Tests. Botham said that, believing his career depended on it, he willed himself to a century. That he was able to do this, after the frustrations of Pakistan, showed what an exceptional competitor he was. 'I thought he had something [special],' John Lever said. 'Once we got to New Zealand, he had a hell of a lot of confidence for somebody on his first tour. You would not say, "Bloody hell, listen to him," but there was a self-belief there that you've got to have at the top level. A lot of people struggle when they step up [to Test cricket].'

What happened next to Gatting demonstrated this point. While Botham cemented his place in the England side, Gatting's fortunes took a different path. He played in the third Test but was out for a duck and did not appear for England again for two years. Even after that it was a long time before he did himself justice. Botham said that Gatting felt overshadowed by him and that there was a tension between them for several seasons. Gatting appeared unnerved by Botham's confidence, which may have only heightened his own doubts. Asked if he felt intimidated by Botham, Gatting said: 'Not particularly. In my eyes, I was a batsman, he was a bowler. I never felt we were competing for the same spot. But he seemed happy mixing in with the hierarchy, while I didn't find it easy.'

Botham was happy to throw his weight around with anyone. Geoff Cope, an off-spinner from Yorkshire, was assigned to share a room with Botham in a motel in New Zealand. No sooner had they got through the door than Botham picked up Cope and hurled him across the room and onto a put-up bed before jumping onto the main double bed and saying: 'Well, if you're having that one, I'll have this.' Cope didn't argue.

Botham's first match back in the Test side did not go well. England lost to New Zealand for the first time in forty-eight years and in humiliating fashion, dismissed for sixty-four in the final innings. The defeat was so comprehensive that England's grievances at some questionable umpiring became irrelevant. To make matters worse, Botham was twice bounced out by Richard Hadlee, a tall, angular and serious young fast-bowling all-rounder whose solitary approach alienated opponents and team-mates every bit as much as did Boycott's. Hadlee's ten wickets won the game for New Zealand and if it was not Botham's recklessness against him that lost it, he was not proud of his double failure. Botham had hooked Hadlee with aplomb in the warm-up at Canterbury and fancied he could do it again, but Hadlee laid his traps well, suggesting Botham had learned little since Brian Close had shouted at him for his irresponsibility against Yorkshire two years earlier.

In fact, this Test defeat proved a turning point. In the next Test at Christchurch, Botham showed great self-restraint as Hadlee, striving to drive home New Zealand's strong start on a greenish pitch, invited him to hook time and again. Botham's progress was slow as he kept letting the short ball go, but he battled away for more than five hours for 103, mainly in company with Bob Taylor. Nervous at the prospect of a maiden Test hundred, he ran out Taylor in search of his hundredth run, poor reward for Taylor's encouragement, but overall it was a superb display from a young and inexperienced batsman.

This was the start of what turned out to be the best game of Botham's life so far, as he went on to take with genuinely fast bowling five wickets in the first innings and three in the second, plus three fine catches. As Botham would acknowledge, his duels with Hadlee – an older, wiser and every bit as ambitious a cricketer as himself – matured him greatly. It was perhaps also significant that the later stages of the game were played in a fractious atmosphere as New Zealand tried to cling to their 1–0 lead; Botham usually played better when he had something or someone to react to. With the final Test in Auckland almost certain to be drawn (as proved to be the case), England had to win if they were to draw the series.

Botham seemed ever more galvanised as hostility thickened the air. After New Zealand avoided the follow-on by sixteen runs, England batted again on the fourth afternoon in search of quick runs. This was ultimately to lead to another notorious incident in Botham's career – the running out of Boycott, the captain, whose slow batting was jeopardising the team's chances – but before that happened New Zealand's spoiling tactics had angered the England camp. They bowled their overs slowly and Ewen Chatfield ran out Derek Randall, England's number three, when Randall – alert to the need for quick runs – was backing up at the non-striker's end. Such an act was widely considered contrary to the spirit of the game.

Botham was next man in but before he left the dressing-room he was involved in a discussion with Bob Willis, Phil Edmonds and Taylor about the need for quick runs. Interestingly Botham, Edmonds and Taylor were all relative newcomers to the England side, Edmonds and Taylor having won promotion following the defections to Packer of Underwood and Knott. Willis was vice-captain and – according to Botham's account –he had muttered to Botham of Boycott, 'Go and run the bugger out.'

In a bizarre aside, Botham later claimed that no sooner had he arrived at the crease than Chatfield warned that he might run him out too – to which Botham replied: 'Remember mate, you've already died once on the cricket field. Anything can happen.' This was a reference to Chatfield having been hit on the temple by England's Peter Lever three years earlier; his heart had stopped and his life was saved only by the quick work of Bernard Thomas, the England physio. But Chatfield denied this conversation ever took place. 'I have no recollection of that exchange whatsoever,' he said in his autobiography.

If Botham had taken Willis's words as a direct instruction he did not immediately act on them. There were about forty-five minutes left in the day and he had been batting with Boycott for twenty minutes before Boycott was run out. John Woodcock in his report for *The Times* described the incident thus: 'Botham called Boycott for what would have been the sharpest of singles into the covers. Loud and clear, Boycott sent Botham back but on he ran, deaf to the injunction until he had passed his dumb-founded captain, thus making sure it was Boycott who was out.' Mike Gatting, who was watching from the dressing-room, said that with both batsmen at the same end 'there followed a hue and cry about who should be out' before a consensus emerged that it was Boycott.

Botham's claim that he deliberately ran out his captain – and indeed his supposed conversation with Chatfield – has stood largely unchallenged for more than thirty years. But would a novice of four Tests, even one as apparently confident as Botham, really have dared do this? Or was it something that just happened naturally, through Botham's search for quick runs and Boycott's in-built aversion to risk?

Taylor faithfully supports Botham's own contention that the run-out was planned. Clive Radley, who was playing his first Test and acquired video highlights of the game from NZTV, had his doubts: 'It was hard to tell whether it was deliberate or not. I'm not sure it was.' John Lever, who also did not play but was present, said: 'Beefy was fairly stirred up, as we all were. We wanted to declare and bowl at them that night but knew Boycott was happy to bat through to the next day. It was just the heady atmosphere of "Let's get on with it". I think it's a horrible thing to say that he'd do that on purpose. I think it just happened and nobody was too upset because it gave us the opportunity to win the game. Beefy had had Goose [Willis] in his ear for an hour or so. Boycs came in [to the dressing-room] and sat in the corner with a towel over his head muttering something like, "He's run me out, he's run me out" ... and nobody was taking any notice.'

Journalists were unsure what had inspired Botham to act as he did. 'It wasn't blindingly obvious that he'd done it deliberately,' Pat Gibson said. 'It was only afterwards that it was claimed that he had. They [the other players] were trying to make a point about the captain, who wasn't making any attempt to win the game.'

John Woodcock in his report said: 'Put it down, if you like, to too much adrenalin. Botham is a young and high-spirited cricketer and he had some reason for thinking that in the time left he could do more for his side than Boycott, to judge from the way Boycott was batting.'

Asked if he himself believed Botham had deliberately run him out, Boycott said: 'I hope that was not the case. If he had done it on purpose I don't think it would be something to be proud of. I think the story acquired something in the telling.' Chatfield was also sceptical, saying only that Botham had dined out on the story and that the words exchanged between Botham and Boycott 'have varied with the telling'.

Botham may have had an ulterior motive. If he did not deliberately run out Boycott, then it must have happened accidently, which might have reminded everyone that Botham himself did not have a great reputation as a runner – as he had shown earlier in the game by running out Taylor when looking for his hundredth run. In the course of the next eighteen months, Botham would be involved in four more run-outs in Tests – with Taylor again, Phil Edmonds, Derek Randall and Boycott himself at the Oval in 1979, when it was Botham who was out. *Wisden* laid the blame firmly at Botham's door on that occasion, saying that he had been guilty of 'neglecting to ascertain Boycott's intentions as he charged up the pitch'.

Brearley was no fan of Botham's running at that time. 'Botham's running-out of people is the worst part of his batting,' he was quoted as saying in 1980. 'He can be selfish. He can get so carried away with his own performance that all he thinks about is getting at the bowlers.' And Willis himself, while laying no claim to instructing Botham to run out Boycott, commented in his autobiography in 1985: 'He [Botham] will tell you to this day that he did it deliberately. Being critical of the running between the wickets of both men, I am not so sure.'

Botham's claims about this incident, as with his assertions that he 'sledged' Ewen Chatfield and that he had been in a 'punch-up'

with Ian Chappell, perhaps highlight the fundamentally contradictory nature of his personality – that a supreme self-confidence
masked a deep-seated anxiety for acceptance. He admitted in
retirement that he had camouflaged his fears with 'bluff and
bravado'. Part of this may have manifested itself in the telling of a
tall tale or two.

Hopes of England declaring in time to bowl at New Zealand that
evening had already died by the time Boycott was run out and his
departure had little impact on the course of the game, even if it sated
the anger of team-mates. After he was out, England added another
29 runs in 25 minutes, most of them from Botham, whose
unbeaten 30 occupied 31 balls. This certainly put in the shade
Boycott's 26 off 80 balls, although Brian Rose, Boycott's opening
partner, scored only seven off 40. It was not until shortly before play
the next morning that a distracted Boycott, under pressure from
colleagues, agreed to declare, leaving New Zealand 280 to win.

In this febrile environment, Willis and Botham saw to it that
England won with all haste. Botham had a hand in six wickets:
one blinding slip catch off Willis, whose ferocious opening burst
claimed four victims; two catches off Edmonds; and the scalps of
Nine, Ten, Jack with his own bowling. Still upset over the run-out,
Boycott refused to talk directly to Botham and conveyed instructions through intermediaries. Botham's one disappointment was
expensively failing to bounce out Hadlee. Even so, New Zealand
were dismissed for 105 with plenty of time to spare.

In the days after the game, Brearley had dinner with Botham
and congratulated him on his tireless bowling, the courage he had
shown against Hadlee and the clipping of Boycott's wings, inten-
tional or otherwise. 'Maybe you have got Chris Old covered,' he
conceded.

Botham had left home merely as one of England's bowling
options but returned with an extra yard of pace to his bowling and
as an all-rounder of exciting potential. He now had the England
captain firmly onside too. The only downside was that he had
been away for nearly four months, during which Kath had been

left alone with their young son Liam. He and Kath agreed that they were not going to be apart for so long again and before touring Australia the following winter Botham asked the TCCB, which discouraged wives from joining tours, to allow her to accompany him for a short period. After initial resistance the board relented and Kath – by then pregnant again – was with him for a period up to and including the first Test.

In the second Test of the English summer against Pakistan, Botham repeated his Christchurch feat of scoring a century and taking five wickets in an innings of the same Test, something only two other all-rounders in history had twice accomplished – Gary Sobers himself and Mushtaq Mohammad of Pakistan.

These efforts ensured Tony Greig's swift eclipse as an England cricketer. Botham's emergence may have been perfect for England but it could not have been worse for Greig, because it meant he was neither missed nor mourned. England's good fortune did not stop there, as Bob Taylor and Phil Edmonds were proving themselves worthy replacements for Knott and Underwood. No wonder England survived the Packer era better than most.

After he had finished with World Series Cricket, Greig settled in Australia and took up work as a TV commentator for Packer's Channel Nine. He acknowledges that he was quickly forgotten as a player because of Botham but maintains their records were on a par. Greig prides himself on having scored a hundred against Australia when they were the best team in the world whereas Botham never managed one against West Indies when they were the best team of the 1980s. 'I don't think Ian would be very proud of his record,' Greig said. 'I would put mine against his any day. There are plenty of all-rounders who have been as good as him if not better. Did England miss me? I don't think you miss good cricketers when you are playing against second elevens. The accolades given him are over the top.'

Botham, of course, did not replicate Greig in every way. Brearley, who played with them both, thought Greig the shrewder man. 'Tony was a more calculating figure, as we saw with his involvement in World Series Cricket. He was a shrewder operator too. He was someone who might not say much but his words and praise counted. He was always trying something. He was provocative, like the way he would signal the fours he hit off Dennis Lillee, encouraging him to bowl short. That showed courage and panache. Botham did not manipulate the opposition as Greig did. Tony was much more capable of cleverness or calculation than Ian.'

Underwood, who bowled at both as well as playing alongside them, thought Greig the better batsman, if not the better bowler. 'Tony was a much underrated cricketer. He had a presence about him, though he was less forthright than "Both". He was more charismatic on the field than off it. He played a number of astonishing innings. He was a versatile player who could play in any conditions, whereas I always thought that "Both" relied more on strength than technique. "Both" was a more dangerous player. He would take on the bowling and suddenly be in control, the luck riding with him. I don't want to understate his ability or credibility [as a batsman] but he was more likely to score runs against the quicks than on a turning wicket. As bowlers there was no comparison. To me "Both" goes down as one of the great bowlers of all time.'

Greig's departure for World Series Cricket did Botham many favours but one of the most advantageous things it did for him was make it easy for Greig to be portrayed as the man who had betrayed English cricket and Botham, by extension, as its saviour.

# 5

## Bouncing against the Framework

'Mike Brearley let him have his head. He didn't discipline him and say you can't do this or that. As long as he was producing the runs and wickets, Brears didn't want to change him. He would have said to himself: "How am I going to get the best out of this player? Is it by disciplining him, or by letting him have his freedom?" And Brears worked it out: give him a bit of space.'

JOHN EMBUREY

Botham had no further need to impress Mike Brearley, but he did his best anyway, dismissing him in the MCC–Middlesex curtain-raiser to the 1978 season at Lord's. Having had Brearley caught behind, he later performed the hat-trick, removing Clive Radley leg-before and then his old friend Graham Barlow, and Norman Featherstone, with successive yorkers.

Six weeks later, he was playing his first Test under Brearley's captaincy for ten months. It was to prove the start of a golden run and a golden alliance. Between June 1978 and February 1980, Botham was to play twenty Tests under Brearley's guidance in which he scored 1,099 runs and took 112 wickets. In only one of those games did he not make a meaningful contribution. He averaged more than twice with the bat (40.7) than he did with the ball (18.4), a rare thing.

Botham was the most influential figure as England won twelve and lost only four of those twenty games, and won five out of six series. The one loss came in Australia in 1979–80 in a hastily arranged series to celebrate the return of the Packer players; three Tests, all won by Australia, were interspersed with one-day matches as well as Tests between Australia and West Indies. In protest at the patchwork scheduling, England refused to put up the Ashes they had retained the previous winter. England also reached the final of the one-day World Cup staged on their own turf in 1979 before being outplayed by West Indies.

This success brought Botham greater financial rewards and began the process which turned him into a national hero. Through Brian Close, Botham acquired his first agent in Reg Hayter, who had handled a number of top England cricketers of recent vintage, including Basil d'Oliveira, Ray Illingworth, Tony Greig and Close himself, as well as footballers and boxers. Hayter had set out as a sports reporter back in the 1930s and was hugely experienced in cricket affairs. He was not an agent in the modern sense but through the agency he ran out of a small office in The Strand was well connected and could offer the best advice available to someone in Botham's position. The scope for sponsorships and endorsements was limited, though growing, and Hayter was as much press manager as commercial agent. He and Botham became good friends, Hayter finding Botham warm, generous and trusting.

One of Hayter's earliest moves was to secure Botham a column with the *Sun*. This proved lucrative and maintained Botham's status as a national celebrity even when his cricket wasn't doing that for him. The *Sun* had long been on a drive under Rupert Murdoch to challenge the *Daily Mirror* and it finally overtook the *Mirror*'s sales in 1978 when both newspapers were selling nearly four million copies daily. Frank Nicklin, the *Sun*'s sports editor, was a close friend of Hayter's and happy to add Botham to his stable of columnists. Nicklin – dubbed by Larry Lamb, the *Sun*'s first editor, as a 'pie-and-pint man' – had a deft populist touch. He recruited George Best and Jimmy Greaves to write on football, Harvey Smith on show-jumping and Mick McManus on wrestling, and Botham fitted the same mould. Nicklin also got on well with Botham's father through their RAF connections; Nicklin had flown fighter planes in the Second World War and twice been shot down.

Botham's attitude towards his column was not untypical of the bigger stars whose time was precious and respect for the written word qualified. Within certain parameters, he was prepared to leave the words and sentiments to the journalist assigned to 'ghost' his piece; as he once said to one of them: 'Write what you like. Just don't land me in it.' Several journalists were to ghost Botham's column but the busiest was Ian Jarrett, who did it for six years. 'Botham was always difficult to track down and often I would end up writing the column with little or no input from him,' he said. 'The column was supposed to be cleared by Lord's and often we did not get it to them until late so it was touch and go whether it would be run with or without permission. My impression was that the column was secondary to the paper having access to Botham during times of drama. One of the rare cases of Botham himself instigating a piece was to complain about the treatment of wives and girlfriends at Test matches and the poor seats they were given. I wouldn't have been surprised if Mrs Botham and the in-laws were behind that story.'

Botham benefited financially from the feverish competition among the popular papers but was to suffer from it in other ways. When in 1980 he put on weight, the papers went to town on the story – running unflattering photographs, copies of Taunton's lunchtime menus and quizzing friends as to his eating habits. It was a sample of what was to come.

Even at this early stage of his career, as his England commitments grew, Botham inevitably had less in his tank for Somerset. There was nothing unusual in this; England cricketers were routinely expected, and expected themselves, to play whenever they could for their clubs, but fatigue was bound to take its toll. This contributed to some painful disappointments. Somerset's captaincy had passed from Brian Close to Brian Rose, but Rose could not at first prevent the team again falling within touching distance of a first trophy when they lost the 1978 Gillette Cup final to Sussex. Botham batted well for eighty, Somerset's top score, but got overexcited after claiming two of Sussex's first four wickets, including that of Imran Khan. His bowling proved expensive and Sussex ran out comfortable winners. The next day Somerset lost their last John Player League match to Essex by two runs when they needed to win to take the title.

Somerset's desperation to win was such that it led them to controversy in May 1979 when Rose, following a team vote, declared an innings closed after one over to protect their run-rate and guarantee them qualification for the knockout stage of the Benson and Hedges Cup. The team were disqualified for bringing the game into disrepute.

Later that season, two days after sending down fifty-five overs in the first Test against India, Botham's wayward bowling in the Gillette Cup against Derbyshire brought him heckling from the Taunton locals. Incensed and frustrated, he swore at the crowd and stabbed a V-sign at them. 'I don't think I've ever come nearer to walking into a crowd,' he said later. But Somerset won the match and went on to lift the cup, their first prize in 104 years. Botham's bowling, ragged against Derbyshire, played a vital part in later victories. He produced some near-unplayable swing bowling in the semi-final against Middlesex, during which Rose posted six slips and gullys, and the final itself against Northamptonshire, who were beaten decisively thanks to a masterly century from Viv Richards and six wickets from the towering Barbados fast bowler Joel Garner, playing his first full season for Somerset after two years of occasional appearances on leave from the Lancashire Leagues.

His batting was even more inconsistent. He was roasted by Rose after a reckless innings against Kent in the quarter-final. Always a brilliant rationaliser after the event, Botham claimed merely that he should have hit out harder, but everyone in the team knew he had done what he did because he was partnering Viv Richards at the time. Botham batted with Richards again in the final, Northants astutely playing on his ego by bringing in the field when he was on strike but not when Richards was, and he was again out slogging. It was already clear that Botham was more comfortable playing for England, where he was at least as good as any other player, than for Somerset, where Richards' superiority was a distraction.

The day after Somerset won the Gillette Cup, they clinched the John Player League at Trent Bridge, Botham claiming the final wicket – and a stump as a souvenir.

Playing for England, though, Botham was at his athletic and competitive peak. He was confident, enthusiastic and strong, and indifferent to physical pain or ailment, while lean and lithe enough to swing the ball at pace. There was a ferocious energy in everything he did, a youthful zest that only a man in his early twenties could display. He was a joyous cricketer, playing for love and glory, with no hint of the jaundice that scarred his later cricket. A perfect example came at the Oval in 1979 when England looked a beaten side going into the final hour of a long and exhausting game. India were 366–1 chasing 438 and on course for a historic victory when in twelve overs Botham roused himself to take a catch, three wickets – including India's linchpin Sunil Gavaskar for 221 – and execute a run-out. The match ended in a thrilling draw with India 429–8, and both sides tantalisingly close to victory. He was an exponentially better cricketer for having two strings to his bow: the better he bowled, the better he batted, and vice versa. Mostly he batted in the top six and always opened the bowling or came on first change. This was what he had always wanted to do and he proved it made him most effective.

In a way he was unlucky that this pomp coincided with the Packer split because he would have been a handful for any full-strength side, as he showed when the Packer players returned for

England's tour of Australia in 1979–80. In his first Test against the full might of Australia, he took eleven wickets from a gargantuan 80.5 overs and conceded barely two runs an over. In his third match, he dealt calmly with Dennis Lillee's skilful bowling on a slow pitch to score an unbeaten century. He did squander his wicket in the second Test, much to Brearley's wrath, but it was not his fault England lost the series 3–0. These efforts were often forgotten when it was claimed that he never did much against the strongest sides.

If there was one area of his game over which there remained a question mark it was how he played spin. New Zealand's left-armer Stephen Boock caused him problems and he got in a tangle against India's spinners – so much so that Viv Richards, watching the second Test on TV, chided him for losing his nerve. Richards encouraged him to remain bold and Botham was certainly that during a rumbustious century in the next Test, a rain-blighted affair at Leeds, where he took 43 runs off the 34 balls he received from Bishen Bedi and Srini Venkataraghavan. It was an exhilarating display in an otherwise forgettable game: Botham scored ninety-nine during the morning session of the fourth day and in all hit five sixes, then a record for a Test in England.

There were other reasons why England did well at that time, just as there were other reasons besides Botham why Somerset were so effective at one-day cricket. The batting acquired two significant additions in 1978. Graham Gooch was recalled as an opener with a new determination based on a strong fitness ethic. David Gower, like so many, had fallen into county cricket happily, unconcerned at the low wages, his enthusiasm sparked at Leicestershire by Ray Illingworth and his academic career having foundered at University College London. 'I was supposedly there to read law but never actually found the library,' he said. 'I wasn't so much reading law as hearing about it.' Gower was an instant success; a silky stroke-maker and athletic cover fieldsman who – and this was to be significant given his friendship with Botham – required little training to stay fit and in form. John Emburey arrived on the scene the same year, giving Brearley a third spin-bowling option alongside Phil Edmonds and Geoff Miller. The fielding was exceptional, with Gower and Derek Randall in front of the wicket and Taylor, Brearley, Botham and Hendrick behind. Boycott, who had been playing since 1964, said it was the best England fielding side he was involved with.

But it was the fast bowling that gave the side its edge. Bob Willis was the spearhead with a style that complemented Botham's perfectly. Taylor saw the effects at first hand. 'Bob bowled wicket to wicket, relying on pace and a quick bowler's length, which was shorter than Beefy's. If you were going to swing the ball like Beefy, you had to pitch it up. Facing him, batsmen were looking to get on to the front foot. No one in England swung the ball as much as he did but he hit the gloves hard too. But against Bob the batsmen needed to be on the back foot, fending the ball off their bodies. It was a good combination.' The best game they had together was at Lord's in 1978 when New Zealand were all out for sixty-seven and Botham, swinging the ball outrageously, finished with eleven wickets.

They were supported occasionally by Chris Old and John Lever, and more regularly by Hendrick. On the day that Botham claimed Gavaskar as his hundredth Test wicket at Lord's in 1979, Botham and Hendrick went for a drink in a pub near the ground called the Artillery. 'It used to do a good pint of Bass,' Hendrick recalled. 'I said, "Well done, 'Both', on your hundred wickets." And he said, "Well, thanks . . . I probably owe thirty of them to you."' Botham had required just nineteen Tests for his hundred wickets, the fewest by any bowler for nearly fifty years.

England were not the only nation well armed in fast bowling. In the 1970s, a whole host of men capable of unusual speed had come onto the horizon and, encouraged by the confrontational style promoted by Kerry Packer, their intentions were rarely anything but hostile. It became generally understood too that without legislation fast bowlers could pretty much batter opponents into submission. Amnesties for tail-enders were sometimes negotiated but any lower-order batsman who hung around was regarded as fair game. When Iqbal Qasim, used by Pakistan as a night-watchman in the first Test of 1978, was hit in the mouth by Willis after resisting for forty minutes, a heated public debate arose about the morals of targeting batsmen of limited ability, but Brearley and his players were unrepentant. 'Qasim was in a negative mood in what is supposed to be a positive game,' Botham said. 'I saw nothing wrong with bouncing him.' England felt their tactics were vindicated when Qasim failed to score for the rest of the series.

Botham loved this new climate. Even before the Tests against Pakistan he had made excessive use of the bouncer in a one-dayer at the Oval and a few days later got into hot water with umpire Bill Alley in Somerset's derby match with Gloucestershire. Alley warned him for bowling too many bouncers at the prolific Pakistan batsman Zaheer Abbas, missing from Pakistan's tour because of his Packer contract. By the time Botham succeeded in bouncing him out, Zaheer had sped to 140. In the same game, Botham committed a rare breach of on-field etiquette by running out from slip opening batsman Alan Tait who, thinking he had edged a catch, was on his way back to the pavilion.

Botham had the mind and the methods to bully tail-enders into submission. Although primarily regarded as a swing bowler, he possessed a deceptively quick ball, and an awkward bouncer. It was a package that was simply too much for many tail-enders. He was also adept at undoing them with changes of angle, squaring them up by bowling at their legs from wide of the crease; he got countless wickets this way. Nor was he afraid of roughing up those who were fast bowlers; the thought that they might retaliate was of no concern to him. Derek Underwood, a tail-ender who faced Botham with trepidation in county cricket, appreciated his talent for laying waste to the tail. 'He would be at you even before you'd reached the crease. He was very forthright and could unsettle you with just the odd comment. He would often take two of the top six wickets but end up with five in the innings.'

Through necessity, batsmen began better arming themselves and by the end of the decade the use of helmets was widespread. Even Botham wore one at times, though less often than many (he arguably batted better without one, the greater element of danger seemingly raising his game). Indeed, the predominance of pace at the expense of spin suited him well. The helmet transformed the batting of many, particularly those late-order players who had previously feared for their safety. It certainly cost Botham wickets: up to 1980, one in four of his Test wickets was provided by numbers nine, ten and eleven, but this slipped to below one in five later. Stories such as those of Iqbal Qasim largely disappeared from the game. Richard Hadlee was among those whose batting was dramatically improved by the helmet.

Brearley's England team were winning and happy. Under him, a sense of collective purpose was forged among a diverse band, a process assisted by Packer having laid siege to the traditional cricket in which they were involved. Boycott was tolerated because he was their most dependable batsman and Brearley made sure that Boycott, like everyone else, felt important and wanted.

Botham was at the heart of this common mission. After returning from New Zealand, he scored a century in the first Test of the 1978 summer against Pakistan at Edgbaston, an innings played with England already well on top against weak opponents. Then, in the next game at Lord's, he dazzled with bat and ball in typically serendipitous fashion. After the first day's play had been not so much washed away as drowned, Botham and Old – his erstwhile rival – were given permission by Brearley to have a drink that evening, everyone confident that there would not be a prompt start the next morning. Their night finished at around 2.30am but to their alarm play began at 11.30am. Brearley took pity on them by opting to bat first but by mid-afternoon Botham was at the crease and in belligerent mood despite England's precarious position at 134–5. His second scoring stroke was a six and he had raced to a hundred shortly before stumps, by which time Old had joined him, still shaking his head at Botham's capacity to play so well after their night out. Three days later, Botham ran amok with the ball after Pakistan, thoroughly demoralised, had followed on more than 250 in arrears. Having previously taken only one wicket in the series, Botham claimed a first victim on the Saturday evening when the ball wasn't swinging and then added seven more during a sensational passage of play on the Monday morning. Even though the skies were clear he managed to swing the ball prodigiously from the Nursery End, where Brearley had originally called on him merely to let Willis change ends. The ball that swung late to take Haroon Rashid's off stump was among the best Botham ever bowled.

Graham Gooch remembered Botham's relish at being the centre of dressing room attention. 'There are characters who have a self-confidence bordering on arrogance. They fancy themselves but they could back it up. Ian was like that. It was good for his cricket. You have got to believe in yourself as a cricketer.'

During this period, Botham was a terrific team man – selfless, popular, mischievous. He got up to any number of pranks inspired by his size and strength. He shoved people into swimming pools (he himself was not, according to some, a keen swimmer), singed their hair with cigarette lighters and, with breathtaking predictability, turned up to Christmas fancy-dress parties as a gorilla. Once, on a coach journey from Newcastle to Sydney, shortly after England had retained the Ashes on the 1978–79 tour of Australia, he was the instigator behind Boycott being stripped of his clothes and his privates covered in shaving foam in a clear re-enactment of the ritual Botham endured on the Lord's groundstaff. When the coach reached the team hotel in Sydney, Botham and the rest of the team disembarked with Boycott's clothes, leaving Boycott threatening to walk into the hotel naked unless his items were returned. In the end, he marched through reception missing his trousers but semi-clothed. Boycott generously did not hold this incident against him, insisting that Botham was one of his three favourite cricketers along with Graham Stevenson and David Bairstow. 'I admired and liked him immensely,' Boycott said. 'He made me laugh and made the game fun to play.'

One of the reasons Botham was held in great affection was because, despite his own enormous personal success, he had the generosity to share in the triumphs of others. 'He was the first guy to go to anyone who did well,' John Lever said. 'When you get to the top level and you're looking after your place, a lot of people have found it hard to be that gracious. OK, his place wasn't in danger, but he showed a lot of others the right way to go.' Derek Underwood noticed that he was particularly good with people who were new to the scene: 'He always noticed and encouraged them.'

A few people, though, felt ill at ease with his high spirits and some were hurt by his teasing. Bob Willis tired of being compared to a wounded camel when he was experiencing injury problems, and Botham was asked by Brearley to desist. Not many were capable of warning him off. One who did was Peter Willey, a powerfully built batting all-rounder who played a full part in the 1979–80 tour of Australia. Asked if he found Botham intimidating, Willey said: 'No, because I stood up to him. I'd first got to know him well in '76, when I got 220-odd against Somerset. We were both young lads and became good mates. I didn't take his pranks or bullshit. Poor old Boycott ... if he [Botham] knew he could dominate them, he made life a misery. I wasn't going to have that. I have never been intimidated by anybody. We had a carry-on in Australia where I was going to hang him [Botham] up on the hooks in the showers because he was messing about.'

The challenge for anyone who captained Botham was harnessing his extraordinary energy and talent. It has been suggested that Brearley received too much credit for Botham's success under him. There is no doubt that Brearley was lucky to have him in his side when Botham was so young, eager and good. Equally, the quasi-magical power of man-management that has been attributed to Brearley owed much to what happened later in 1981. But it is only necessary to survey how things went wrong when Brearley was not around to appreciate that his relationship with Botham must have been something out of the ordinary.

As England captain, Mike Brearley held some clear advantages in his relationship with Botham when they were reunited in 1978. The first was his seniority. At thirty-six, he was thirteen years older than Botham and older than every man in the team except Boycott, who turned thirty-eight that year. Boycott, of course, was unable to command Botham's respect in anything like the same way, so age in itself was not enough but, unlike Boycott, Brearley naturally possessed the bearing of an elder statesman and, also unlike Boycott, he was the officially appointed captain. He wore his authority lightly but was very clearly in charge.

Even at this relatively early stage of his captaincy, Brearley's record as a cricket leader was impressive. Middlesex had not been the easiest team to take charge of – older pros such as Fred Titmus and John Murray made sure of that – but he had led them to the championship in 1976, and in 1977 he not only led them to the championship again, as joint winners with Kent, but also the Gillette Cup, while at the same time England regained the Ashes under him. His reputation was quickly to grow too, as England continued to win regularly under him. Few questions were going to be raised while he, and the team, were doing well.

Brearley's intellect was another means by which he could assert his position. Unlike most cricketers who went to Oxbridge, he had been serious about learning, taking a First in Classics and a 2:1 in Moral Sciences before undertaking postgraduate work while developing a career as a lecturer. When he took up full-time cricket, this unusual past cast him as a man apart among the more utilitarian minds on the professional circuit, but his articulacy gave him a distinct advantage. When Brearley's authority as England captain came under threat through his poor form with the bat, it was his capacity as a thinker that kept him in command.

Had Brearley been overbearingly clever, it could have backfired, but he was well grounded and pragmatic – he was a doer as well as a thinker. His antecedents were far from grand and – perhaps helpfully as far as Botham was concerned – from the North. His grandfather, who came from Heckmondwike in Yorkshire, had been an engine-fitter as well as a lively fast bowler; his father Horace, while maintaining the family passion for cricket as a batsman, became a teacher in Sheffield and then London. Brearley himself seemed happiest surrounded by hard-headed Northern cricketers such as Hendrick, Miller, Randall, Willey, Boycott, Taylor and (if family origins count) Botham, while one of the few players with whom he failed to hit it off was Phil Edmonds, born in Zambia and every bit the bolshie ex-colonial. What he may have liked about his 'Northern' players was that they were generally more prepared to execute his strategies without question. In his way, Brearley was as tough a leader as the Yorkshire pairing of Close and Illingworth – 'just with a different coating', according to David Gower.

As far as his relations with Botham were concerned, Brearley had already demonstrated his largesse by admitting, after Botham's star performance at Christchurch, his mistake regarding the relative merits of Botham and Chris Old. This may not have been the hardest thing for him to do but, Brearley being England captain, it would have been an important moment for Botham. Before that he had felt that Brearley was primarily responsible for his omission from the Test side in Pakistan and that the decision may have been as much a verdict on his behaviour off the field as his abilities as a cricketer. That Brearley's support had been initially withheld only made it more precious once it arrived, particularly given that Brearley's judgement and intellect were so highly regarded. Botham was flattered that such a clever man as Brearley was now taking a close interest in him. Botham was impressed by successful people – and, to the young Botham, Brearley was certainly that.

John Lever thought that Brearley's support, once it came, was crucial. 'I always thought that he [Botham] needed someone to believe in him in a big way. Brears was the perfect person for that, encouraging him with little comments like, "We need a bit of magic now, 'Both'." "Both" would always respond.'

Brearley was Gower's first England captain too. Gower said that Brearley made it clear that he was in charge, and working to well-thought out plans, while at the same time treating everyone as adults, whatever their age or experience. 'Brearley worked with Beefy to build that respect, to affirm the fact that he was in charge,' Gower said. 'Beefy would want to bat, bowl and catch all day but Brears would say, "Now, hang on, that's enough for now, I need you for later," and that would work.

'Beefy had immense respect for Brears through those first years. He was a young man, a colt. And when you are that age, I know from my own experience, you just think the man's God. There's a sort of automatic, "He's captain, he's in charge, I'll do what he tells me," type thing. And that's enhanced when that same captain treats you as a rounded individual, not as a young hothead who needed to be kept out. There were some captains who'd say, "Well, let's do this then." Why? If you wanted to ask Brears, he'd tell you why. He might even tell without you asking. That's the gift of someone who knew his subject intimately.'

But the relationship went beyond that of captain and star player. Brearley said that they soon found that they liked each other, and got on well. 'He was always bouncy, ebullient,' Brearley said. 'He gave his opinion if asked. He wasn't arrogant, but confident, likable.' Nor did Brearley have any problem with Botham's proclivity for mickey-taking. 'He was a very rumbustious character. He would tease, but in the friendliest way. He had a zest for life and one would happily take things from him. He wasn't cruel, he wasn't unkind. He was a great piss-taker.' Brearley conceded that there might have been something of a father–son aspect to their relationship but felt this was an easy conclusion to draw given the age difference. Botham himself rejected this sort of claim. He felt they were more equal than that. Brearley thought a key element in the relationship was a common sense of humour. They were, too, both sociable people.

Perhaps the biggest threat to their relationship was Brearley's form with the bat. By the start of the 1978 season, he had played fifteen Tests, mainly as an opener, and was averaging twenty-seven without one century. When the low scores continued that summer he dropped himself to number five, just one place above Botham. He began by making fifty but there was to be no long-term improvement; indeed, during the twenty Tests in which he led England from 1978 to 1980 he averaged twenty-one, even fewer than before. And still there was no hundred.

This personal crisis amid the success of the team created plenty of media debate, and perhaps some whispered comments in the dressing room, but publicly the team remained strongly behind their captain. Gower put the team's backing for Brearley at 110 per cent. And, for all that he could be harsh in his judgements of some players who failed to cut it at Test level, Botham's support was firm, something that Brearley appreciated. 'I wasn't always comfortable about batting [in Test cricket] or sure I quite belonged,' Brearley said. 'He [Botham] relished it. It was his stage. Like a lot of the best players he would be nervous before a Test but as soon as he walked onto the field he would feel great. But if he had respect and liking for you he was a good friend, and to the ordinary person who worked hard at his game and did his best, he was generous. There was absolutely no sense of arrogance or superiority. Oddly enough, a word of encouragement from him meant a lot.'

But for all Botham's talent and instinctive desire to do well, Brearley had to find ways to motivate him at times when, for whatever reason, Botham ran low on creative energy or a game had reached a critical juncture and Brearley needed something special. This was where Brearley's famed understanding of what made his players tick – what Gower called 'his ability to look into people' – became so important.

And what Brearley concluded with Botham was that here was a

person with extraordinary pride and competitiveness. There were times when it needed tempering and times when it needed galvanising to its absolute peak. Brearley had seen how persistently indignant Botham had been about being ranked below Chris Old; he had seen how the rivalry with Richard Hadlee had concentrated Botham's mind over several weeks in New Zealand. He had seen how well Botham had played amid the acrimony and niggling in the Christchurch Test, and he saw how he relished the bouncer wars with other fast bowlers. Brearley reasoned that, provided the right way could be found to activate it, Botham's competitiveness was a natural resource that could always be tapped.

That Botham possessed an almost atavistic desire to outdo everyone and anyone was not in itself an extraordinary insight. What took skill on Brearley's part was deciding when and how to fire it up. It was a dangerous game, rather like shoving a stick into a wasps' nest with the aim that someone other than yourself gets stung. It was a trick that could only be played so many times, and in between it was necessary to convince Botham that deep down his captain still regarded him as a 'colossus', the word Brearley used to describe him after his unprecedented all-round feat against Pakistan at Lord's.

The words 'provoke' and 'provoked' frequently crop up in Brearley's own assessments of his relationship with Botham. Asked how the two of them had interacted, Brearley said: 'He provoked, enlivened, amused, stimulated and irritated me. I provoked, stimulated and occasionally moderated him.' In commenting on his decision to pick Old rather than Botham in Pakistan, Brearley said he was acting on a genuine belief that Old was the better bet: 'I wasn't being provocative.' But provocative was what it was – and it ultimately helped Brearley crack Botham's personality code. Another time, Brearley said that Botham 'needed a framework against which to bounce'. Off the field, that framework was the family structure; on it, it was Brearley's calculated provocations.

Brearley gambled that if Botham thrived on confrontation with opponents and team-mates who were rivals for his place, he might thrive on confrontation with his captain. The possibility that Botham might turn on him and reject what he had to say did not appear to worry Brearley, who for all his quietly spoken ways, and mild and thoughtful manner, was not averse to the occasional contretemps. In fact, Brearley himself seemed to thrive amid hostility, three of his four half-centuries as Test captain between 1978 and 1980 coming in Australia where he was baited by the crowds as either a haughty Pom in the mould of Douglas Jardine, or as unfathomably remote a leader as Iran's Ayatollah Khomeini, to whom they reckoned Brearley, with his thick beard, bore a resemblance.

And so Brearley would at times chide, harass and insult the most important member of his team. So would others, commandeered to the cause by their captain. If Botham's bowling lacked spark, or Brearley needed a big spell of bowling, a scathing comment about the speed of his delivery would be passed – 'My aunt could bowl faster than this,' or, worse still, 'Chris Old could bowl faster.' When Botham had had to go into a second spell in search of his hundredth Test wicket against India at Lord's, Brearley admonished him from slip: 'Let's see some aggression this time . . . Come on, where is all this fire we hear about?!' When Botham was carving India's bowling to ribbons at Leeds in 1979, Brearley stood on the dressing-room balcony making mock appeals for him to get his head down, knowing full well that this would only provoke him to keep swinging, which Brearley was happy for him to do. When Botham developed a kink in his approach to the crease in 1981 – when Brearley was briefly, famously, recalled to the captaincy – Brearley called him the 'side-step queen'. 'He hated that,' Brearley recalled. And, roused to anger, Botham would bowl better.

It became a standard tactic on the tour of Australia in 1978–79, when Botham was especially eager to show the Australians how good he had become since his time in Melbourne club cricket. On the final day of the first Test – ahead of which Botham had been violently ill from a bad oyster – England were labouring to dismiss Australia a second time when Bob Willis resorted to shouting an insult at Botham from mid-off. 'Call that quick? You're bowling like an old tart. You couldn't knock the petals off a tulip!' The very next ball, Rodney Hogg, a short-tempered fast bowler with whom Botham had struck a bet as to which of them would dismiss the other more times, was clean bowled. Another wicket followed in the same over. Perhaps because he was a fast bowler himself, Willis's insults were often the most effective.

Botham's rivalry with Hogg was a ready-made motivational aid for Brearley to exploit. In the fourth Test in Sydney, where Botham bowled heroically through the heat while Willis and Hendrick were unwell, Brearley encouraged him to keep going with the words, 'Two more wickets and your mate Hoggy's in.' Later in the same game, with England well behind on first innings, Botham was persuaded that the team needed him to bat as long as possible with Derek Randall and got his head down for ninety minutes, during which time he scored six runs – probably the slowest innings of his life. During a difficult period in the fifth game in Adelaide, Brearley got the whole England team to stir Botham up in the dressing-room. 'The result was amazing,' Boycott wrote in his tour diary. 'It was the old belligerent Botham steaming in uphill, hostile and aggressive ... he was positively intimidating.'

The two of them also regularly bickered about Botham's style of fielding in the slips. Botham's favourite position was second slip, to the right of Brearley at first, and his habit was to creep forward, standing closer to the bat than was customary, often half-standing with hands on his knees rather than crouched and hands held out. He didn't miss much, but he did once strain his friendship with Hendrick by putting down a catch off him in Adelaide. Brearley, fretting, would implore him to move back. Again, after initially resisting instructions, Botham often relented. Whether it was Brearley's intention or not, the whole process served to keep

Botham on his toes and determined not to give his captain justification for saying, 'I told you so.' In truth, Brearley rated Botham as second only to Greig as a slip catcher and, as an all-round fielder, the best he had seen.

Gooch said: 'No one could match Brearley's knack of getting the best out of Ian. If he thought there was more in the Botham tank, he'd wind him up on the field with a few tart comments and would deflate him in the dressing-room if Ian started horsing around at the wrong time. In the verbal battle between those two, there would only ever be one winner.'

If he disagreed with Brearley about tactics, Botham might vehemently argue his corner, but would often go away and reflect more carefully than he let on and then revise his opinion – just so long as he was able to do it discreetly. The very obvious backdown was not his style, implying as it did an earlier error of judgement. There was a time during a Test in Australia when Brearley told Botham he'd be better off going out to bat in spikes than normal training shoes. Botham refused but Brearley later saw him quietly putting on his spikes at the next interval.

'Though sometimes initially reluctant to listen, he does take a point,' Brearley said. 'He would get angry but that was fine. He was a young man with hot blood in his veins. He was rebarbative, he would jib against instructions or criticism, but would come round.'

One time when Botham didn't come round was during the second Test of the 1978–79 Ashes. The pitches in Perth were famous for their bounce and Botham's fondness for the short-pitched ball got the better of him. Taking the new ball for the first time in a Test, he bowled wastefully, especially in a failed attempt to bounce out early Peter Toohey, a compulsive hooker. Botham's justification was that Toohey had top-edged a ball to precisely the spot where he had been denied a fielder by Brearley. Botham was furious with Brearley, Brearley with Botham. 'We had a right row,' Botham said. 'One of our best.' Botham did not take a wicket in the game, his one blank Test under Brearley.

Some of Botham's argumentativeness must have stemmed from having to so doggedly follow Brearley's dictat, just as he had once jibbed at Close's commands. Following Brearley's word may have been easier because he would answer Botham's 'Why?' with more fulsome explanations than Close's cussed 'Because.' But for someone of his personality, Botham must have found it hard to accept Brearley's word without a fight.

To sweeten the pill, Brearley offset the stick with the carrot. He cut him some slack – quite a lot of it in fact. He indulged him with regards to net practice, believing that a man who was in form – as Botham always was during this period – did not need to work as hard as someone who was struggling. 'He didn't always want to practise, and sometimes I'd tell him he had to and he'd bowl bouncers at me and be a little flamboyant with his batting,' Brearley said. 'I thought that was better than him doing nothing. I gave him licence because he might have bowled fifty or sixty overs in a match and scored a hundred runs. Why would somebody like that need to practise? He just needed to get loose. At the beginning of a tour he had to do what everyone else did, as did Gower. But once the Tests started, there was no point making them practise much. On the other hand you couldn't go too far in that direction because of the [rest of the] team. I trusted them to manage their own games.' Brearley would also sometimes allow himself to be persuaded by Botham's opinion on whether to bat or bowl first on winning the toss.

It is beyond dispute that Botham put a lot into his matches for Brearley. He bowled an average of thirty balls per match more under Brearley than he did under any other official captain, and some (including Willis) accused Brearley of over-bowling Botham to the detriment of his future career. But it would be wrong to think that Botham got away with murder in terms of practice under him. Geoff Boycott noted how much less practice Botham did when Botham himself was captain, and harked back to the Brearley era as the blueprint for Botham's success. 'What makes Botham what he is, is hard work, a tremendous pride in his physical presence, an appetite for hard going,' Boycott wrote in his 1981 West Indies tour diary. 'When he slacked before, he was made to toe the line and took a great pride in showing that he could bowl longer and work harder than anyone else.' On the 1978–79 tour of Australia, when his preparations were affected by a wrist injury and his fitness criticised by Bill O'Reilly, he stayed off drink for a few weeks until the Ashes were won. It was a self-discipline much less in evidence later.

As Brearley would have seen it, the carrot was an essential part of the deal if he was also going to be using the stick. John Emburey, who played under Brearley at Middlesex and came into the England side in 1978, understood the rationale. '"Both" was full of fun and Mike Brearley let him have his head. He didn't say you can't do this or that. As long as he was producing the runs and wickets, Brears didn't want to change him. He would have said to himself: "How am I going to get the best out of this player? Is it by disciplining him, or by letting him have his freedom?" And Brears worked it out: give him a bit of space.' In Botham's own words, Brearley let him be a free spirit.

Brearley's support was total. He may have chivvied Botham on the field but at other times, in other ways, he made it clear that he would go out of his way to do a lot for Botham, in return for Botham doing a lot for him. When Somerset were trying to win the John Player League in 1979, they needed Kent to lose their final match. Kent's opponents were Middlesex and Brearley promised Botham he would see to it that Kent were defeated. And he was as good as his word – Middlesex beat them.

Botham's most joyously uninhibited performance came in the twentieth and last Test match he played under Brearley during this period. It was a match in Bombay to celebrate the silver jubilee of the Indian cricket board. With both England and India teams weary – India had played sixteen Tests in the previous seven months – the game was played in a relaxed manner, neither team really being up for the challenge – with the exception of one player. To most people, including Botham, it was a fairly inconsequential fixture but a Test match nonetheless – an occasion to be enjoyed rather than agonised over. Amazingly, the pitch was as grassy as an English county ground in April, sparing Botham the worst kind of ordeal from India's spinners and making Brearley's inclusion of two spinners, Underwood and Emburey, irrelevant (and rather odd). Underwood bowled seven overs, Emburey none.

This Test saw Botham in excelsis. His all-round contribution of a century and thirteen wickets – eight of them caught by wicket-keeper Taylor and four lbws as the ball seamed about to his delight – remains unmatched in the history of Test cricket; it was also the third time he had scored a century and taken five wickets in an innings, another unique feat. Barrington said Botham's innings was the most mature he had seen him play and his bowling the most hostile and intelligent since Fred Trueman and Brian Statham fifteen or more years since.

Although the pitch was tailor-made for a bowler of Botham's type, the conditions were not; it was hot and humid and bowling fast was hard work. But he thought nothing of it. He bowled twenty-three overs on the first day and took six wickets. The next day was a rest day, due to a total solar eclipse. The day after that, he scored 114 to rescue England from 58–5 through another big partnership with Taylor worth 171. The third day of the game saw Botham's most extraordinary effort as he bowled twenty-four overs unchanged for another six wickets, a second-innings tally he raised to seven on the fourth morning before England cantered to a ten-wicket win. It was a demonstration of stamina that marked him as a bowler out of the ordinary. 'It's not only skill, pace and intelligence that make a great bowler, it's the ability to bowl a lot,' Graham Gooch said. 'When asked to keep going, or keep coming back, you do it. Some bowlers are not capable of that, but Botham was.'

Even more amazingly, this was one of those games where Botham was burning the candle at both ends, a process assisted by the team – well, Botham – having arranged for copious amounts of beer to be brought in from Australia. Not that he stuck to beer; shorts were consumed as well. 'It was very easy to get caught up in the swing of things with Ian,' said Underwood, who had the misfortune to share a room with him during this Test. 'His capacity [for drink] was ten times mine and making the decision to duck out was crucial. I treasure those moments rooming with him in Bombay ... But we kept different hours.' Underwood actually sought to switch rooms, unsuccessfully. 'I don't think Ian had a lot of sleep during that match,' recalled Lever, who himself bowled more than forty overs. 'That for me was Beefy ... he enjoyed the crack. It was a Test match, but it was also a show-game, and he performed brilliantly.'

Bombay 1980 was the ultimate expression of Young Botham – implausibly brilliant heroics on the field, fun and games off it, superhuman staying power in both arenas. It was the greatest game of his life to date, and it may have been no coincidence that it happened when it did. Life was about to get a lot more complicated. Things would never be so perfect, or so free, ever again.

Botham's great game in Bombay did two things. The first was that it anointed England's young star as the world's best all-rounder. No one else playing at that time could have done what he did. It conjured up memories of Gary Sobers at his best in the 1960s, bowling left-arm fast, stroking glorious back-foot centuries and taking feline catches. Barrington, whose opinion was important to Botham, said after the game that only Sobers compared with Botham.

There were other all-rounders on the horizon though. One had recently emerged from northern India, Kapil Dev – like Botham, he bowled marathon spells and hit the ball prodigiously hard. He, like Botham, had already topped 1,000 runs and 100 wickets, although he was a less versatile batsman and in their personal meetings Botham had kept Kapil quiet with the ball. Pakistan's Imran Khan had developed into a bowler of genuine pace and hostility, but his batting remained immature, although it had

improved since Imran had taken to wearing a helmet. Like
Richard Hadlee, he found protective headgear gave him fresh
courage. 'The advent of the helmet made a great difference to
Hadlee and Imran, whereas it didn't make any difference to
Botham,' Brearley said. 'He had no fear, whereas they did. Botham
would run at them and when he had a ball in his hand they were
nervous of him.' When New Zealand toured England in 1978,
Hadlee had not yet worn headgear and Botham cleaned him up
three times.

Kapil, Imran and Hadlee had not made the impact on Test
cricket that Botham had. While they had all played about the
same number of Tests by early 1980 – their appearances ranged
from 25 to 27 games – he had scored the most runs and taken the
most wickets at the best averages; in fact, no one in history had
reached the 1,000 run/100 wicket double in fewer matches than
Botham's 21. He had also helped his team win many more
matches. The notion that there was rivalry between this quartet
was talked up by the media until it became something very real,
particularly for Botham, who liked to demonstrate his superiority
once a challenge became public.

Botham had another rival in county cricket in Mike Procter,
exiled from Test cricket through his South African nationality.
Their duels aroused much interest in the West Country. Procter's
car sponsors arranged two single-wicket tournaments at Bristol
plus a double-wicket event between Botham and Viv Richards and
Procter and Zaheer Abbas. Procter won all these events, prompting Botham to arrange a clay-pigeon shooting match instead. 'I
wasn't very good at shooting,' Procter said. 'But he had to find
something he could beat me at.'

The second thing Botham's performance in Bombay did was
greatly boost his chances of taking over the England captaincy.
Shortly before arriving in India, Brearley had informed the selectors that he did not wish to tour again. He was about to turn
thirty-eight and although by his own standards he had not done
badly in the recent Tests in Australia, scoring two half-centuries,

he had not otherwise passed thirty runs. He had tired of year-round cricket and felt his captaincy was deteriorating. He intended to continue captaining Middlesex but outside the English season he wanted to developed a career as a psychoanalyst.

The timing of his decision was unfortunate, with England facing a difficult five-Test series at home to West Indies – a very strong side with their Packer players restored – followed by a Test against Australia to mark the centenary of the first Test on English soil, then a return series with West Indies in the Caribbean. It left the team, coming off three sound beatings by Australia, in a vulnerable position. Brearley recognised as much by offering to stay on as captain for some or all of the home Tests, a point which runs counter to later assertions that he was getting out while the going was good. In the light of subsequent events, this was a significant proposal which should have been taken up.

The choice of captain fell to a four-man selection panel chaired by Alec Bedser and also comprising Ken Barrington, Brian Close and former umpire Charles Elliott. Bedser, an experienced servant of English cricket who had carried England's bowling in the immediate post-war period and had chaired the selection panel since 1969, would have had no qualms about appointing someone as working class as Botham; he was of similar background. He had fought in the Second World War alongside his twin brother Eric as a sergeant and played frequently under Len Hutton, England's first modern professional captain. Bedser had also had chance to observe Botham at close quarters as tour manager in Australia and India, as had Barrington as his assistant.

Bedser, as chairman, was obliged to remain open-minded. Elliott, too, was reckoned to be open to persuasion. Barrington favoured giving the job to his young protégé Botham but Close was dead against. Close's opposition had Botham's best interests at heart, his former Somerset captain fearing what detrimental effect the responsibility might have on his game. 'I said something was going to suffer,' Close recalled. 'He couldn't be expected to get all the wickets and runs, and run the side as well. Ian was a doer and things happened for him. How was he going to make them happen for other people? He hadn't learned that. And when you are captain the game comes first, the team second, other individuals third, and you're last. Ian was a front man. He hadn't worked out how to look after everybody.'

Bedser was later to describe the options as limited. Those candidates to whom consideration was given apart from Botham included – intriguingly – Botham's captain at Somerset, Brian Rose; Keith Fletcher, captain of the county champions of the previous year Essex; Roger Knight, a capable leader of Surrey; and John Barclay of Sussex. But each of these men, while armed with experience of leadership at county level, had question marks against them as potential Test cricketers. Knight and Barclay had never played for England. Rose, though he had played a handful of Tests, had not cemented a place. Fletcher, a gifted but understated individual from a rural background, had played more than fifty Tests but the last of those was three years earlier and his technique against the fastest bowling had been exposed. Close also raised the name of Lancashire's David Lloyd, a former county captain and former opening bat in eight Tests.

Bedser concluded that the sheer power of the West Indian bowling meant that the captain had to come from within the existing team. This was a reaction to what had happened with Brearley, who had struggled to justify his place as a batsman even against weaker opposition. It was an understandable ambition but ruled out some capable candidates. It brought the choice down to Botham, Willis, Gower or Boycott. Willis was a regular member of the side with more than fifty caps, but had gone through a tough time in Australia, and there were reservations about specialist fast bowlers making good captains. He was a good first lieutenant. At twenty-three, Gower was even younger than Botham and like Botham had never yet captained in the county championship.

Boycott was in many ways the obvious choice, an experienced player and former county captain with Yorkshire, but he was an awkward character who polarised opinion. The Establishment could not bring itself to gamble on him and Close knew him too well to want to back him. 'It was obvious that the selectors didn't want a senior player like me taking over and I was not angling for the captaincy,' Boycott said. 'It had passed me by. I'd have loved to have been official captain of England. But I was thirty-nine and wasn't going to play much more. I had enough on my plate working on my fitness and my game.'

This left Botham himself. There were obvious shortcomings with him too. He, like Willis, was a fast bowler. He was the team's all-rounder and – as Close pointed out – was already shouldering an enormous burden. He had next to no experience of captaincy at any level since his schooldays and no one had seriously thought of him as captaincy material before England. But he had played twenty-five Tests and understood the game and its tactics. Whether he understood people was less clear but there had been a few encouraging signs. He had been part of the team's management group in Australia – for which he was narrowly chosen ahead of Gower – and when Brearley and Willis were rested against Queensland between the first and second Tests, he had led the side. Having got through a lot of overs in the first Test, he was instructed not to bowl, and did as he was told. He duly led England to a comfortable victory. Bedser considered this all part of his forward planning. 'His appointment was far from a snap decision . . . Botham had been marked as a potential captain. For all that, when the time came we were very conscious of the magnitude of his task, particularly as he had not captained his county. But he was not the first player to be asked to do this.'

What Botham also had in his favour, crucially, was Brearley's support. Brearley's recommendation to Bedser was that Botham be given the job. Given Brearley's intimate understanding of his players, and the respect his judgement and captaincy record commanded, his opinion was bound to carry weight. But in advocating Botham, Brearley's analysis was – by his own subsequent admission – coloured by his own experiences as captain. He was grateful to Botham for what he had done for him: without Botham, Brearley's record would have been much worse. Asked what Botham's credentials for the job were, Brearley said: 'He was shrewd. He was absolutely no fool tactically. He was aggressive. He always wanted to try and find a way of getting a wicket. He was likable, confident, gregarious. He was totally different from me.' The liberal in Brearley may also have wanted to see the England captaincy go to someone who was deserving but also socially against type. But however persuasive the arguments, it was to prove the worst error of Brearley's career.

Ultimately, what persuaded Brearley and the selectors was the sheer allure of Botham's talent and personality. They forgot about the classic captaincy virtues of experience and tough-minded professionalism that had made Illingworth and Brearley the successes they had been, and went for the man with the star-appeal that would satisfy the media. 'Botham had seemed the perfect antidote to me,' Brearley said. 'He was charismatic and of heroic stature.'

Botham was appointed to captain MCC in the opening fixture of the season against the champion county. With Fletcher leading Essex, there was an element of leadership showdown to the occasion, so Botham would have been well satisfied that his side had the better of a draw. Knowing what course of action the selectors were set on, Close visited Botham during this game and tried to talk him out of it. 'When I knew I was going to be defeated, I went to Ian at Lord's and pleaded with him not to take the job,' Close said. 'But I couldn't stop him ... Anyone offered the England captaincy was going to grab it.'

Botham was initially appointed only for two one-day internationals that preceded the Tests. Given Brearley's record in the one-dayers in Australia there was a logic to this, and it did not necessarily preclude Brearley from being retained as Test captain for the time being, as he had proposed. David Lloyd was also included in the one-day side. 'I got a tip-off that I was in the mix [for captain] but I was not good enough to be in the team,' Lloyd recalled.

'I was actually looking to retire but was persuaded by the secretary at Lancashire to carry on. I didn't think I could play for England again. I got one-day hundreds against Derbyshire and Scotland when nobody else was scoring runs and I read the build-up in the papers and thought, "I'm going to get picked." But the ambition had gone.'

As it happened, an injury to Brian Rose meant that Botham was briefly deputed to lead Somerset's one-day side shortly before the West Indies matches; one of these games was against Middlesex, so Botham and Brearley were pitted against each other as captains for what proved to be the only time. In a thrilling finish, Middlesex won by one run. The prospect of captaining England did little to affect Botham's form. In his last championship appearance, he gave a bravura performance against Gloucestershire at Taunton, achieving the highest score of his career, 228, in just over three hours of unbridled ferocity which included numerous hooks off Mike Procter. 'Ducking was never part of his repertoire,' recalled David Graveney, off whom Botham was dropped during this innings. 'Lots of times he might have got bored but on this occasion he seemed determined to stay in.'

The one-dayers went pretty well. Botham did enough with bat and ball to suggest that his game had not been unduly affected by the captaincy. The first game in Leeds was lost, but not badly so, West Indies winning a low-scoring game by twenty-four runs. Lloyd lasted only eight balls during which time he was hit on the elbow by Malcolm Marshall and bowled by Gordon Greenidge to give him his only wicket in international cricket. Botham saw England home in the second match at Lord's with a brisk unbeaten forty-two that included a six off the miserly Garner. His own bowling was unusually expensive but he removed Viv Richards before he could do much damage. Vic Marks remembered Botham doing an impressive all-round job and passionately spurring him on towards the end of England's run-chase; there wasn't the normal Botham jocularity. There was, though, an odd moment when England's seventh wicket fell with only five needed and Botham signalled to the dressing-room for John Lever to come out and join him rather than Chris Old.

The next day, with Botham back in Taunton for a championship match, he received a call from Bedser confirming his appointment as Test captain. As it happened, Somerset's opponents were Middlesex, so Brearley – who had also been phoned and told by Bedser that the selectors were going to 'give Ian a go' – was on hand to offer congratulations. When Botham came out to bat, Brearley greeted him mid-pitch with a little gesture of namaste, an Indian greeting of respect: recognition of Botham's new status but perhaps also of his meteoric elevation. Brearley's genuflections did not go down well with all his Middlesex players; some felt he was showing too much deference to an opponent. Such disgruntlement hardly evaporated when Brearley put down Botham in the slips second ball and Botham proceeded to rattle up eighty-nine runs from seventy-six deliveries. But Brearley redeemed himself by scoring ninety-eight, despite Botham 'running in appallingly fast' at him according to Mike Gatting, and leading Middlesex to eventual victory.

Brearley thought the decision to go with Botham was neither unexpected nor personally unwelcome, but he thought it a mistake to not allow a period of transition. 'I thought it was very hard to put him straight in,' he said. 'They should have kept me on for a few Tests. If things went well, all well and good. If things went badly, they would bring Botham in. Make Botham vice-captain and make it clear he would be the successor, but don't throw him in the deep end. He could have learned from me as well, but that was not the main thing. For anyone, it was going to be an almost impossible year.'

That Botham was thrown in at the deep end showed just how much everyone had bought into the dream. Brearley, Bedser and Barrington had seemingly returned from the winter tour in thrall to him. That he might fail, and how that might affect him, was officially raised by no one except Close. Peter Roebuck reckoned that those who knew Botham best at Somerset had had their doubts: 'It was a fantasy really, that this mighty figure that had saved the team so often could save them as leader as well. Everyone at Somerset wished him well but I doubt that many thought he'd succeed.' Geoff Boycott thought Botham too young and too ebullient. 'It was ridiculous,' he said. 'He had been playing for England for three years. It was a bad misjudgement. There were two sides to him – him talking sense and then the larger-than-life personality. Whenever I heard him speak sensibly about cricket and he was not acting about, he showed he understood cricket, but he was an outgoing individual.'

It was his maturity as a person rather than as a cricketer that ought to have been questioned. A clue might have been gained from an incident three weeks after Botham had come off tour. Attending the England rugby team's last match of the Five Nations championship at Murrayfield as the guest of Tony Bond, the injured England centre, Botham and Bond had attempted to join a post-match party put on by the Scottish RFU only to be told by an official that they were not welcome. Their protests that they were there at the invitation of Billy Beaumont's grand slam-winning team cut no ice. Botham's response was to pour his gin and tonic over the official's head, which led to him being frog-marched from the room. Although Beaumont, who had witnessed the exchange, came out and joined them for a drink, Botham's way of dealing with the situation was neither sensible nor the behaviour of someone about to lead his country.

Botham revealed no doubts about taking on the captaincy. When Brearley first broached the subject in Bombay, he was in Brearley's words 'unambivalently keen to do so'. If he had any doubts about maintaining his form, it appears he firmly suppressed them.

Regardless of how he was going to cope, he wanted the job for what it was, for its status and cachet. As England's best player, he felt he had earned it. He would have had a sense of entitlement. Being England captain also meant, importantly, acceptance from a cricketing Establishment that he felt had looked down on him ever since he had served on the MCC groundstaff all those years ago. For a former comprehensive school boy from Yeovil, the position of England cricket captain was an extraordinary thing to attain. He would be England's youngest captain for almost a hundred years. He would be a Test captain ahead of Viv Richards. It was an offer he was never going to turn down. He had, too, chafed against Brearley's strictures long enough. Now it was his turn to call the shots.

# 6

## Friends

'He used to try to bait you and get you away from your game. I used to say to myself, "Beefy, you can't get me into a conversation with you. You can't get me bowling where you want me to bowl. I've got the ball and you have got to worry about me." Maybe he got the best out of himself by engaging other people, but we never really got to that point ... All I needed was five and a half ounces of leather in my hand.'

JOEL GARNER, WEST INDIES FAST BOWLER, ON
PLAYING AGAINST BOTHAM

Botham, England captain and star all-rounder, had so far been fortunate. He had been mentored by some of the canniest minds in cricket. The Packer crisis had given him opportunities with the England team while sapping the strength of some of their opponents. He had played in a strong England side under the intelligent and attentive leadership of Mike Brearley. And when a successor was needed, there were few strong alternatives to himself. Not yet twenty-five, he stood near the summit of the game. He had been handed a very big chance.

And yet even in the moment of his ascendancy, fate presented circumstances that conspired against him. The captaincy had come his way just as England were about to play home and away series against West Indies, whose amazingly talented team had been inculcated with a fierce discipline through their involvement with Packer. Clive Lloyd's side were about to prove themselves to be not only the best team in the world but arguably the most formidable in history. As if that was not enough, within the team were two players, Viv Richards and Joel Garner, who through their time at Somerset possessed an intimate knowledge of how Botham functioned. If he was to prosper in the long run he would have to survive this sizable short-term obstacle.

Some awkward personal challenges also lurked. In three years as an England player, Botham had never experienced anything like a poor run of form. He had rarely had a quiet game. This was not entirely a good thing. How was he going to cope when, with expectations so high, the unfamiliar happened and he finally went through a bad trot? As chance would have it, he was also suffering from back trouble. During an early-season game against Oxford University at the Parks, he had bowled in cold weather without loosening up sufficiently beforehand; this triggered spasms which he struggled to shake off. He finished the game bowling off-breaks and gave up bowling altogether for two weeks. Infuriatingly, this problem, which Bernard Thomas, the England physio, put down to a kink in the vertebrae, would reappear at unpredictable moments and played a part (not to be underestimated) in shortening Botham's temper.

His desire to be captain was a two-edged sword. He may have considered the job to be his by right but his inexperience of captaincy left him vulnerable. Was he prepared to acknowledge his deficiencies and seek advice from senior players? Was he secure enough to detach himself from the other players so it became clear he was their leader first and friend second? And if he was to retain his full potency as a player he was going to have to work out how to balance the need for responsibility as captain with the willingness to take the risks that had underpinned all his great performances. As captain he was going to have to think twice occasionally; as batsman or bowler, it often served best if he barely thought at all. This was the biggest circle to square.

There was also the question (not that it was one Botham would have put to himself) as to what framework he could bounce off now that Brearley was gone. Who would dare insult and cajole him now that he was captain? Who, knowing that England needed him to go up a gear with the ball, would tell him he was performing like an old tart? This was a facet of his personality that Brearley and the selectors had overlooked when they concluded that Botham was the right man to take over.

To make matters trickier, Botham's public profile had never been higher. With the national football team at a low ebb, he was arguably the best-known sportsman in the country. British sport was generally short of heroes but he was undoubtedly one. His ordinary background, and his column in the *Sun*, made him a figure with which the man in the street could identify, even if his extraordinary deeds did not. As England captain, he was an even more familiar figure and one of whom high standards were expected. It was a job that required discretion. He found this out at an early stage when, on the eve of his first Test as captain, he was caught speeding and, despite pleading that he was 'a little excited', served with a one-month driving ban.

Botham's capacity for self-analysis, self-belief and self-discipline faced the stiffest of tests. Captaincy, he did not yet know, could be a lonely position. He was running the very real risk of tasting two kinds of failure at once – failure as a captain in terms of results, and failure as a player in terms of performance. He was about to find out whether it was indeed a tragedy for someone to be given everything he wished for.

His Test captaincy started off quite well. In the first Test of the series, England ran West Indies very close at Trent Bridge; had they held their catches they probably would have won.

In his first innings, Botham escaped giving a chance on twenty to score an enterprising half-century which prompted *Wisden* to comment, 'Botham demonstrated he could cope with the responsibility of leading a Test side without losing his belligerence.' Although he failed in the second innings, he gave a strong performance with the ball despite wearing a corset to support his back. He claimed four wickets, including that of a rampaging Viv Richards, trapped leg-before with a leg-cutter, as West Indies chased 209 to win. Led by some hostile bowling from Bob Willis, England fought tenaciously before West Indies got home by two wickets. With thirteen runs needed, David Gower's normally safe hands let him down when Andy Roberts offered a chance at cover. It was an incident Botham never let Gower forget.

There was nothing so encouraging about the remaining four matches. All ended in draws but, after batting first, England had to fight their way out of difficulty each time and but for rain would surely have lost at Lord's and Headingley. At the Oval, where for the second time in the series they fielded Brian Rose, Botham's Somerset captain, as one of four opening batsmen by trade in an attempt to stymie their opponents' fast-bowling battery, they took a first-innings lead of 105. At least their stubbornness with the bat spoke of a team working together.

Botham, though, struggled. He fell for six single-figure scores in the series, and his two other innings ended in the thirties. This was a marked fall from grace. With West Indies batting only once in each game, his opportunities as a bowler were limited but he never got on a wicket-taking roll. For someone used to taking wickets by the bagful, to not take more than three in an innings was a new experience. After Trent Bridge, he dismissed just one tail-ender, another rare departure. West Indies were a strong batting side but it was not that Botham was incapable of getting out good players – he removed Richards three times – but that he seemed unable to sustain his aggression. His back was one reason; another was that he had given up cigarettes and had put on weight. Neither development was conducive to him swinging the ball as he had. He bowled fewer championship overs in the season for Somerset than he had ever done.

There were no extenuating circumstances to his failures with the bat. The bowler who caused him most difficulties was Garner, at this time perhaps the best bowler in the world. At six-feet-eight, he generated steepling bounce that pinned batsmen on the back foot and made aggressive shot-making next to impossible. Garner had taken 94 wickets for Somerset in all competitions in 1979 at just 12.4 runs apiece and a fraction over two runs per over. In the five Tests he took 26 wickets at 14.2 each and an economy rate of 1.7. He dismissed Botham four times.

The way Garner and the rest of the West Indies attack – Andy Roberts, Michael Holding, Colin Croft and a young Malcolm Marshall, all exceptional fast bowlers in their own right – unpicked the England captain's mind and method was brilliant. Naturally they raised their game for him, knowing that they could hurt the England team if he was made to struggle. 'Ian had a big reputation at that time,' Croft said. 'He had made runs against Australia, Pakistan and India. Him being captain made a massive difference. The captain was always earmarked for special treatment [by us]. The two batsmen we targeted were Geoff Boycott, as the best batsman, and Botham as captain.'

Richards concurred. 'We didn't want him to get a start because we knew how dangerous he was. Because of his strength and the way he played, this was one individual we had to target. We always targeted the captains. To me, Beefy was always the danger. Having played with him at Somerset, I knew he was a guy who if he spent half an hour at the crease could be very destructive. The bowlers gave a hundred per cent to him more than anyone else.'

Richards and Garner had seen in county cricket how Botham liked to attack. He was capable of defending, but it was rare and not his preferred way of going about things, certainly not when Richards himself was on the field. Then, almost as a matter of course, Botham had to try and dominate, just as Richards himself sought to dominate aggressors like Willis, whose bowling he tore into during the Old Trafford Test. West Indies had also gained a few pointers as to how Botham liked to play from the World Cup the previous year and some one-day internationals in Australia in the winter just gone. Botham had not passed forty in those games.

'Beefy's way of dealing with fast bowling was to attack,' Garner recalled. 'Fast bowlers are aggressive and he always tried to counterattack. If you fell into the trap of bowling bouncers you could waste a lot of time. If you gave him room to swing his arms, he gave you problems. We stuck to our plan. It was all about patience. We aimed to take away his freedom to play shots and keep him quiet for as long as possible. You pay more attention to the people who are the dangerous players.'

Drying up Botham's runs was seen as the best way to undermine him. 'We knew he liked to drive and weren't going to give him too many drives,' Holding said. 'Beefy was an excellent front-foot player and always looking to hit through the line, and over the top, especially over extra cover. He was very good in that direction. Beefy wasn't too fussed about driving the ball along the ground, which made it more difficult to know what length to pitch to him because he would just hit through the line. So we made sure that he had to play a lot of back-foot shots. He got so many short balls that he was quite often a bit late coming forward [when he had the chance to]. That was the tactic. We all knew what the plan was: no drives.'

Pinned on the back foot, and deprived of the boundaries that made him feel in control, Botham was now vulnerable to fending off the short ball and being caught in the arc of close catchers, or leg-before to the odd full-length delivery. During the 1980 series, he was five times caught by the wicketkeeper, slips or gullies, and four times lbw.

'His technique was not that correct,' said Croft, a tall bowler who awkwardly angled the ball into right-handers from the edge of the crease. 'Feet and bat were never working together. You could get away with that if bowlers did not bowl quickly or consistently the same line, but if they bowled at express pace, maybe just short of a length on off stump, then eventually you're going to get caught in the gully or third-slip region. If you brought the ball back into him you could get him lbw because he played a lot away from his body, but most times it was a case of hitting the top of the bat and looking for catches to gully or slip. He tried to hook but didn't hook well. He needed to play exuberant shots but he could only do that if the ball was outside off stump. He wanted to carry the fight to West Indies – too much sometimes.'

Peter Willey, the grittiest of batsmen, spent most of the 1980 series as next man in to Botham – Botham mainly batted six and Willey seven – and it was an exhausting experience. 'Beefy had to take on everybody,' Willey recalled. 'Some games you'd be up and down like a blue-arsed fly. That game at Trent Bridge which we lost, he got a few runs there. I must have been in and out of my seat so many times. 'Where's he hit that one? Oh no, we're all right ...' I was exhausted before I even got to the wicket. You never knew what he was going to throw at you.'

Depriving Botham of the chance to play his favourite shots was one method Lloyd's team found to counter him; another was refusing to engage in the banter of which he was so fond. Botham would have seen matches against West Indies as opportunities to verbally spar with players who were familiar to him from county cricket, particularly Richards and Garner. This was not as innocent as it looked. Botham liked to wind up an opponent and talk him into an undisciplined move.

Lloyd's men had no intention of falling for such tricks, with Richards leading the way. 'I tried to keep things as far away as possible from how close we were as friends,' he said. 'When we were out there he was just like any other individual [to me]. Friendship should never be allowed to overpower you. Beefy was competitive and what he did was try to get into your head. It may be said in a jovial mood but deep down he meant it. Once, I was coming in to bat and I needed maybe another four runs to get to a milestone, and he passed me and said something like, "You're not hoping to get that record today? Maybe some other time, but not today ..." He was trying to plant something in your mind.

'When he was batting, basically I'd walk past him, or I'd go and stand near where he was standing [in the batting crease], basically invade his space, and I'd shout things like, "Well bowled Macko!" Clapping my hands. "It's coming . . . this time!" And he'd say out of the corner of his mouth, "Fuck off, Smokey!"'

Croft witnessed these exchanges and detected that while to Botham they were essentially jocular, to Richards – who stood in as captain for most of the fourth Test and all of the fifth after Lloyd tore a hamstring – they were an opportunity to deliver a warning. 'Viv and he were always teasing each other on the field and yet Viv was serious about it. Viv would shout from second slip, "Come on, Crofty! Let's get his neck broken," or something like that. And it worked, because he would hear that, and would sometimes react to it, which we wanted.'

Richards might have baited him back but conversation-wise Botham got next to nothing out of the West Indies fast bowlers. Croft hated talking to opponents at the best of times – 'anybody I played against was never my friend' – and was not overly keen on speaking with team-mates for fear it would disturb his focus. 'He would try to talk to you,' Croft said of Botham. 'But the more he talked, the more angry I became. He didn't understand that.'

Holding, too, wasn't a friendly presence on the field, perhaps for the same reason that he didn't want anything to affect his focus. Because of his friendship with Botham at Somerset, Garner had to fight harder to not get drawn into disarming chat. 'He used to try to bait you and get you away from your game,' Garner said. 'I used to say to myself, "Beefy, you can't get me into a conversation with you. You can't get me bowling where you want me to bowl. I've got the ball and you have got to worry about me." Maybe he got the best out of himself by engaging other people, but we never really got to that point. I didn't need to be motivated like that. All I needed was five and a half ounces of leather in my hand.'

What the West Indies did to Botham was the reverse of what

Brearley had done. Like Brearley, they provoked a reaction. But whereas Brearley galvanised Botham into proving himself by judicious use of a teasing insult, the West Indies players antagonised him into an intemperate response by being pointedly, chillingly hostile. 'They thought they could psyche him out,' said Willey. And they were right.

Botham's first season as England captain ended with a Test at Lord's against Australia to mark the centenary of Test cricket in England. Blighted by bad weather and unruly crowd behaviour towards umpires who seemed insensitive to the need to get play started again after rain, the game failed to replicate the drama of the centenary game in Melbourne three years earlier, and failed to see Botham return to form. He led England to wins in the two one-day internationals that preceded the Test but he did little himself and made alarmingly little impact on the game at Lord's either. His bowling had never looked so innocuous for England – he was lucky to be awarded an lbw decision against Kim Hughes, the star of the game – while Len Pascoe, a feisty new-ball partner for Dennis Lillee, dismissed him for nought, an indignity he had not suffered even against West Indies, during a collapse that left England trailing by 180 on first innings.

Most revealingly, when England reached 124–3 in pursuit of 370 with nearly three and a half hours remaining, Botham disappointed the crowd by not sending himself in to have a fling. It was, after all, supposed to be an exhibition game. In times past, he would have leaped at this chance. Instead, he instructed Boycott to stay in as long as possible. 'He said to me, "Don't get out, Fiery, or we'll lose the game,"' Boycott recalled. Botham's nerve, it seemed, was failing him.

During the last three weeks of the season, Botham led Somerset in the championship for the first time as Brian Rose – to whom he was now vice-captain – was ruled out of three matches through injuries. Botham himself was suffering with his back and bowled only occasionally in these games. The gung-ho manner in which Somerset chased 302 against Leicestershire at Taunton perhaps betrayed his eagerness to get a meaningful win under his belt as captain, especially as Richards was playing under him. Botham hit a low full toss to midwicket off Nick Cook, a young spinner who claimed five cheap wickets, as Somerset collapsed to 144 all out. There was more frustration at the end of an epic contest with Gloucestershire which ended with the scores level after Somerset were left to score 200 in 38 overs. The pursuit faltered as Botham and Richards were both caught on the fence off David Graveney.

Botham's unhappy season came to a disturbing conclusion when under him Somerset lost to Warwickshire by ten wickets. Apparently annoyed at something that had been written about him, Botham attacked the press box at Taunton. 'He came round and shouted, "Three cheers for the press," and threw a chair at the press box window,' said Jack Bannister, who was covering the match for the *Birmingham Post.* 'He was upset about something. We thought about taking it up with the club, but in the end decided against, and we also decided that none of us would write about the incident.'

Botham in his autobiography said this incident took place in 1983, when he was annoyed at press coverage about his wife's miscarriage, but Bannister remembers it occurring in 1980. Despite what had happened, he still dined with Botham that evening, and they discussed selection issues for the forthcoming winter tour.

By the time Botham next led England, things had got worse. When he and the team left for the Caribbean in mid-January he did so in the extraordinary situation for an England captain of having an assault charge hanging over him. Botham had already pleaded not guilty and elected for trial by jury, but this meant the case being adjourned until after the West Indies tour was over. It was an uncomfortable situation and it had required the negotiation of his solicitor Alan Herd to ensure that the hearing would not be set for a date when his client was still away on tour. Needless to say, Botham's masters at the TCCB were not best pleased. Those who might have thought that Botham was not made of the right stuff to be national captain had been handed ammunition.

The trouble arose from an evening in Scunthorpe that Botham spent with his friend Joe Neenan, a 21-year-old Scunthorpe United goalkeeper. Botham had continued to play occasional football for various teams throughout his professional cricket career. He had made seventeen appearances for non-league Yeovil Town during the previous three years and towards the end of the 1979–80 season had played centre-half in a couple of first-team games as substitute for fourth division Scunthorpe, with whose squad he sometimes trained outside the cricket season. He remained a registered player with the club and would play more games for them in future.

Botham had accompanied Scunthorpe players on an outing two days before Christmas. Unfortunately for Neenan, who had previously kept goal for York City, he had made a catastrophic error the previous week in an FA Cup replay against non-league Altrincham. By losing his temper and inflicting a crude tackle on Johnny King, the Altrincham captain, Neenan had needlessly conceded a penalty from which came the only goal of the game. The prize was an away tie at Liverpool, so the stakes could hardly have been higher, and Neenan was rightly blamed for having blown his team's chances.

During the evening, Neenan was taunted by disgruntled Scunthorpe fans, while Botham was approached outside a nightclub by Steven Isbister, a nineteen-year-old apprentice seaman, who asked if Botham would like his autograph. When Botham said, 'Not particularly,' Isbister had replied that he did not want Botham's either and walked off, shouting as he went. This culminated in Neenan and Botham giving chase – Botham saying later in court that he had wanted to find out what Isbister was talking about – and catching up with him in an alleyway. According to Botham's account in his 2007 autobiography, Neenan caught up with Isbister and thumped him. 'Honour was satisfied and we walked back and caught a taxi home,' Botham wrote. However,

Isbister went to the police, claiming that during an attack by Botham and Neenan he had suffered injuries to the head and body and lost a tooth. The upshot was that Neenan and Botham were interviewed by police, cautioned and charged with assault occasioning actual bodily harm. On 14 January 1981, Neenan pleaded guilty at the local magistrates' court and was fined £100 with £100 costs. Botham denied the charge, chose to go to trial and was granted unconditional bail. In the end the trial itself did not take place until September.

The incident created a frenzy of interest. It was shocking on two fronts. First, it was then much less common than it later became for sportsmen to have their names linked to public disorder offences. Should the England cricket captain be treated in the same way as any other citizen? Was it reasonable for his case to be put off for what transpired to be eight months? Dennis Canavan, MP for West Stirlingshire, protested to the Attorney General Sir Michael Havers. 'It would be very unfortunate if the public was to get the impression that there is one law for England cricketers and another for the rest of us,' he said.

The episode also touched a raw nerve. There was already general disquiet about social unrest in the country. Unemployment had been on the rise since Margaret Thatcher had come to power in 1979 and there was an ongoing debate in some quarters about whether Britain was in a state of suppressed civil war. Concerns that the government's tough economic policies might trigger violent opposition had been fuelled by a riot in the St Pauls district of Bristol in April 1980 – and more inner-city riots were indeed on the way. There seemed to be no end of evidence that violence was lurking just beneath society's surface.

This, really, was the start of the bad publicity that was to become a common feature of Botham's playing career. Before this, his life on and off the field had aroused relatively little controversy and certainly nothing that might be termed a scandal. Shortly before he left for the 1978–79 tour of Australia, he had cut his left wrist on a glass-panelled door at a pub in Epworth and there had been rumours (never remotely substantiated) that it was caused in a fight. Reporters had turned up at his home and sought confirmation from his wife, much to the distress of her and her husband. There had been unkind pieces written about his increased weight. But nothing so adverse as this.

What the incident also appeared to do was encourage some mindless elements with a few drinks inside them to think that Botham might be worth baiting if they came across him in a pub or club late at night.

Then, within days of his arrival in the West Indies and with the assault charge hanging over him, Botham was involved in an incident in a bar in Antigua, the team's first port of call, which could have cost him dear. BBC radio reporter Don Mosey described Botham's behaviour as 'crass idiocy'.

A group of cricket writers were in the bar at the time but they again decided not to make public what happened. They chose to protect Botham – for his sake and the sake of the team, and the harmony of the tour (even today no-one will go on the record about what happened). This showed that the ties of friendship between players and pressmen remained strong, although they were not to do so for much longer. 'He was more indiscreet than most,' said one journalist on the tour. 'Initially at least, he was indiscreet, naive and gullible.'

England's chances of avoiding defeat in the West Indies were slim. As captain Botham could hardly say as much, nor was it his way. As ever, he talked a good game and at one point publicly stated that Clive Lloyd's team could be beaten.

As had been the case with previous captains, he was broadly given by Alec Bedser's committee the players he wanted, and the players he wanted were middle-order shot-makers and fast bowlers rather than spinners. Essentially, he wanted a team in his image. Roland Butcher, his old friend from MCC groundstaff days, was taken ahead of a stodgier accumulator of runs, Bob Woolmer, who had been an unhappy member of the side for the first two games in the series in England, selling his wicket dear but grinding out runs at twelve an hour. Time would show that this was actually the best way of countering the West Indian fast bowlers.

The tour party also included another old mucker of Botham's in Graham Stevenson, who was to be a support fast bowler behind Botham himself, Willis, Old and Graham Dilley, a promising young bowler of genuine speed. Botham would say later how he had come out of the selection meeting delighted that there had been no place for Robin Jackman, a heavy wicket-taker for Surrey whom he had taken against some fifteen months earlier when Jackman had dismissed him in a match at Taunton. Jackman recalled: 'He had to walk past me to the pavilion and I said something like, "And how does it go?" And I whooped my arms up in the air, which is what he used to do when he got a wicket. It didn't go down well. He said later that he had wanted to flatten me. He thought I was an "arrogant poser".'

Curiously, the three spinners who were taken were all off-spinners, even though the value of off-spin was questionable given the shortage of left-handed batsmen in the West Indies side. Some interpreted this decision as confirmation of Botham's reliance on Brearley for advice, as Brearley had a difficult relationship with Phil Edmonds, the leading left-armer. But Botham generally did not hold spin in high regard, even though he came unstuck against it. He thought it was there to be hit. John Emburey, the team's frontline slow bowler, felt Botham was among the less sympathetic of the eight Test captains he played under.

In the event, England could make insufficient impression on either the West Indian batting – which posted first-innings scores in excess of 400 in three of the four games – or fast bowling, which laid them waste in the first two games in Trinidad and Barbados, before England mounted stronger resistance to earn draws in Antigua and Jamaica. The most dangerous bowler this time was Croft, who took twenty-four wickets in the four Tests and nine more in two one-day internationals. He was backed up by Holding, whose eighteen Test wickets included Geoff Boycott three times in the space of eleven balls. Garner, the star in England, took only ten wickets but again gave away precious few runs.

To lose 2–0 was not a disaster but the tour, lasting three months, proved far more traumatic for Botham and his team than the bald scoreline suggested. The Test in Guyana – supposed to be the second – was scrapped when the government there, in a random act of political interference, objected to the connections with apartheid South Africa of Jackman, who had flown out to join the tour party after Willis went down with a knee injury, which was a big blow for the team. The Jackman Affair led to a tortuous two-week hiatus during which England played just one one-day match.

Then, after the team eventually moved on to Barbados, Ken Barrington, the assistant manager who had found the crisis in Guyana so stressful, died of a heart attack on the second night of the Test.

This was a particularly devastating blow for Botham, who had so valued Barrington's paternal interest in his welfare since coming into the England side four years earlier. Barrington, who won a reputation for treating every player the same regardless of ability or background, had never wavered in his support. With Brearley out of the team, and Botham himself captain, Botham would have regarded Barrington as the main person to whom he could turn for the encouragement, support and belief that was so important to him. His death therefore presented Botham with a major challenge. In the midst of this crisis Botham received invaluable help from the tour manager, A.C. Smith, whose silk scarves and Oxbridge education had previously aroused Botham's suspicion; his friend Graham Stevenson; and Peter Willey, who went round the team on the morning after Barrington's death in an effort to get everyone focused on the match they had to complete. This was a job that might, in other circumstances, have been done by the captain.

In the absence of Willis, Botham carried the attack manfully, although without his old rhythm. He bowled the most overs and took the most wickets, and at times bowled superbly at Viv Richards, but against a strong team he found success hard to come by. The frustration showed. 'He was not a patient man . . . His attitude was, "If you can't do it, I'll do it",' Roland Butcher remembered. 'So you would find that he would be bowling when he shouldn't have been. He always believed that he could get the batsman out. He'd want to bowl all the time.' He overdid the short ball, forever trying to bounce out Desmond Haynes, who opened the batting and relished the hook shot, but at least his old knack of cleaning up the tail returned: eight of his fifteen wickets were those of the four fast bowlers who propped up the West Indies batting order.

His batting was worse than ever. The tactics the West Indians had used in England worked even better than before, as the England captain was restricted to seventy-three runs in seven innings. Croft and Holding accounted for him four times. He was never out to Garner, although he said that one ball he received from him in Barbados was the fastest he had faced. Again denied the drivable balls he thrived on, he hit just six fours in the four Tests. Croft had him leg-before to his second ball of the series but after that he was routinely caught in the close cordon. Although run-scoring was naturally hard work for everyone, Graham Gooch (twice), Geoff Boycott, David Gower and Peter Willey all scored hundreds. Holding said that these four were the only good batsmen in the England side. Botham's one real success with the bat was an innings of 60 in a one-dayer in St Vincent but England, chasing only 128, still lost by two runs. By the final Test, he had demoted himself below Willey in the order.

All this was bad enough but Botham did not help himself in other ways. His comment that the teams would struggle to get a result on the Trinidad pitch even if the match lasted ten days came back to haunt him when England were beaten in half that time, as did his warning that if they lost, heads would roll. As he got out slogging at Viv Richards' part-time spin, it was his head that was left looking most vulnerable. 'It was the first time that I'd seen him almost in half-shock,' Brian Rose said. 'It was the first sign that the captaincy was affecting him. He was already under pressure.' Nor did he send a good signal to his players by throwing down his bat and glaring at the pitch in Barbados.

'You could see then that we had the upper hand,' Michael Holding said. 'It was as if he was not too sure what was going on.'

Even during this most difficult period, Botham never publicly questioned his own ability. 'He would not admit to self-doubt,' David Gower said. 'Every time he had a crunch [bad trot] in his career the last thing he would do was admit a problem. In the West Indies in 1981 you could see him coming back in [to the dressing-room], shaking his head in disbelief, refusing to admit that there was anything but bad luck out there. There were times when it would have been handy to admit that a re-think was needed and that pure instinct wasn't enough. I once asked him, "Are you honestly telling me that at no stage did you have even a fleeting moment of self-doubt?" It was a categorical "No". I would say there must have been some at some stage. The ability to deny it to everyone else is one thing; whether you ever fully deny it to yourself, who knows?'

If Botham's struggle to keep his own game going was one problem, another was how he looked after those playing under him. If some of his actions on the pitch failed to inspire confidence, he also struggled to understand that some players needed coaxing. Like Brian Close, he found it hard to hide his feelings as captain. There was an early issue over his treatment of Dilley, who was twenty years old and on only his second tour. The abrasiveness between them was plain. With Dilley finding his rhythm elusive, Botham's response was to make a series of leg-pulling remarks that Chris Old believed were actually meant in a serious way. Old suspected Dilley felt worse because of them and he suggested to Botham, without success, that he try encouraging Dilley instead. Old believed that his frank comments to Botham when the team reached Guyana were a contributory factor in him never playing under Botham again, although Botham himself attributed Old losing his place in the next Test to a late withdrawal by Old due to a mysterious malady. Livid at what he saw as someone bottling it, Botham had bawled Old out. Botham knew that Mike Brearley would have handled the incident more sympathetically but said that he did not have the time or inclination to go down that route.

Old was not the only player to question Botham's methods. Peter Willey took his captain aside in Guyana and advised him that he might do better to keep a greater distance from his players. Being one of the lads was undermining his authority, Willey suggested. Botham admitted that this conversation made him stop and think, but it does not appear it made him change. As a captain himself at county level, Brian Rose appreciated Botham's predicament. 'Beefy was such an outgoing bloke. He was always the centre of things. But when you are captain it is completely different. People become wary of captains because captains take decisions. They cannot go on being everyone's mate. That was a difficult thing.'

Opposition to Botham's style of captaincy appeared to emanate from Gooch and Emburey. Gooch felt that Botham failed to understand that it was necessary to appreciate the needs of each player if he was to get them playing for him. 'We had problems on the tour in terms of Gooch and Emburey,' Butcher said. 'They felt that "Both" wouldn't listen, that he'd just do what he wanted. There were some shouting matches and "Both" a couple of times told them to shut up. He probably thought he could deal with it but I feel that because of his value to the team as bowler, batsman and fielder, the captaincy was too much. But he would never have thought that.'

Botham and Gooch had a serious falling-out in a team meeting in Barbados about training methods. Although Botham's personal regime was not really the point at issue, it may have been an unspoken factor in the argument, because since becoming captain Botham had cut back on practice, as Geoff Boycott noted in his tour book *In the Fast Lane*. 'It is noticeable that he doesn't spend as much time bowling in the nets or throwing himself into the warm-up exercises,' Boycott wrote. 'Some of the players comment on it. Botham may now feel that he has to save himself for the Test matches, if so he is doing himself a disservice.' Perhaps the slackening off in training, along with the fewer overs he had bowled in England, had contributed to him looking like he was carrying a few more pounds. Meanwhile, Gooch, still striving to fully establish himself as a Test cricketer, having scored only one hundred in twenty-six Tests before the two he made in this series, had realised that if he was to open the batting successfully he needed to be stronger, fitter and more mentally alert, and had committed himself to a strict training regime.

When Botham saw Gooch fall asleep at the dinner table one evening, he decreed that Gooch should cut out his early-morning jogs along the beach. '"It's making you tired," he said,' Gooch recalled. 'I was trying to do my bit to keep fit and it worked for me. So we had a row. It wasn't in jest. But I carried on jogging. The fact was that I was in the habit of falling asleep in the evening if I'd had a couple of glasses of red wine.'

This spat came to epitomise the different ways Botham and Gooch approached the game. While Botham was to increasingly demonstrate an extraordinary capacity for getting by on a regime of modest practice and excessive late-night socialising, Gooch was happiest going to bed early and rising with the sun to get in a training session before the day's regular work began. While Botham's lifestyle had not mattered when he was playing brilliantly, training harder and not captaining the side, now that he was struggling for runs and other players were looking to him for a lead, it became a talking point.

Gooch felt Botham undermined his own captaincy by failing to set the right example. 'Tactically he was fine,' he said. 'The only issue I had was the way he lived his life. It's difficult to call the shots when you [the other players] know what they [the captain] get up to. I'm not saying that I didn't have a drink with them. Of course I did. He was one of the few cricketers I played with who could enjoy life to the full and turn up next morning and still run in all day. John Lever was another one like that. It [drinking] didn't seem to affect them.'

Willis's view was not dissimilar to Gooch's. He felt that Botham was not mature enough to cope with the off-field role of captain, a role that had grown a great deal since the mid-1970s. Ironically, after Willis went home, Botham wanted Gooch to take over as vice-captain but the TCCB ruled that Geoff Miller, who unlike Gooch had captained in county cricket, should do the job, even though Miller wasn't certain to play in the Test side.

Emburey recalls with wry amusement Botham's optimistic tactics during a match against Jamaica shortly before the final Test. 'At times he didn't endear himself to the side,' Emburey said. 'We were getting smashed around but he still had an attacking field, and he kept bowling bouncers at a guy called Tucker, and Tucker just kept slogging him for six or four. And then the ball was driven back past him, and he turned round, and there was no one there, so he had to chase it himself. He got back to his mark, and we were all laughing in the slips, and I shouted across, "Shall we get one of the slips out and put him out there?" He just pointed at me and said, "You!" ... and motioned a zip across his mouth and a finger across his neck. It was quite funny.'

Even the West Indians could detect the divisions in the rival camp. Viv Richards said: 'He was not supported well enough as captain by some of the senior guys. You didn't need to be in the same dressing-room to find that out. You could see that just from looking at the way they responded to him. There were some clashes ... Beefy was too casual in some ways.' With the local crowds sometimes getting on Botham's back, Richards noticed how during one-day matches Botham would, in later overs when he might be fielding on the boundary, edge around the fence trying to pick out who was harassing him. Richards shared a drink with Botham and listened to him insist that he didn't mind the criticism he was getting; Richards was not fooled.

Nor did the troubles within the team go undetected by the English cricket writers, who in print pored over Botham's struggles with the bat and his qualities as a leader. They may have protected him over incidents like the one in Antigua but they now had plenty of ammunition to question his future as England captain on cricketing grounds.

Astute as ever, Boycott in his diary expressed the fear that the captaincy was stripping Botham of his potency.

> *Quite simply we lost him as a player. Hard as he tries – and let nobody doubt his commitment – I do not believe that England can afford a captain with L-plates ... By his late twenties he would have been experienced and weathered enough to have taken it in his stride and done it without attracting the controversy which sometimes dogged him on this tour ... Not long ago, Botham was being hailed as the greatest all-rounder since Keith Miller: I should hate him to lose the substance in search of a dream he may not yet be ready to achieve.*

As the players prepared in their hotel rooms for their flight home from Jamaica, Robin Jackman got a phone call from his captain. Given what had passed between them, Jackman found it a moving moment.

'He said, "What are you doing?"

'"Well, I'm just packing a few things," I said.

'And he said, "I've got a bottle of whisky in the room. Do you want to help me with it?"

'So I went straight down and we sat and talked about the tour. He wasn't in a good space because of the criticism that he was getting and it was probably the closest to tears I have ever seen him, if I might not have detected the odd one. I felt chuffed that I was the one he had called on, hardly to cry on my shoulder but just to talk to on his own. That was very unlike him. He was such a gregarious guy.'

Even the journey home was fraught. In transit at Bermuda airport, Botham accosted Henry Blofeld of the BBC, *Guardian* and the *Sunday Express*. Blofeld had written that Botham 'captains the side like a great big baby'. Graham Morris, the photographer, recalled: 'I was stood in the corner of the lounge and heard these players saying, "Go on, go over and stick one on him." Bairstow and Stevenson were egging Beefy on. The next thing I knew, Beefy had gone over and was holding up Blowers against the wall ... It was probably drink-fuelled, like many things that "Both" now regrets, I would think.'

Blofeld, who happily dines out on the story, said: 'Botham was upset at my criticising his captaincy. He was encouraged by David Bairstow and that well-known Yorkshire intellectual Graham Stevenson. He tried to punch me, missed and I ended up on the floor.' A.C. Smith was horrified. 'I kept telling Ian not to read the papers,' he said, 'but he's fundamentally insecure and very sensitive about criticism.'

Again it was agreed among the cricket correspondents that the story would not be written. But other journalists got to hear about it and the *People* called Derek Hodgson, who had been covering the tour for them as well as the *Star*. Asked directly whether the incident had happened, Hodgson felt he could not deny it. On 26 April the *Sunday People* ran the story on its front page, claiming Botham had jostled Blofeld 'with one fist clenched', leaving Hodgson to defend himself from another cricket correspondent who felt he had given the game away. The TCCB investigated the incident and cleared Botham of wrongdoing.

How things had changed in the year since Botham became England captain. Someone who had forgotten what it was like to have a poor match was now battling to retain his self-belief. He was not playing well, the team were not winning, and relationships with some team-mates were fragile. He had become fiercely sensitive to criticism from fellow players and journalists with the result that he was starting to cut himself off from some of the most helpful sources of advice. The famed confidence was gone and it must have stung his pride to know that everyone could see it had gone too. He was in an emotionally vulnerable state.

'The pressure of ongoing criticism and failure, personally and for the team, got to him more than I would have predicted,' said Mike Brearley, who would have heard first-hand accounts of the tour from four Middlesex team-mates. 'I didn't expect that within the team he would get rather huffy and sensitive. People would be nervous about giving their opinions if they were different from his. That is a terrible situation to get into and it happened within quite a short time.' One England player told Brearley that he had been physically afraid to pursue a suggestion once Botham disagreed with it.

Botham's 1981 home season began miserably. As luck would have it, his first two championship appearances brought him back into contact with West Indian fast bowlers who had been making his life a misery. Nor did they spare him again. Out to Malcolm Marshall for five at Southampton, he faced Michael Holding on a lively pitch at Old Trafford with a sense of foreboding. Vic Marks, who was in the dressing-room shortly before Botham went out to bat at 47–4, said that this was a rare instance of Botham being beaten before he had started. When he got to the middle, Botham told his batting partner Peter Roebuck: 'I'll never survive this over.' And he didn't – he was out first ball. As he walked back through the crowd to the pavilion, Botham shouted: 'It's just like the bloody winter!' They laughed. Botham was not yet so demoralised that he couldn't fight back with the ball – his back was feeling good for the first time in a year – and he and Joel Garner bowled unchanged as Lancashire were dismissed for 121 to give Somerset victory by 33 runs. Holding was one of Botham's four victims. A week later, he batted skilfully in a tricky run-chase in a Benson and Hedges Cup match against Kent at Taunton, his unbeaten fifty-seven winning Somerset the game by five wickets.

For all that had happened, Botham was hardly likely to give up the captaincy yet. The chance to lead England in an Ashes series was not one to pass over and there was good reason for thinking he could fare better at home to Australia than he had against West Indies. With Ian Chappell having retired (for a second time) and

Jeff Thomson and Len Pascoe overlooked, Australia did not look as strong as when they had beaten England 3–0 in Australia eighteen months earlier, or at the Centenary Test the previous year. Moreover, they were being led by a novice. With Greg Chappell pulling out of the tour to attend to his young family and business affairs, the captaincy went to Kim Hughes, the star of the Lord's showpiece in 1980. Hughes had never led a full-strength Australia side before and his appointment had not gone down well with all the players. Rod Marsh and Dennis Lillee, who knew Hughes well from Western Australia, felt the captaincy ought to have gone to Marsh himself. Hard-bitten pros and – unlike Hughes – former Packer men, they thought Hughes was gifted but undisciplined, lacking maturity and responsibility. They wanted to win at all costs; he seemed to want to entertain and have fun. These divisions, known about in English ranks at the time, were potentially far more incendiary than Botham's differences with Gooch and Emburey, although Hughes, a pacifist by inclination, accepted Lillee and Marsh's hostility and their skipping of the first leg of the tour to Sri Lanka with mild good grace. Nor was he too proud – possibly unlike Botham – to accept advice from players with whom he did not see eye to eye.

The England selectors were naturally concerned that their giant had turned to journeyman, but were sympathetic too. They felt he had been unlucky in the West Indies; the Guyana crisis and Ken Barrington's death were events that would have sorely tested any leader. A.C. Smith, the tour manager, had been kind on him too; despite Botham's foolishness in making his 'heads will roll' remark and grabbing a critical journalist by the collar, Smith said in his tour report that the captain had done well to keep the side together in the face of unnatural adversities.

Even so, the support for him was now qualified, an admission that selectorial doubts did exist. Brian Close, who had never wanted him to be captain in the first place, would have welcomed Botham being relieved of the job. In the event, Botham was appointed captain only for the three one-dayers against Australia that presaged the six Tests. Unfortunately these did not go well, despite Australia's warm up matches being blighted by rain. England comfortably won the first game at Lord's but the series turned on their failure to capitalise on a commanding position in the second at Edgbaston. With six overs to go, Gatting, batting with authority, and Botham were together with only twenty-six runs needed and five wickets in hand. Botham then skied an awkward catch to Hughes and in the last over Gatting was caught equally well by Geoff Lawson. In the end, England lost by two runs, and Australia went on to take the decider at Leeds with ease.

With ten days to the first Test, the selectors decided that they could not appoint as captain for the entire series someone whose form was so obviously not what it had been. They announced that Botham would captain on a match-by-match basis, effectively placing him on trial. BBC TV's fledgling magazine programme *Newsnight* entered what was now a lively media debate as to whether Botham should continue as England captain by holding a mock 'Trial of Ian Botham' – an echo of the actual trial still hanging over him – even while the first Test was going on.

This cannot have been an easy time for Botham and he hated it. The mood between himself and the authorities (in the shape of the TCCB and the selectors, at least all of them bar Brian Close) was now one of grave unease. Bedser wrote of Botham in his autobiography: 'His inexperience as a captain began to show when the situation soured, the problems mounted and some critics went over the top.' His captaincy was breaking down. The team had stopped practising their fielding drills or holding regular team-talks, which Botham dismissed as boring and counterproductive. He hardly ever addressed the team about tactics and if he did speak to them it was to deliver short up-and-at-'em imprecations. His view was that players should psyche one another up 'over a beer or two'.

Not much happened in the first Test at Trent Bridge to improve things. On a damp, seaming pitch, Australia won a tight, low-scoring match late on the fourth afternoon – the first Sunday on which Test cricket had been played in England – largely because they held their catches and their non-practising opponents didn't. The worst error was committed by wicketkeeper Paul Downton, who put down Allan Border ten runs into his innings of sixty-three, the only half-century of the match, but two inexplicable errors were perpetrated by Botham, who provided further evidence of not being himself by waiting until the fifty-fourth over to give himself a bowl in conditions tailor-made for him.

This was not the man England had made captain.

# 7

## Lightning Strikes Thrice

'We were about to go out and Beefy was putting on his
Nike tennis shoes. Mike Brearley saw him and said,
'What are you doing?' So Beefy – strong character as he
is – said, "You're all right, captain, you don't want me to
bowl." Brearley said, "Get your bowling boots on." We
were all waiting to go out. And he tried it again. "You
don't want me to bowl, do you?" And Brearley's voice
changed. "Get your bowling boots on." So he had to hurriedly get them on ... A lesser captain would have
ducked down to him and Beefy would have got away
with it.'

BOB TAYLOR ON THE FINAL AFTERNOON
OF THE EDGBASTON TEST, 1981

Although the job had perhaps brought out the worst in him –
making his forcefulness and impatience more apparent, to the
detriment of his generous and caring side – the loss of the England
captaincy was the greatest tragedy of Botham's career. That he had
failed at the game's highest level as captain would define him
almost as much as the triumphs that came before and after. And
although he tried, it could not be brushed off as anything but a
failure. He may have been unlucky to come up against a West

Indies team in their pomp, but he did little better against Australia and struggled to carry his players with him.

To not win one of twelve Tests in charge was a spectacular disappointment that hurt all the more because he had been so desperate to do well. Like Geoff Boycott before him, Botham had wanted the England captaincy and yet when it came to it his personality, like Boycott's, proved unsuited to the challenge. Both of them, too, insisted afterwards that they were eager to have it back one day. Neither would admit that the job had beaten them (albeit that Boycott had only been a stand-in captain), but it had. It was this unsuitability, rather than a supposed tendency to self-destruct, that cost Botham the job.

Botham took the loss badly. He blamed both Alec Bedser and the media, although Bedser was never less than sympathetic or generous, even at the end calling Botham a 'great bloke' whom he expected to one day return as captain, while the media scarcely gloated; they had protected him in the past and their response to his going was, according to one, a feeling of 'relief tinged with compassion'.

By the end, Botham's mood was uncharacteristically introspective. Mike Brearley thought his view of the media had descended into near-paranoia. Botham himself would admit that the captaincy made him 'withdrawn and moody' and put up an emotional wall that prevented even his immediate family from sharing his difficulties or helping him find a solution.

What may have hurt most was a sense of the cricketing Establishment gradually withdrawing its support. From the moment that his Test captaincy switched to a match-by-match basis until the axe fell on the final day of the second Test against Australia, it must have become increasingly clear that he was no longer viewed as the right man for the job and that, perhaps, the old class prejudice was kicking in. For Botham, the feeling of power slipping through his fingers must have been torment. He may have sensed too that his own players thought it best if he went back to concentrating on his own game. Cricket writers were reporting as much and Bob Willis had even said on radio that he felt Botham was too young to be given the captaincy – and been fined £25 by the TCCB for saying so. Everyone could see it. Botham was too much one of the boys. Defeatism was in the air.

Although in the end the selectors stuck by him until the end of the second Test, Botham was nearly replaced beforehand. Around the time play was starting on the final day of the first Test – with England facing probable though not certain defeat – Mike Brearley was approached by Alan Burridge, the Middlesex secretary, before a home match against Leicestershire in the Sunday league. At Bedser's request, Burridge asked if Brearley would captain England again. Brearley said yes. When that time might be was not clear. Unfortunately for Botham and Bedser, a newspaper got wind that something was afoot and reported that Botham had been sacked that morning by the selection panel only for them to change their mind in the afternoon. If that was indeed what they did, they presumably changed their minds because of how hard England fought to deny Australia that afternoon. Botham was confirmed as captain for the second Test as soon as the Trent Bridge Test ended.

Despite Bedser's denials regarding the press report, Botham now strongly suspected that the selectors (consisting of Bedser, Brian Close, Charlie Elliott and John Edrich, the replacement for the late Ken Barrington) were preparing to remove him. He would have only had to speak to Close, his former mentor, to find out which way the wind was blowing, and his subsequent comments suggested that he had. He sensed 'rumbles from Lord's' about his captaincy, and feared a rug was being pulled from under him. Friends noticed he seemed distracted and detached. Brearley believes Botham knew in advance that the selectors were intent on sacking him.

He was in acute need of support in the ten days between the first and second Tests. In Swansea for a championship match, he sought out Tom Cartwright, now Glamorgan's manager. 'He was badly in need of reassurance,' Cartwright said. 'I suggested he came off the field with boot trouble so we could talk ... It was really a matter of giving him a boost and getting him to feel that he could still go out and do it.' During the same game, Botham spoke at a dinner in Cardiff and took with him a couple of team-mates, including Vic Marks. 'It was a grand affair,' Marks recalled. 'People like Phil Bennett, Max Boyce and Mike England were there. "Both" was going through complete hell and we worried about how he'd cope. I don't suppose he'd written his speech but he carried it off well, telling stories against himself. He was incredibly impressive. Basically, he fronted up in a difficult situation.' Back in Swansea, he scored his first century in thirteen months. The old magic was clearly still there, somewhere.

He went through the Lord's Test in something of a daze. Bob Taylor, returning to the team for the first time since Botham had taken over, was immediately struck by how flat the players were and how listless was their captain. Botham was out third ball for nought as England squandered a good position by losing six first-innings wickets for twenty-seven runs and, after three rain-interrupted days, the match hung uncomfortably in the balance. That evening, at the team hotel, Botham met David English, an executive at RSO Records who had managed the Bee Gees. Conscious of Botham's troubles, English, a former bit-part actor, used his flair for humour to entertain Botham and his family, who as usual were in tow for a home Test. 'I told them my best jokes for about three hours and he said it was great,' English recalled. 'I said, "That's OK. I was trying to cheer you up." He said, "Now what you doing tomorrow? ... I've got to be at a Saab showroom in Piccadilly at 10am. You can come along." And so we carried on drinking and I became his new best friend.'

In what was far from a unique experience, English felt so ill from spending an evening socialising with Botham that he spent the morning throwing up, including in a taxi with Botham and his wife. Botham teased him for his weak constitution – 'He was showing me his cruel side now,' English said – but he never forgot English's kindness of the previous evening. Botham even used his contacts with Saab to fix up English with a car. 'He used to take me everywhere,' English added. 'I became the Loon, the sidekick. It was great fun but he did get boisterous – he was big on ear-chewing and headlocks – and there were people like Derek Randall who were scared of him. He was wary of new people but once you were a friend you were a friend forever. He would have been hurt if you let him down.'

English fitted a specific type of friend that became important to Botham, the ever-present court-jester. The incident in Scunthorpe had served as a reminder that Botham had to be careful when he went out in public. If he was therefore to sometimes stay in, or at least confine himself to controlled environments, then he needed people who could keep him entertained. Not everyone was cut out for this role. 'We used to take it in turns to go to his room, keep him company and get drunk,' one England team-mate said. 'But most of us found it boring, sitting there watching TV and talking rubbish. Did he like his own company? No. He was an action man who needed action going on. The trouble was, some members of the public wanted to provoke him into showing he was an action man, and he didn't suffer fools gladly. Maybe he didn't fancy himself in verbal combat, so he was quick to temper.'

When the game resumed after the rest day and England lost two cheap wickets after conceding a first-innings deficit of thirty-four, they were in danger of losing again, and it was not until lunch on the final day that England dared take the initiative. Several players – including Botham, out for a second duck, sweeping at his first ball from Ray Bright – sacrificed their wickets in the search for quick runs before Australia were left under three hours to survive. The whole strategy looked like too little, too late. The game petered out into a draw.

Afterwards, Botham made much of the stony silence from MCC members that greeted his return to the pavilion after he had collected his second duck. 'It was the feeling of being deserted which affected me so deeply,' he said. 'I've never felt as lonely as I did that day.' But what else, really, did he expect? A few miles away at the *Sun*, the editor Kelvin MacKenzie was shouting at the television: 'Whose idea was it to sign this guy?!'

After the match, Botham and Bedser met in the attendant's cubby-hole outside the England dressing-room where they immediately agreed that Botham's captaincy was at an end. Bedser, in fact, had already met with his fellow selectors during the morning – on the pavilion balcony, in full view of Botham, who guessed he was the subject of their conversation – and decided that Botham should be sacked. Only Close, bizarrely given his original opposition to Botham's appointment, spoke up in favour of him being given one more match. 'We knew what Ian's failures meant to him but we saw a dream fading and our plans falling apart,' Bedser explained. 'We decided, reluctantly, that we had to ditch Ian.' Botham, for his part, had discussed his future as captain earlier in the day with Bernard Thomas, the team's physiotherapist and confidant, and Bob Willis. Willis thought quitting was the only option available to Botham. 'The job was plainly not only having a detrimental effect on Ian's cricket but on his whole life,' Willis reflected years later. 'The myth that he has an indestructible temperament was quickly crumbling.' Botham told Bedser that he wanted to quit unless the selectors made him captain for all four of the matches that remained, a request he must have known they would not meet.

Botham's thoughts quickly shifted to damage limitation. He asked Bedser if he could announce to the press that he had resigned. 'By all means, if that's the way you want it,' Bedser replied. 'You say it that way ... [But] if I'm asked a direct question, I'm going to give them a true answer.' Inevitably after Botham, armed with a smouldering cigar, had made his resignation statement in the writing-room downstairs, Bedser was indeed asked if Botham would have been sacked anyway; he replied in the affirmative.

Botham was devastated at what he called Bedser's 'petty pointscoring' and some believed he never forgave Bedser for not allowing him to make a dignified retreat. But in truth this was next to impossible, as Bedser had originally recognised. The truth was going to come out and attempts at hiding it would have soon come unstuck, particularly as Bedser's panel had already shown a tendency to leak. Botham's later claims that he had decided to resign even before arriving at the ground that morning were surely an attempt to pre-empt the selectorial conference on the balcony. While few doubted the true chronology, it was important to Botham to be able to maintain, even if only to himself, that he had chosen this course of events, rather than it being thrust upon him.

Bedser told reporters that Botham was all but certain to retain his place as a player, although privately the selectors would agree that he would be given only two more matches to rediscover form. It was Bedser's assessment that had Botham been dropped after Lord's 'it would not have created a sensation'.

Botham said that when he told his players in the dressing-room that he was going their reaction had been 'a little bit shocked, surprised'. Later, in a television interview, he said that he was willing to play on under anyone but, specifically, that he would happily play under Brearley. Here was more evidence to suggest that he knew about the plan to replace him dating back to the last day of the first Test.

Only then did Bedser phone Brearley – from a pub on his way home – and confirm his appointment. Uncertain as to his chances of success, Brearley asked to be put in charge for the next three matches only. He was worried about the reception awaiting him in Leeds, wondering how many there would feel that Boycott had again been denied due recognition – 'and that I had been brought back solely because of the advantages of a university education and a southern accent.' In fact, in the minds of the selectors Brearley's main rival had been Keith Fletcher, who unlike Brearley was available to tour and therefore offered a long-term solution. Close argued against Brearley on the grounds that it was Brearley's championing of Botham as captain that had created this present crisis. Only when Brearley met Edrich at a Test match in 2009 did he learn how close the call had been between himself and Fletcher.

'He [Edrich] intimated that it was almost a toss-up between us,' Brearley said.

Having left the press conference, Botham returned to the England dressing-room. By the time Ian Jarrett arrived to speak to him about his *Sun* column, he found only Botham and Boycott still there. 'Boycott had stayed to console Botham,' Jarrett recalled. 'I found that quite admirable from someone who had always carried the reputation of being selfish.' The rest of the team had done the same as the MCC members, and left Botham to his disappointment.

Botham then got into his car, in which Kath was patiently waiting, and dropped her off at the hotel, having peremptorily told her that she could not now accompany him as planned to Taunton, where he was playing in a Benson and Hedges Cup semi-final the next day. Kath was devastated. She had arranged for the children to be looked after by their nanny so she could join her husband for a few days, and now that he had lost the captaincy he did not want her help. He later conceded that his treatment of her that night scarred their marriage for years.

Arriving late in Taunton, he met his Somerset team-mates in the Four Alls pub and drowned his sorrows with Viv Richards. His famed powers of recovery were never better in evidence than the next morning, when the front pages of the newspapers carried news of his 'resignation' along with reports of the latest inner-city riots. Violence on the streets of Southall and Toxteth over the weekend had sparked copy-cat sprees across the country; Molotov cocktails had been thrown and CS gas used against demonstrators for the first time on mainland Britain. Compared to this, Botham's argument with the cricket authorities was relatively small beer.

'He turned up at the ground at 8.45am looking absolutely dreadful,' Nigel Popplewell, a team-mate, recalled. 'He was drawn, pale, a shadow of his real self. Yet he still managed to contribute, despite his desperate psychological condition.' He dismissed Kent's openers in the course of three maiden overs and finished with 3–23 to pave the way for a five-wicket win.

A few days later in the championship, Botham dismissed four of Sussex's top six in 22 balls before dazzlingly striking 72 with the bat. 'He was happy to come back and that was reflected in the way he played,' Brian Rose, the Somerset captain, said. 'He was relieved, I think. He was back in a side where we were all his mates.' But Peter Roebuck believed that, whatever the short-term benefits, the loss of the England captaincy had a permanently deleterious effect on Botham. 'He had craved the captaincy more than he'd ever admit. Here was a comprehensive school boy from Yeovil, a backward town in Somerset that is not even as big as Taunton or Bridgwater, in charge of all England. The captaincy was a mighty thing in his mind and losing it was an enormous blow. He was never quite as free with the world after that.'

Botham was to be remembered best for what happened next, but what had come before could not be forgotten. That the 1981 series went down as 'Botham's Ashes' was chiefly but not entirely recognition of the starring part he played in the next three games, all won by England to ensure that the Ashes were still theirs. The series became synonymous with him specifically because he was a champion reborn; what he did sprang directly out of the humiliations he had endured as England captain. The series encompassed his lowest and highest points. This was what gave the story its depth and drama. It was Botham Unbound.

Put simply, he played decisive parts in the winning of three successive matches with three inspired passages of play – passages that occupied remarkably little time given the impact they had on the series, on the English national psyche, and on Botham's future. The first lasted approximately 120 minutes late on the fourth day at Headingley, during which he swung the bat wildly in raising his score from 39 to 145 and English hopes of victory from near-impossible to slim. The second encompassed barely 40 minutes on the fourth evening at Edgbaston, when he capitalised on Australia's jittery nerves to snatch their last five wickets when they had been within 37 runs of victory. And the third spanned about 55 minutes either side of tea on the third day at Old Trafford during which he plundered 90 runs from 48 hell-raising deliveries.

Botham made contributions at other times – he finished the series with 399 runs, 34 wickets and 12 catches – but it was these three extraordinary periods, totalling less than four hours, that enabled England to win games that they might very well have otherwise lost, indeed certainly would have lost in the case of Headingley. But it was not all Botham. Bob Willis, who feared his career was coming to an end, bowled with demonic purpose on the final day at Headingley; John Emburey took as many wickets at Edgbaston as Botham, and scored more runs; and Chris Tavare held England together twice with two great defensive innings at Old Trafford in only his third Test appearance. But partly because of the exuberant way he played, partly because his reputation preceded him, and partly because in the end the Australians came so visibly to fear him, it was Botham's efforts that stole everyone's attention.

Of course, many inconvenient truths quickly got shelved during a summer that was more concerned with fairy tales than facts. People wanted to believe in the magical powers of Botham and Brearley just as they wanted to believe in the romance between Prince Charles and Lady Diana Spencer, whose marriage took place eight days after the Miracle of Headingley. Of course, if Botham really had been Superman in white clothing and Mike Brearley really had been able to toy with Australian minds like a cricketing Svengali, the England team would not have got into the difficulties they did in the first place. Australia too were unlucky with injuries. Dennis Lillee was struggling to shake off viral pneumonia for most of the series – hence his habit, so annoying to England, of leaving the field to change his shirt – and Rodney Hogg and Geoff Lawson were both ruled out of the later stages with back trouble. 'Some of the Ashes '81 was a bit apocryphal,' said David Gower, who played in five of the six matches.

Along with the Royal Wedding, 'Botham's Ashes' provided

some much-needed respite from the country's desperate economic and social problems. Within days of the riots that appeared to be tearing the fabric of the nation apart, came two events that brought the nation together again, even though they were watched by vastly different audiences (28 million viewed the wedding, but only a tiny fraction of that the later stages of the Headingley Test). That both were plainly never-to-be-repeated occasions only made the memories sweeter and, in the long run, all the harder to let go of, even when it was perfectly obvious that Charles and Diana's marriage was a sham, and Botham was a shadow of the cricketer he had once been.

Botham's heroics were born out of desperate situations, at least in the first two games, and probably would not have happened if they had not been. Aggression was not only permissible but to be encouraged as the best chance of escape. He was not required to worry about the consequences – as he had been on an hourly basis when captain – but simply to take a chance and see what happened. This was exactly the basis by which he had achieved so much of his earlier success. Circumstances had thrown him a lifeline: don't bother thinking too much about what to do, just do it. And he duly did.

Nor did it do any harm that he chose to bat without the protective headgear that he had automatically donned against West Indies. Australia's bowlers may not have been as hostile but they were lively enough to bowl nasty-looking bouncers, even in Geoff Lawson's case two beamers. Botham thought little of it: he either evaded them or, more often, batted them off his face – and into the stands – as the best means of self-preservation. Such adrenalin-rush cricket suited him. Bare-headed, bearded and shaggy-maned, there was more than a touch of the caveman about him when he was batting in this series.

If, after his long run of failure, the Australians had forgotten how dangerous he could be, they made a serious mistake. In fact, for large parts of the series, Australia – in particular Lillee and Terry Alderman, whose natural wicket-to-wicket line was one

Botham didn't like – bowled immaculately on pitches that were awkward to bat on. Despite Botham telling team-mates that the Australian fast bowler was not as fearsome as of old, Lillee dismissed him five times, including for scores of three, nought and three. But when the pressure was on the Australians fell apart against him in the field – and it cost them the series. The series was, in fact, as much a story of Australian failure as English triumph. Kim Hughes became overly reliant on Lillee and Alderman, his match-winners at Trent Bridge; he condemned them to exhaustingly long spells while overlooking the value of his other bowlers. But just as Rod Marsh was ready to question Hughes's tactics, so Lillee was a hard man to prise the ball off. Brearley was sympathetic: 'He [Hughes] came up against Botham in his glory, whose impact would have thrown any captain's tactics into confusion.'

But as the team assembled at Headingley on the afternoon before the third Test, Botham's glory needed some finding. Brearley noticed Botham trying to hide his unease with jokes and vitality, which included turfing Gatting out of the dressing room seat he wanted for himself. Botham also warmly welcomed Chris Old, who had been recalled to the side; Old found this strange given Botham's antipathy towards him since their run-ins in the Caribbean. Brearley soon got to work on his provocation. At practice, he asked casually whether Botham actually wanted to play – and duly got the response he wanted. 'Of course I want to play,' an incredulous Botham replied. Then, as Australia, capitalising on English errors that included two dropped catches by Botham, amassed a big score on a spicy pitch, Brearley noticed that Botham was not charging in with the ball as he used to; he was stepping in close to the stumps just before delivery. So out came the insults, Brearley calling him the 'side-step queen' and a 'middle-aged swinger', and by the second afternoon Botham was getting back some of his rhythm. In a long spell he worked his way through the last five wickets and the crowd began to cheer him again, the first time this had happened for months.

Brearley's advice to Botham that he needed to play straighter and with less conservatism on such an awkward batting surface also paid dividends. Botham rode his luck to reach a first half-century in twenty innings, but no one else prospered as Australia bowled straight and full throughout the third day, dismissing England for 174 and Graham Gooch cheaply for a second time in the follow-on. Botham may have been finding his form but the team were not; the loss of the Ashes looked inevitable. That night, with the Sunday a rest day, Botham put on his now customary barbecue for the teams at his home in Epworth, where there was no disguising the disparity in morale between the camps. Gower said the mood among the England players was fatalistic and several of them stayed up drinking beyond 3am, with Botham as usual the last to bed. Sunday involved resting plus a couple of pints at Botham's local.

The sheer hopelessness of England's position – reflected in the bookmaker's odds of 500–1 – was central to how events unfolded on the fourth afternoon, from the carefree way England batted to Australia's slowness to respond. With Australia again bowling well, an English defeat looked certain when Graham Dilley joined Botham at 135–7, still 92 in arrears, half an hour before tea; it was certainly a conclusion the public, numbering only 7,000 inside the ground, appeared to have drawn. Dilley, convinced he would be dropped for the next Test after bowling poorly, decided he might as well hit out; he was a talented but inconsistent striker of the ball. By the interval he had scored twenty-five and was closing in on Botham, who had been batting nearly an hour and a half for thirty-nine.

To this point, Botham's strategy, such as it was, was simply to bat. When Brearley teasingly asked him why he was going so slowly compared to Dilley, Botham said that he was playing for a not-out; it was said as a joke but after the tough times he had been through no one would have blamed him if he had taken an unbeaten half-century as England slid to an innings defeat. But when Dilley continued hitting the ball imperiously after the resumption, Botham felt compelled to try to match him.

This was how the unlikely revival started, just as it was how Botham's famous stand with Hallam Moseley began in the Benson and Hedges Cup in 1974. The situation was so hopeless that there was no pressure. Dilley said that during their partnership the game resembled a benefit match in which there was no gameplan, and no responsibility, just one batsman trying to out-hit another for the hell of it. Brearley, seeing the advantage of this, waved at Botham from the pavilion balcony to keep going. Botham said later that he was oblivious to the match situation; he did not know whether England were still behind Australia's score, or had gone in front. It was irrelevant to his thinking, which was focused on out-doing Dilley and, after so long in the doldrums, enjoying himself. Chris Old, who put on 67 with Botham after the stand of 117 with Dilley had been broken, said that Botham was beginning to get a grip on the shifting state of the game by the time he joined him.

When his score was in the thirties, Dilley was nearly caught at gully and then almost became another of Botham's run-out victims as Botham dithered over a single; a shy from Trevor Chappell, a good fielder, that would have left Dilley for dead flew for four over-throws. As the boundaries flowed, the Australians could not drag themselves away from their old tactics. The way to keep Botham quiet was to bowl straight at his body, yet they repeatedly bowled wide of off stump, giving him room to free his arms and swing through the ball – hence the large number of boundaries he hit through the off side. That said, he was lucky, mis-hitting many balls off thick outside edges that flew through or over the slips and thick inside edges that squirted past the stumps or away through square leg (ten of his twenty-six fours came in these ways). That Dilley and Old were both left-handers made it harder for the bowlers to maintain accurate lines, but even so the brainless, pan-icky way they bowled would have left the West Indians incredulous had they been watching. Good judges such as Alec Bedser and Richie Benaud, commentating on BBC TV, were baffled by how much width Lillee, a class bowler, allowed Dilley and Botham.

'We kept thinking we'd get him out,' Geoff Lawson said. 'Even when he got to his hundred off me – I've seen the film plenty of times – we had two slips and a gully. We still thought he'd nick one.'

Hughes's most glaring error was to persevere with his three exhausted seamers rather than call on Ray Bright's left-arm spin. With hindsight, Bright would not even have played, as a fourth seamer in Rodney Hogg would have been a better bet, but even so he was needlessly denied what could have been a decisive role. He had dismissed Botham at Lord's and Botham remained a chancy player of spin. Keith Fletcher as Essex captain always brought on a spinner when Botham came in because he knew Botham found it hard not to go on the attack; 'We always gambled with "Both" because we knew he wouldn't block and you always had a chance.' John Emburey, England's twelfth man and an off-spinner himself, felt Hughes definitely missed a trick. 'A left-arm spinner turning the ball away from him [Botham] would have caused problems. "Both" tended to go leg-side against the spinners and with Bright he would have been doing that against the spin. The way he was playing he wasn't going to block.'

In the end, Hughes – by now being ignored by Marsh and Lillee – brought on Bright late in Botham's partnership with Old. Straightaway Bright nearly bowled Botham, but he was given only four of the 27 overs bowled in the final session from which England plundered 175, a remarkable rate of scoring in any era of Test cricket. At stumps, England led by 124, which they extended to 129 the next morning before last man Willis was out. Botham finished unbeaten on 149.

That Botham was still in an emotionally fragile state was clear from his refusal to speak to reporters after play that evening, a message he reinforced by walking to his car with a towel stuffed in his mouth. He was simmering at what he saw as his unjust treatment by the media, which included journalists attempting to question his three-year-old son Liam and reports of the party he had held two nights earlier, but also comments suggesting that he would never be the same player again (some of these remarks had come from ex-players).

If Botham had given England an outside chance of victory, it was Willis who actually delivered it with just as extraordinary a performance with the ball as Botham had produced with the bat. Brearley gave Botham the new ball – something Botham had given up on towards the end of his captaincy – and it quickly brought the wicket of Graeme Wood, who was considered unlucky to be adjudged caught behind, but even Botham's ambition now seemed sated and he had nothing left to offer. It was left to Willis, steaming down the hill, to cut swathes through the shell-shocked ranks of Australians who really could not fathom how they had got into the position of needing 130 to win.

Minutes after the game had reached its astonishing conclusion, with England victors by eighteen runs, Willis launched his own impassioned attack on press treatment of players – especially Botham but also himself, as Willis had been written off after bowling poorly in the previous game and had only narrowly avoided being dropped at Headingley.

Feelings generally ran high in the aftermath of this incredible game. The small crowd that had turned up in the hope of seeing a miracle sang 'Jerusalem', an unheard-of event at that time, and Brearley and Hughes praised Botham's innings as one of the greatest in history, but even so Willis's outburst – though typical in some senses of an unpredictable personality – reflected a genuine feeling among England players that they had been pilloried. After years of largely cordial player–press cooperation the relationship had entered a crisis and before the next Test reasonable men from both camps, Brearley and Peter Smith, cricket correspondent of the *Daily Mail*, held clear-the-air talks which led to most players agreeing to cooperate again with newspapermen. Botham, however, held out for a few more days before relenting, although typically all was soon forgotten.

Four days later, Botham helped Somerset win their first trophy since their double of 1979 as they crushed Surrey in the Benson

As a member of MCC's groundstaff, one of Botham's duties was crowd control during Lord's finals. Here (jacketed, right) Botham – aged 17 – patrols the field after Kent's Benson and Hedges Cup victory in 1973

It took Botham nine innings in competitive county cricket to establish a reputation for match-turning, odds-defying heroics. Here he leaves the field after taking Somerset to a one-wicket win over Hampshire in 1974

In his first Test at Lord's, Botham scored a century and took eight for 34 – the best ever bowling figures in a Test on the ground – including Haroon Rashid bowled by this sumptuous late outswinger

Mike Brearley said of Botham: 'He provoked, enlivened, amused, stimulated and irritated me.' In return, Brearley got more out of him than any other England captain

Botham batting against India in Bombay in 1980 during a brilliant all-round performance that sealed his elevation to the England captaincy

The England team line up before Botham's first Test as captain at Trent Bridge in 1980

Botham was England captain in the Caribbean in 1981 but it did not prevent the usual horseplay. Here he hugs Geoff Boycott, someone he loved to bait

Botham walks off amid stony silence among MCC members at Lord's in 1981. Within hours his departure as England captain had been confirmed

Botham acknowledges applause for his century at Headingley in 1981 and the thought starts to form that all might not be lost for England

Hoist the flags: Botham, Geoff Boycott and Bob Taylor fight their way from the field as a nation starts to celebrate their team's astonishing win

Botham, who had not wanted to bowl, takes his fifth wicket in as many overs at Edgbaston in 1981 and England have stolen another victory over Australia

Botham raises aloft the NatWest Trophy at Lord's in 1983, one of only
two trophies he won as captain of county or country

Elton John with the England team in New Zealand in 1984, a tour that drew wide-ranging allegations of off-field shenanigans

Botham, with his wife Kath, recovers from knee surgery in 1984 days after returning from Pakistan and publicly denying allegations of drug-taking

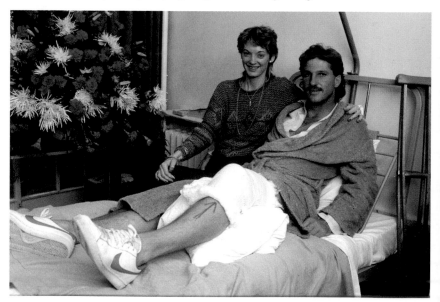

Tim Hudson (centre), whom Botham appointed manager in 1985, achieved a lot of publicity for his client – ultimately of the wrong sort

Botham's recovery programme bore little resemblance to that of the modern-day player

If Mike Brearley got the best of Botham as captain, David Gower had the worst.
Gower led England to only three wins in 21 Tests in which Botham took part

The West Indies pace attack bowled brilliantly at Botham, who reached 40 only five times in 38 innings. Here he is caught behind off Malcolm Marshall's bowling in Trinidad in 1986

Botham sitting in the stands alongside Mick Jagger, Barbados 1986

Botham is toasted by Somerset team-mates on his England recall following his drugs ban in 1986. Within days it emerged that Joel Garner and Viv Richards had been sacked by the county and that Botham was intent on leaving

A fishing trip with Eric Clapton (left) and David English

Botham, seen here batting with Graeme Hick, helped Worcestershire to win several trophies between 1987 and 1991

Botham's time with Queensland started well but quickly nosedived. He and Queensland captain Allan Border (left) disagreed about a drinking ban

Botham's son Liam played four matches for Hampshire before pursuing a successful rugby career

Wasim Akram, the bowler, and Imran Khan, Botham's long-time adversary, celebrate Botham's wicket during the World Cup final, Melbourne 1992

As a television commentator Botham had his run-ins with England coach Duncan Fletcher

Botham, at home with his dog Pinot, celebrates his knighthood for services to cricket and charity

Botham has raised about £12 million for Leukaemia and Lymphoma Research, mainly through long-distance walks

and Hedges Cup final at Lord's. With Viv Richards and Joel Garner available all season, Somerset had high hopes of doing well in all four competitions and this performance showed why. Garner took five wickets and Richards contributed an imperious 132 not out to make ridiculously light work of a target of 195. Botham's involvement was relatively low-key, but he batted with Richards while the last eighty-seven runs were scored and for once matched his friend shot for shot without coming unstuck.

Botham was still not his old self. He was quiet for most of the fourth Test at Edgbaston, even though it was a fractious contest of the kind that usually brought out the best in him. He was bowled by Alderman in the first innings playing an indeterminate shot that he would have hated, and was caught behind in the second attempting an ugly heave at a wide ball from Lillee that would have made him even angrier. His first – and for a long time only – wicket of the game was that of Ray Bright, Australia's night-watchman. He was unable to do much to stop Australia assuming another commanding position: when he was out to Lillee, England were effectively 47–6.

Fortunately the tail wagged and Australia were left 151 to win, which on what was still a good batting surface would have been a formality had it not been for what had gone before at Headingley. In two brief spells Botham extracted little swing or bounce and it was left to Willis, waspishly fast again, to spearhead England's slim hopes of a second salvation. By lunch on the Sunday – this was another game that experimented with a full weekend of play – Australia had crawled to 62–3, but they still appeared to be on course to go 2–1 up. At this point, Botham had apparently concluded that he would not be bowling again. In truth he had not bowled well since the first innings in Leeds and had in the interim taken just two wickets in thirty-six overs.

Taylor was now witness to just how reluctant Botham was to bowl again. 'We were about to go out [after lunch] and Beefy was putting on his Nike tennis shoes,' Taylor recalled. 'Mike Brearley saw him and said, "What are you doing?" So Beefy – strong character as he is – said, "You're all right, captain, you don't want me to bowl." Brearley said, "Get your bowling boots on." We were all waiting to go out. And he tried it again. "You don't want me to bowl, do you?" And Brearley's voice changed. "Get your bowling boots on." So he had to hurriedly get them on … A lesser captain would have ducked down to him and Beefy would have got away with it.'

Australia's progress remained slow but they lost only one wicket in the next hour and with Willis's energy finally spent Brearley asked Botham to take over. Botham was still reluctant – Brearley described him as 'strangely diffident' – and suggested instead that Peter Willey partner Emburey, who was bowling immaculately. But Emburey then claimed the key wicket of Allan Border and Brearley was convinced that Botham had to bowl. Even after taking the ball, Botham said to Old: 'I don't know why I've come on – you're doing so much better than me.'

But Brearley's instincts again proved sound. His final instruction to Botham was also straight out of the Little Book of Provocation: 'Keep things tight for Embers.' Botham must have thought, 'I'm damned if I'm bowling for Emburey's wickets.' With the ball doing little, and Australia needing only thirty-seven more, his best option was to bowl as fast and straight as he could. He also knew better than most how to bowl at the tail and after Rod Marsh was yorked heaving across the line at his third ball the first of the tail-enders arrived. Cheered on by a crowd of 10,000 in a much more raucous finale than was seen at Headingley, Botham's uncertainty suddenly evaporated as he smelled Australia's fear. Bright was plumb leg-before first ball. Lillee – chasing a wide delivery just as Botham had against him – was caught behind at the second attempt by Taylor. Martin Kent, the one remaining batting specialist, was bowled off his pads and last man Alderman also bowled, in more comprehensive fashion. While it took Botham fourteen balls to account for Kent, another fourteen balls saw him remove four of the last five in the order. He had bullied tail-enders into submission many times before, but never in such a tight corner as this. 'He plucked that game from nowhere,' said Graham Gooch. 'He won it with sheer magnetism. He got into the Australians' minds again.' But it took him an inordinate time to get there.

Only now was he more at ease. Before the Test series resumed at Old Trafford, he had an excellent game against Northants at Weston. Bowling with his rediscovered fire, he broke Peter Willey's thumb – putting him out of the last two Tests – and almost snatched victory for Somerset with a late burst of three wickets that hinted at a reprise of Edgbaston. Earlier he had top-scored in both innings with forties.

At Old Trafford itself, after the unpromising start of a first-ball duck, he gave his most assured performance of the series. He had a part in six first-innings dismissals – three catches off Willis and three wickets of his own – as Australia, their morale close to collapse, folded in just 30.2 overs on the second day. Botham then scored a spectacular and well thought-out century that turned the game England's way after Australia's bowlers had fought back on the third day. Botham later admitted that it was only after Old Trafford – not Headingley or Edgbaston – that he felt the relief of knowing that the good times had finally returned. Paul Allott, who made his debut for England in this game, was struck by how cavalier Botham and the other players were in the dressing-room. He saw Botham throw a fully kitted Boycott into the bath, and was surprised by the amount of drinking that went on in the evenings. But Brearley seemed content as long as his players performed.

What stood out about Botham's century at Old Trafford was its good judgement and maturity. This was not an innings fashioned out of thoughts of a not-out or out-hitting a partner for fun, but out of the urgent need of his team. When he went in, twenty minutes after a lunch that in Botham's case involved two large steaks, Australia had clawed their way back into the game with some terrifically disciplined bowling. Chris Tavare, Botham's partner, who had been brought in for this game with the express instruction to hold firm at number three, was virtually scoreless and after 69 overs on a true pitch England had scored just 104–5. With a spinner already bowling and only eleven overs to the second new ball, it must have been tempting for Botham to get after Ray Bright, but the light was not good and Bright had men round the bat, and Botham chose to bide his time. It was 34 balls before he hit his first boundary and after 50 deliveries he had still scored only 21.

It was then, with three balls to go until the new ball, that he went on the attack, reckoning that the harder ball would be his best opportunity to put the game beyond Australia's reach. He may also have sensed that after what he had done to them at Headingley and Edgbaston, the Australians might wilt in the face of another counterattack.

If so, he was right because Australia's determination and control, so impressive throughout the day, crumbled almost the moment he swung in anger. Having hit Alderman's first delivery with the new ball for four, Botham skied the second over deep mid-off where Mike Whitney, a left-arm seamer making his debut following the injuries to Lawson and Hogg, put down a difficult chance. Moments later, Botham was facing Lillee, whose tactics were as unfathomable as they had been when the flak flew in Leeds. Banging the ball in short, Lillee was twice hooked for six by a batsman whose decision to forgo a helmet must have seemed like an act of provocation. Lillee's first over yielded nineteen to Botham and he quickly conceded another twenty-four to him, including a third six, before finally accepting that he should come off, having refused Hughes's first request to do so. A rare bright spot for Lillee, in one of the darkest days of his career, was almost having Botham caught at third man on ninety-one.

Lillee took the brunt of the punishment but Alderman was also hooked into the crowd and when Hughes brought back Bright the left-arm spinner was swept for six to give Botham his hundred off eighty-six deliveries, one ball fewer than he had needed at Leeds. He then hit him over the sightscreen for his sixth six. When Alderman finally remembered to bowl at middle and leg rather than outside off stump, Botham found scoring less easy, but generally the Australians bowled too short and too wide. Botham's hitting was much cleaner than at Headingley, with only one of his boundaries plainly coming off an edge. When he was finally caught behind off Whitney, he had scored 118 out of a stand of 149 with Tavare, whose contribution was just 28. Botham did not share in many memorable partnerships, but this was certainly one, and it was an authentic one at that, the two batsmen complementing each other in the way they played.

'I tell people that was the most extraordinary moment in my career,' said Tavare, who played all his thirty-one Tests alongside Botham and later became a master at Sevenoaks. 'If I do an assembly at school, it's the one I always show the film of. It was a joy to watch. I remember the sixes he took off Lillee. Lillee had put two men back and I thought, "Well, that's out." And the ball just kept going. I also remember Alderman dropping one short and Botham pulled it and it sounded like a rifle going off. If you listen to the film it sounds like that. It was the most fantastic experience. I found it an advantage batting with him. I could just potter along at the other end. If I'd had to score quickly it would have put more pressure on me. It suited us both to play the way we did.'

Botham's spectacular hitting triggered further displays of patriotic fervour. Having shed some inhibitions over the Royal Wedding and Headingley, the British public were becoming used to cheering and waving flags, which seemed the only reasonable response to the drama being played out. That there was still so much regularly disturbing news from everyday life – unemployment was precipitously climbing towards three million and Margaret Thatcher's spending cuts were causing divisions even within her own cabinet – may have only encouraged the feverish mood.

Certainly, Botham's heroics were met with wild enthusiasm, and hyperbole was in the air. Jim Laker, an illustrious former England spin bowler turned commentator in his sixtieth year, hailed Botham's innings as the greatest he'd ever seen, and John

Woodcock, cricket correspondent of *The Times* for more than twenty-five years, claimed it was the greatest ever innings 'of its kind', adding: 'I refuse to believe that a cricket ball has ever been hit with greater power and splendour.' There was no doubting it was a wonderfully measured innings, but plenty of hundreds had been made against teams with stronger attacks and sturdier morale, some by Botham's team-mates in the Caribbean earlier in the year.

With England going on to win the game and the Ashes, Botham's confidence was now sky-high. He produced some euphoric hitting for Somerset, striking nine sixes in a weekend against Hampshire and another eight in the course of two championship half-centuries against Essex and Warwickshire. During the sixth and final Test at the Oval, his appetite for bowling, which had been so meagre at Edgbaston, was voracious. Despite suffering from a sore knee and trapped nerve he got through 89 overs, which brought him ten wickets and the record for the speediest 200 Test wickets in history.

After the game, Kim Hughes – who had been confident towards the end of the Headingley Test that he had secured the Australia captaincy for good but was now destined to make way for Greg Chappell again – claimed reasonably enough that, had it not been for Botham, Australia would have won the series 4–0 rather than lost it 3–1. In the House of Commons, Charles Morrison, a Tory backbencher disaffected with Margaret Thatcher's leadership, noted that the England team's fortunes had improved following a switch in leader and asked: 'Was this not a good example of a change of tactics which we might emulate?'

So the legend of Botham as miracle-worker was born. Before 1981, Botham had been an exceptional cricketer who achieved striking things, but he was now elevated onto another plane altogether. He had seized the imagination of the nation and for his bravery, intelligence, skill and gambler's instinct deserved much of the praise that came his way. But he was thrust atop a pedestal on which it was almost impossible to remain. Being cast as the single-handed winner of such a high-profile Test series as the Ashes was not quite accurate and certainly not helpful. Being portrayed as someone routinely capable of retrieving hopeless causes, while flattering, was bound to end in disappointment.

None of this seemed to matter in the immediate aftermath. Being a national hero could only be good news. He was the best-known sportsman in Britain and a celebrity around the world. His feats had even attracted attention in the United States, a point that would ultimately prove significant.

Although Botham might deny it, the triumphs of '81 fundamentally changed his outlook. Crucially, coming so soon after the captaincy disaster, it allowed him to brush off his year of failure as an aberration, a freak loss of form for which there was no longer need for contemplation. In future, his attitude was that any bout of poor form could be overcome as long as self-belief was maintained; things would inevitably come right in the end. If luck could deal him such an outrageous hand, he would trust in luck again. He could turn on his talent 'like a tap'.

Not everyone agreed. 'The great deeds of Botham and Willis in 1981 only served to muddy the waters in English cricket,' Gooch said. 'The belief lingered that the top players could coast in the minor games and time their commitment to the appropriate moment in a Test series or tour.' Gower agreed that Botham's thinking did not change for the better. 'He was billed as the single-handed winner of an Ashes series and on the back of that sort of fame there is no criticism. That fuels the self-confidence. He could have climbed Everest, flown single-handedly round the world, fought polar bears, and wrestled alligators, and the world would have loved him. But maybe from that you get an air of invulnerability – the feeling that you can do no wrong.'

In fact, Botham had already taken up flying lessons, although he was to be denied his chance to pilot long-distance flights – let alone fly around the world – because of his colour-blindness.

Confidence restored, he started to think again about getting back the England captaincy. During a drinks break in the final innings of the Old Trafford Test, when it was announced over the public address that Brearley would captain England at the Oval, Botham, in Brearley's phrase, covered up his ambition by saying: 'All names in the hat for captain in India by Friday, please.' But by now even Brearley, his former advocate, was convinced that Botham was best kept away from the captaincy: to give him back the job would, Brearley wrote at the end of the series, 'run the risk of reducing the greatest English cricketer since W.G. Grace from genius to mediocrity.' One of Alec Bedser's final tasks as chairman of selectors was to name Keith Fletcher as Brearley's successor as England captain. Not only was he not chosen, Botham was apparently not even considered. While this would have been a disappointment to Botham, Fletcher was thirty-seven years old, only two years younger than Brearley, and was unlikely to be around for long. Botham could have reasoned (rightly as it turned out) that a new captain would be needed again soon.

Captain or not, Botham had acquired folk-hero status. It was hard to know who were the more fanciful, the youngsters who aspired to be the next Botham, or the coaches who thought he could be copied. Darren Gough, who was ten years old at the time, had his cricketing ambitions fuelled by Botham's heroics: his first bat was a Duncan Fearnley because that was what Botham used and even after he became an established England player Gough still tingled at being in Botham's company. Graham Thorpe, who turned twelve the day before Botham's match-winning spell at Edgbaston, viewed him as the mightiest of cricketing gods. And among a captivated huddle of pedestrians following one of Botham's *tours de force* on a television in a Manchester shop window was a thirteen-year-old grammar school boy, Michael Atherton. At Lord's, Don Wilson, who had succeeded Len Muncer as the head of the MCC groundstaff, implored his young charges – among them a future England team-mate of Botham's in Dermot Reeve, then aged eighteen – to take inspiration from their most illustrious predecessor. 'Just look at what Botham's done,'

Wilson said. 'That could be you!' Reeve was never one to under-estimate his own abilities but even he found the idea ludicrous.

Botham was to find it increasingly difficult to conduct a normal social life. It proved a stressful and miserable experience. 'He and Viv [Richards] could not go out to pubs in the normal way because they would be pestered for autographs,' Dennis Breakwell, their friend and Somerset team-mate, said. 'It was sometimes different in Taunton where they were known, but he'd be set upon by people for no reason. He was a big bloke who was a star and some people were not happy with someone being a success.' Joel Garner, another county colleague, added: 'A lot of people did a lot of things to try to provoke him because they knew he had a short fuse. Quite a few things happened. You'd just say, "Beefy, don't worry about it, let them go." It was difficult for him not to react.'

Gower felt that Botham tended to forget the more pleasant spin-offs of being famous when he found himself in company he did not like, and to overreact if people set out to rub him up the wrong way in a bar, 'as many have'. '"Both", he concluded, 'is quite a vulnerable character.'

In the week after the English season was over, Botham appeared at Grimsby Crown Court to face his charge of assault occasioning actual bodily harm to Steve Isbister. With Botham even more famous now than he had been, there was enormous public interest in the case. During his cross-examination, Botham said that during the evening he had drunk about two pints of beer and six gin and tonics, and while he admitted that Isbister had got under his skin, he denied punching or kicking him. When asked by Graham Richards QC for the prosecution if an aggressive nature had played a part in his success in sport, Botham had agreed that it had, but added: 'That does not mean to say I hit the umpire if he gives me out.' After a three-day hearing, and after deliberating for almost five hours, a jury of six men and six women failed to reach even a majority verdict. With the prosecution deciding not to offer fresh evidence, partly on humanitarian grounds, and partly because of the difficulty of finding a fresh jury after the case had been given such huge media coverage, Judge Hutchinson declared that a 'not guilty' verdict should be entered.

As soon as the case was over, Botham was due to fly to Los Angeles to take part in a testimonial match for Norman Gifford, accompanied of course by his ghost from the *Sun*. 'I had been sent to Grimsby to cover the case, although in effect I was there to keep the other papers away from him,' Ian Jarrett said. 'We left the court to catch a helicopter to Gatwick and I recall us travelling very fast to the airport when we were overtaken by a police car with blue lights flashing. They thought it was a big joke because they waved as they overtook and carried on.

'In the helicopter with us were Botham's solicitor Alan Herd and his barrister. We were somewhere over east London when Herd said he lived locally and could the pilot drop him off.

'"Where?"

'"The local cricket club. I'm the chairman, so you have permission."

'With that we landed on the cricket ground and Herd and the barrister alighted to the bemusement of locals.

'Botham and I continued to Gatwick but by the time we arrived there were no flights so my wife Jackie picked us up and he spent the night at our house in Haywards Heath. Next morning, Roger Bamber, our photographer, arrived to get a picture. I was searching for something to say for the column when I noticed the rhubarb in my garden. I got Bamber to take a picture of Botham holding sticks of rhubarb and I made up a quote, "I'd rather face Dennis Lillee with a stick of rhubarb for a bat than go through another court case like Grimsby." The following day newswires around the world were using that quote in their stories.

'We flew to Los Angeles via Atlanta. The flight to Atlanta was a very boozy affair, I fell asleep and when I woke Botham told me I was two bottles of red wine behind him.'

The cricket match turned into a double-wicket competition at the Rose Bowl in Pasadena in which Lou Ferrigno, who played the Incredible Hulk, also took part. 'Cricket's not as easy as it looks,' said the Hulk afterwards. Botham said that it was during this trip that the Dodgers offered him an eighteen-month trial but it was not something he seriously considered. Probably the Dodgers were not serious either. Baseballers were developed through vast training schemes and there was little scope for an outsider being fast-tracked into the professional system.Botham had the ability to make it in baseball but not the inclination to invest the time necessary for such a career-change. He had lived enough dreams for one year.

# 8

## Cashing In

'The team dinner was boozy. He [Botham] took the
mickey out of the selectors, Peter May and what have you,
and then said to me after the meal, "Come to the bar, you
need to have a beer or else you won't sleep well." We had
a few beers in fact and we'd already had several wines. I
probably didn't go to bed much before a quarter to midnight . . . it was no different from what we did in county
cricket.'

DEREK PRINGLE ON MAKING HIS TEST DEBUT
ALONGSIDE BOTHAM IN 1982

Botham faced a problem in the aftermath of the 1981 Ashes: what
do you do when you have played the series of your life at the age
of twenty-five? Bob Willis observed during the tour of India and
Sri Lanka that followed, that Botham the Megastar was capable of
'anything' in the next four or five years. But what was that anything to be? As Andrew Flintoff found after acquiring similarly
heroic stature after the 2005 Ashes, extraordinary success brings
extraordinary challenges. While it was easy for others to predict
further triumphs, the man himself has to make hard choices and
find fresh aims. The temptation to bask in the adulation needs to
be resisted.

This was easier said than done. With so many people patting Botham on the back and telling him how amazing he was, it would have been hard for anyone to not think that the mass worship entitled him to do what he liked when he liked.

His competitive instincts remained sharp and his capacity for work huge. He had not missed a Test or one-day international for almost four years, and nor would he for a couple more years yet. This was a staggering record of service of which he was rightly proud. He expected to be at the heart of every England game and it took a lot to keep him from the field. He never doubted his strength to play through aches and pains. When he fell ill in India, there was a genuine doubt as to whether he would make the fifth Test in Madras; in the event, he declared himself fit, took the new ball with Willis – and duly squandered some good bowling conditions. In hindsight it would have been better if Paul Allott had opened the attack. But here was the old problem with Botham: who was strong enough to control him? Keith Fletcher, who knew Botham a little but had never played alongside him before, expressed his disappointment with the way Botham used the new ball, but only after the game was over.

Beyond remaining in the England team, what might his specific ambitions have been? He would have been eager to take revenge on West Indies, but England were not due to face them again in Tests until 1984. The next Ashes series was more than twelve months off and it was eighteen months until the next World Cup in England in 1983 (not that the World Cup was then the big prize it later became). He had already helped Somerset win three one-day trophies. The one thing he wanted that he had not got was the England captaincy.

In this respect, his future prospects did not look bright with Peter May as the new chairman of selectors. May hardly seemed the type to hand Botham a second chance. He was a deeply Establishment figure. His own education, at Charterhouse and Cambridge, could hardly have been more different from Botham's. He had married into the Gilligan family, which had provided two former England captains. And, after cutting short an illustrious career as the finest England batsman of his generation, he had lived a life of quiet suburban rectitude with his wife and four daughters while working in the City as an insurance broker and Lloyd's underwriter. May's recent involvement in cricket had been small, although he had observed Botham's troubles and triumphs at reasonably close quarters as MCC president in 1980–81. He was something of a stickler for proper conduct and his brief as chairman included getting a grip on the behaviour of the players. He did not like them showing dissent or pressuring umpires. He was also wary of newspapers making mischief.

Good judgement and good advice had never been more important but almost immediately Botham came close to a catastrophic mistake. The England team had been secretly approached during the West Indies tour when Botham was captain about playing a series of sanction-busting matches in South Africa. The sports boycott of apartheid South Africa had been in place for more than ten years but the country's appetite for international sport had been whetted by New Zealand hosting South Africa's rugby side. A tour by an England cricket team would be highly incendiary. Indeed, the England cricketers had been warned by the TCCB that a rebel tour of South Africa would prompt repercussions. But the money being offered was such that the players had signed letters of interest in Trinidad.

Plans had hardened and before the England team left for India a group of players met in a London hotel. Botham, however, was holidaying in Antigua with Viv Richards and was updated through a lengthy phone call from Geoff Boycott, who was acting as chief recruiter. Boycott's view was that if enough players signed up the TCCB would have been unable to ban all of them because it would destroy the national side. To those organising the tour, Botham's involvement was central to their strategy: if one of the best cricketers in the world was prepared to go to South Africa, then why wouldn't anyone else?

The players' interest started and finished with the money, which for most compared very favourably with what they were earning through conventional channels. Despite his special status, even Botham's earnings, although healthy compared to most, remained unremarkable despite the improved appearance money since Kerry Packer. By this stage, Botham earned in the region of £10,000 a year from Somerset. For every Test he received £1,400 while his base fee for touring India and Sri Lanka was £8,650. On top of this he had a newspaper column with the *Sun* worth about £15,000 and a long-standing bat sponsorship with Duncan Fearnley worth around £5,000 (Fearnley said he never paid Botham more than £10,000 a year even in years of high-profile tours, partly because Botham generously never demanded as much from him as he might have done). He also had a deal with Saab which provided him with regular new cars. With prize-money and other add-ons his annual earnings might have been £60,000. This was good money in a country in recession and where the average pay of unskilled workers was £5,800, but perhaps not as much as some footballers, whose basic salaries were £50,000.

Reg Hayter, Botham's manager, was more of a press agent than commercial manager; and corralling fresh endorsements and sponsorships was not really his speciality, although Alan Herd, Botham's solicitor, did help make some deals. When he stopped to consider it, Botham might have felt that he was missing out financially.

It was while the England team were in Bombay for the first Test that the South African deal took real shape. It transpired that Botham would be paid at least £45,000 for the tour, the same figure later proferred to Keith Fletcher, the England captain. Set alongside his existing earnings it was a sizable sum for two months' work and it was an offer to which he gave serious consideration. It was Boycott's belief that Botham intended to sign up. Given the magnitude of the decision, though, the South African representatives suggested he discuss the offer with his advisers and Botham duly phoned Hayter and Herd to tell them what was afoot.

Hayter had given Basil d'Oliveira sensible and disinterested advice in 1968 when the first great cricketing crisis over South Africa struck, and he was to offer Botham a similarly invaluable service now.

This was perhaps the point at which Botham, Hayter and Herd woke up to the commercial possibilities available to the player. By the time Hayter and Herd flew to Bangalore to dissuade their client from joining what they were convinced would prove a disastrous enterprise, Botham risked losing not only existing sponsorship deals but also two sizeable ones that were in the process of being secured for him. Quite apart from any other considerations that might have affected his thinking, he stood to lose out significantly in financial terms. Before the negotiating was over the South Africans had increased their offer, although reports of the final price varied – Botham himself at the time publicly stated the offer amounted to £50,000 (a more reliable estimate than the £85,000 claimed in Botham's book).

It was really from this point that the 'Botham brand' became much more of a business than it had been. This was partly a reflection of the times, with Margaret Thatcher's government encouraging entrepreneurial flair and popular capitalism as Britain emerged from recession, but also a realisation of how marketable he really was. Geoff Cook, a team-mate of Botham's on the 1981–82 tour and again in Australia the following winter, said that he noticed a big difference in him between these two tours. 'By Australia it was Botham the business rather than Botham the professional athlete,' Cook said. 'He had become more independent.' In India, Botham brought out Kath and their children for a relatively brief stay in Madras; but for Australia they came on an extended trip and effectively set up home in a house in Sydney. By Australia, too, his deal with Saab had been extended to give him the use of a car in each city.

The rebel tour was announced to immediate and widespread condemnation shortly after the players returned from the subcontinent. The level of hostility was not the only thing that took the players by surprise: Boycott's hopes that bans might be avoided if enough players signed up were dashed when only five of the ten players in India who had shown a firm interest actually signed up – Boycott himself, John Emburey, Graham Gooch, John Lever and Derek Underwood. Given Peter May's brief to deal firmly with indiscipline, the TCCB had no choice but to hand out severe punishments and the players were excluded from international cricket for three years. Boycott, at forty-one, was approaching the end of his Test career but the loss of the others – plus the likes of Mike Hendrick and Chris Old – was to have a material effect on England's performances.

Botham had had a lucky escape, for which he was indebted to the swift response of Hayter and Herd, and he did not endear himself to some of those who did make the rebel tour by the way he dissociated himself from the project. A comment widely attributed to him at the time was that he had pulled out of the tour because he would have been unable to look Viv Richards in the eye had he joined. He later claimed that this was a remark passed to the press by Reg Hayter without his consultation but it was actually a phrase used in his own newspaper column in the *Sun* on 3 March 1982, a few days after the rebel tour began. Ian Jarrett, who ghosted the article, recalled that contrary to his later claims Botham himself was indeed consulted. Jarrett said: 'I suspect that I put the words into Botham's mouth, although as I recall we did have a chat about it and he sanctioned the quote before it appeared.' The article was actually run under a heading that said: 'I Could Never Have Looked Viv in the Eye Again'.

This aroused the ire of Gooch, who was surprised to find Botham citing a moral argument after originally explaining his withdrawal in purely financial terms. What upset Gooch was Botham stating: 'I didn't want to risk my Test career and, quite frankly, I am surprised that certain others have chosen to do just that. I had to consider my own future, the future of my wife and children . . . and the future of English cricket itself.' Gooch said: 'I could not understand why he did not come out with the entire story.' Ten days after his *Sun* column appeared, Botham sent a message of support to the anti-apartheid movement which was read out during a rally in Trafalgar Square.

In his 1994 autobiography, Botham began a chapter entitled 'The Lure of the Rand' with the claim: 'Three times the gold of South Africa has been waved in front of my nose and three times I have had a hard look at it before deciding to put country before cash.'

Botham's newspaper column, which had begun as an innocent and lucrative sideline, was becoming a growing source of trouble. A fierce battle was raging between the red-tops, and the *Sun* had responded to a fall in sales by appointing Kelvin MacKenzie editor. Under him the newspaper was to indulge in ever-greater excess and achieve ever-greater readership figures. If bingo and stories about the Princess of Wales were its staples, Botham, with his colourful life on and off the field, was also a perfect subject, far more so than any personality from football, which saw league gates fall 25 per cent from 1979 to 1983. He liked a drink and he liked adventure – apart from his flying lessons, he had recently made his Football League debut for Scunthorpe in a 7–2 defeat to Wigan – and had a talent for winning cricket matches with extraordinary storylines. 'He was the most theatrical personality of the era,' said Matthew Engel, who set out as a sports writer on the *Guardian* at around this time. 'He was the biggest thing on the sports pages after Mohammad Ali.'

The difficulty with the *Sun*'s sports coverage was that it was not satisfied with match reports: it led the field in wanting behind-the-scenes stories that in the past had remained well-guarded secrets. Botham rarely gave away much but his column raised the stakes for everyone. If the *Sun*'s rivals were denied full access to England's biggest sports star, what could they do in response? Ted Corbett, cricket correspondent of the *Daily Star*, said: 'My sports editor said to me, "You'll have to develop a strategy [to counter Botham's columns]." And I said: "Well, I'll just attack him for whatever he does." And that was what I did. News desks were convinced this man was a story every day of his life.' Botham's celebrity was also a big factor in the Press Association's decision to start regularly covering England cricket tours from around this time.

Press–player relations remained largely cordial in India, partly because the cricket was uneventful, partly because the reporters got no scent of the plans afoot for the rebel tour, and partly because the subcontinent was not the sort of place where there was much scope for headline-making extracurricular activities. Press and players continued to stay in the same hotels and when by necessity they were billeted together in lodgings for up-country fixtures they routinely ate together before whiling away the evenings as best they could, sharing games of cards or snooker, or complaining about boredom and the difficulty of getting hold of a decent drink. Botham found it easier to ignore criticism of his cricket than what he may or may not have done off the field, although he was always sensitive to charges of being a slogger. When Richard Streeton of *The Times* likened his batting in India to that of a village blacksmith, Botham came after him, but they made things up over a bottle of Scotch.

Some events were players-only occasions. One was the traditional Christmas Day fancy-dress party, although even then the press joined the players for drinks beforehand. At the party itself, Botham mocked Boycott again by dressing up as Boycott himself, wearing a shower cap punctured with holes and tufts of hair protruding – a reference to Boycott's recent hair implants – and a nappy, an allusion to his sensitivity to Delhi belly. Botham's bare torso bore the words, '8032 I Love Me', Boycott having two days earlier achieved his great ambition of passing Sir Gary Sobers' world Test run record. Boycott took it in good part. Later, the team staged a mock 'This Is Your (Real) Life' for Botham, who had recently gone through the actual experience on TV. Special guests included A Former Australian Captain, A Scunthorpe Soccer Player, the Highland Keeper of Fisheries and Wild Life and the Nervous Flying Instructor.

In the Tests in India, Botham had a mixed experience. He took more wickets for his side than anyone and scored more runs for them than anyone except Gooch, but more than half his wickets came in the first Test in the only conditions which really favoured bowling. He gave an amazing exhibition of stamina, bowling unchanged for four and a half hours on the first day, but he was still outperformed in the game by Kapil Dev, whose all-round contribution was the main reason why India won by 138 runs. With the five remaining games ending in sterile draws, this result – admittedly achieved with some questionable help from local umpiring – was enough to give India the series.

With the pitches slow in pace, there were opportunities for big scores but Botham squandered several good starts, passing 50 four times but never getting beyond 70 until he finally played one of his most mature and responsible innings when promoted to number five in the sixth Test in Kanpur, where he batted nearly six hours for 142. He did his best to set up a position from which England might win but was frustrated by rain and an Indian over rate of just 12.9 per hour. At one point during a drinks break, Botham had charged off the field and into the dressing-room where he told team-mates that he was on the verge of thumping someone, so angry was he at India's blatant time-wasting.

With India's great spin bowlers either retired or out of favour, the challenge of batting in India was not as stiff as it had been, although Dilip Doshi, the left-arm spinner, proved a worthy opponent. When Botham had first seen Doshi on the tour he had smiled and raised his arms in a mock signal for six. They had already crossed swords in county cricket and both knew Botham's main tactic was going to be attack, although he showed immense discipline in keeping out Doshi and Ravi Shastri for three and a half hours in Madras; it was the slowest innings above fifty he ever played for England. 'He played their spinners all right,' Fletcher said. 'But to be fair, compared to those of the seventies, they were only average. You would have expected him to be able to deal with spinners of their quality.'

There was one worrying indication that Botham's focus was waning. As he had done during his own time as captain, he showed a reluctance to practise. Once the Test series was under way he played in only one practice match, in which he clubbed 122 off 55 balls – including 13 fours and seven sixes in the space of 36 balls – and bowled nine overs. Mike Brearley, who happened to be in Bangalore for the second Test, criticised Fletcher for apparently allowing Botham to go ten days without bowling a ball in anger, and speculated that Fletcher, as a new captain, might have felt unable to insist on Botham bowling in the nets. 'He [Botham] bowled rubbish in Bangalore,' Brearley said. 'I would have insisted that he bowled in the nets at least twice before a Test.'

This was to become a common situation for anyone captaining Botham. It was as though he had decided that if he could not be captain he at least would demonstrate his independence and power by leading the life he wished. If this meant spending little time in the nets, then that would be the way it was. Botham gained a reputation for being reluctant to practise, but it was not a reputation he held before his time as England captain.

In the case of Fletcher, it did not help that he came from a county where attitudes to practice were relaxed, as Essex often played on outgrounds with no net facilities. 'We generally turned up at 10am for an 11am start,' he said. 'We'd have twenty minutes of fielding and then thirty minutes to motivate ourselves and plan what we wanted to do.' Fletcher said he couldn't recall giving Botham leave to not bowl but said Botham was not a great person for nets. 'I would have shared Brearley's view [when Brearley was captain] that "Both" needed to conserve his energy for playing,' Fletcher said. 'I never had a problem with him. You forgot what he did off the field. He always gave you everything on it.'

Fletcher also rejected suggestions that he abandoned the traditional eve-of-match dinner at which tactics were discussed: 'What we usually did was hold a meeting at around 5pm to talk through things we wanted to put into practice but in India it was rarely wise for us all to sit down and eat the same thing the night before a game – for obvious reasons.'

Keith Fletcher paid for England's defeat in India with his job. His sacking came as a surprise and he was never officially told the reasons for it, but Peter May may have believed he did not have a firm enough grip on the team. Fletcher had set a poor example by knocking off the bails with his bat in disgust at being given out in Bangalore and the TCCB's top brass were suspicious about Fletcher's protestations (honest though they were) that he had known nothing about the rebel tour until he was invited to join at the eleventh hour. Even then he might have tipped off May as to what was happening, but had chosen not to.

The captaincy passed to Bob Willis, the team's elder statesman and regular vice-captain. Willis benefited from two former Warwickshire players sitting on May's selection panel in A.C. Smith and Norman Gifford. Willis had done himself no harm by turning down the rebel tour and making a rousing speech at a critical juncture of the inaugural Test in Sri Lanka; England had promptly turned round an awkward situation and won the game. Willis spoke his mind and was, in Gower's words, 'a forthright character who liked to take charge'. Willis had, too, some experience of captaining Warwickshire, whom he had led since 1980. Not only did May appoint Willis for the home series against India and Pakistan but he dropped a clear hint that David Gower was heir apparent by inviting him to lead MCC against the Indians in a curtain-raiser to the summer.

Botham's name would have been quickly passed over. With more than 800 runs and 40 wickets in eleven Tests since last captaining the side, he would have been a brave choice; the selectors would have thought it far better to leave well alone than risk jeopardising his form for a second time. Four days before Willis's appointment, Botham twice crashed a Saab he was racing at Thruxton; two days after, he smashed 105 against Derbyshire in the Sunday league.

Botham would not have been unhappy with Willis as captain. They were close allies and had been England's chief wicket-takers since Botham had come into the team; Willis was unlikely to demand dramatic changes in the way Botham went about things. Willis was aware of this: he conceded that his team talks might not be of much interest to the likes of Botham but could be of value to the less experienced. Willis was a conscientious leader; he knew he had been insular as a player but was determined as captain to take a paternal interest in his charges. However, he encountered the same problems as many fast bowlers when they become captain: they struggle to have enough energy for themselves and the team. Journalists were surprised at how amenable Willis was given his attitude towards them in the past, but he worried a lot and clearly did not find the job easy.

Willis would be criticised for not controlling Botham better, but he was not alone in that. Mike Brearley said that both Willis and Gower 'appeared to be bulldozed' by Botham. Tony Greig, commenting generally about Botham's time in the England team, said: 'Had I been captain, I wouldn't have tolerated some of the things that went on in the dressing-room when he played ... I wouldn't have tolerated any of that stuff.' And Brian Close, in characteristically sweeping fashion, suggested that many of those who played with Botham after 1981 failed in the way they treated him: 'They encouraged him to be stupid. Not just the media, but the players and the captain as well. It was all bravado ... He was provoked into thinking the impossible was always possible.'

Willis was unlucky. The bans on the South African rebels meant seven uncapped players were brought into the side in as many Tests. This was a test not only of his powers of inspiration but of the maturity of these young players, who received Test match fees that were nine times what they had been a decade earlier.

One of the newcomers was Derek Pringle, a Cambridge undergraduate who had yet to make much of a mark with Essex. He was chosen for the first Test of the summer against India at Lord's. Pringle had had an awkward first meeting with Botham the previous September when Essex had played in Taunton. On a night out, Botham had wanted to throw Pringle out of the car he was driving – John Lever had successfully pleaded for leniency – but was now very welcoming at the eve-of-match dinner. 'The team dinner was boozy,' Pringle recalled. 'He [Botham] took the mickey out of the selectors, Peter May and what have you, and then said to me after the meal, "Come to the bar, you need to have a beer or else you won't sleep well." We had a few beers in fact and we'd already had several wines. I probably didn't go to bed much before a quarter to midnight.' Asked whether he felt better for it, Pringle replied: 'I don't know. It was no different from what we did in county cricket.' Pringle scored seven the next day, Botham a rumbustious sixty-seven.

In the circumstances, it was to the credit of Willis and his team that India were beaten 1–0 and Pakistan 2–1. They owed much to Botham, who despite some mutterings from former players about his physical condition had a very good summer, his return from six Tests being 566 runs and 27 wickets. He scored most of his runs against India – including his first and only double-century for England – and took most of his wickets against Pakistan, but either way made his influence felt in each of the three matches that were won.

He batted as well against India as he ever had for England and fully justified his presence at number five. India lacked depth in their bowling, which relied heavily on Kapil Dev and Dilip Doshi, but no batsman in the world at that time could have matched the way Botham mixed defence with attack. His innings of 128 from 169 balls at Old Trafford and 208 from 226 balls at the Oval were readily identifiable as coming from the same player who had torn apart the Australians with such measured ferocity in Manchester the previous summer.

Coming off 220 balls, his double-century was the fastest in Test history to that point but he never indulged in frenzied slogging. His only blemish was sacrificing Allan Lamb, a refugee from South Africa playing his first series since qualifying for England (and someone with whom Botham would get into more scrapes than anyone else), who became the latest team-mate to suffer at the hands of Botham's dodgy running. He himself was out attempting a reverse sweep, a shot he was becoming fond of using against spin, but abiding memories were of the purity of his hitting. Bob Taylor, who played alongside Botham during the 1982 Tests and in fifty-one Tests in all, said that he could always tell how well Botham was playing from where he hit the ball. 'Although he was a big hitter, he wasn't a slogger,' he said. 'Of course he had his off-periods. If he hit over long on or midwicket you knew he was hitting across the line. If he hit straight, and he was a beautiful straight hitter, you had confidence he was in control of what he was doing.' Botham hit one six off Doshi so straight and high that it damaged roof tiles on the Oval pavilion.

Even in the defeat to Pakistan at Lord's, where England followed on 201 behind, Botham tried to kindle the spirit of Headingley the previous year by refusing to accept that defeat was inevitable even when England slumped to 9–3 in the second innings. Having only just come into the side, Derek Pringle was amazed at Botham's attitude: 'I remember him saying, as we followed on and were not doing very well, "Don't worry, lads. We can still win this." His self-belief verged on the delusional. It was a childlike, bulletproof self-belief. "Childlike" may be the wrong word but there was a naivety to it. Most people would have said there has to be cause for doubt here. The hardest person to fool is yourself. He pushed that to the bounds of credibility.' Despite struggling against Abdul Qadir, virtually the only leg-spinner operating in Test cricket at the time, Botham battled for more than three hours for sixty-nine, but with only Chris Tavare also making a score the match was ultimately lost heavily.

Botham was hardly in a position to take things for granted – his status as the world's number-one all-rounder was coming under threat from Kapil Dev and Imran Khan, two all-rounders whose games had greatly improved. Kapil Dev hit quick-fire half-centuries for India in all three Tests and struck the ball every bit as spectacularly as Botham, even if he was not as disciplined. Imran was lithe, fit and physically in his pomp and as potent a fast bowler as there was in the game outside the Caribbean; he was also capable of resourceful fifties in the lower order. This was his first taste of captaincy and he took to it more readily than Botham. Crucially, his performances did not suffer and he was not afraid to take difficult decisions – one of his first acts was to drop his cousin Majid Khan – but tactically he was shaky and he was every bit as wilful as Botham.

If Botham had Kapil Dev covered statistically in the India series, the same could not be said of Imran, who scored 212 runs to Botham's 169 and took 21 wickets to Botham's 18.

That Botham held on to his position as the king of the all-rounders was partly down to his team, and not Imran's, having won the series. But he now had a fight on his hands for a position he clearly cherished. That Imran seemed to lead Pakistan so effortlessly while maintaining his own game cannot have escaped Botham's attention, but it was not just Imran's abilities as a player that set him up as a rival to the England player. Away from the cricket field, the Oxford-educated Imran led every bit as colourful a lifestyle as Botham. One England team-mate recalled: 'All you had to do to wind him [Botham] up was say what a marvellous player Imran was. If you wanted to get him going, that was the sort of comment you made, even if you tended to make it from the back of the dressing-room rather than the front! You only had to suggest someone was a really good all-rounder to know what reaction you would get.'

The duel with Imran, and the requirements of carrying the bowling with Willis, took their toll. In the three Pakistan Tests, Botham got through more than 150 overs, which was not as many as Imran but still represented an enormous workload. It was probably one reason why he did not maintain the batting form he had shown against India. The Pakistan captain had his own views on Botham's problems. After the series, he wrote: 'I admire Ian for getting to the top while still remaining true to his individualistic instincts ... He's a dynamic cricketer ... He attacks in his bowling as well, giving the batsman a chance by pitching it up and trying to experiment ... Although he's supposed to have a bad back, I don't believe his action has suffered because of that. His main problem is that he's overweight.' Imran put this down to a lack of discipline in training.

The Pakistan series was among the most acrimonious Botham had played in and it ushered in years of ill-tempered encounters between the teams. Whereas the Pakistan team that toured in 1978 had been supine, this one displayed the belligerence of a group no longer prepared to go down without a fight. Under Imran they believed they were good enough to win, which they might have done with better luck from the umpiring. Imran had the English umpires in his sights from the start and before the series Pakistan requested that David Constant should not stand. The TCCB refused, despite having agreed to sideline him for India's matches. Imran proceeded to grumble about umpiring for the rest of the tour and was given every reason to complain when Constant committed two errors, both of which favoured England, in the tight deciding Test at Headingley. Afterwards, Imran publicly complained that Constant cost Pakistan the match.

Botham, as it happened, was involved in several flashpoints. He was the beneficiary when Mudassar Nazar was questionably given out lbw to the second ball Pakistan faced in the series and while batting in the follow-on at Lord's he clashed directly with Imran over the condition of the ball. Ball-tampering was not then the controversial issue it later became but English suspicions were aroused by the amount of swing achieved by Mudassar, who was only a part-time bowler, and Sarfraz Nawaz, who would later be acknowledged as the modern inventor of the mysterious art of reverse swing. At one point, Botham, who claimed he could see that the quarter-seam was coming up, had shown the ball to umpires Constant and Dickie Bird. He said they were 'clearly worried' about the state of the ball. A few moments later, he spoke to Imran about it. According to Botham, Imran replied that

England's bowlers might get the ball to swing if they looked after it a bit better. Whatever England's suspicions, the umpires took no action and Donald Carr, the TCCB secretary, examined the ball in question and declared that he had no complaints.

Botham batted under a degree of provocation from the fielding side during this innings. At one point, Abdul Qadir continued to demand that Constant give out Botham leg-before even after Constant had turned down his request, prompting Constant to threaten to suspend play if the Pakistanis did not refrain from their frenzied appealing. Botham also had to deal with Javed Miandad, crouched a few feet away at silly point, making high-pitched bird noises in an effort to distract him. Javed, who was from a modest background and appeared to be motivated by a sense of grievance against most of the world, regularly irritated opponents and the previous year had been involved in a mid-pitch fracas with Dennis Lillee during a Test in Perth. He certainly got under Botham's skin now. 'He [Botham] wanted to fight him because Javed was winding him up,' Derek Pringle recalled. 'At one point Beefy went to sweep, the ball bounced off his pad and Javed, while appealing for lbw, picked it up and threw at the stumps. It hit Beefy and there was a bit of squaring up. A few overs later, he was out and Javed gave him a send-off. Beefy came back threatening to do him serious harm.'

During this match Botham was rumoured to have been spotted by team-mates in the dressing-room with a gun in his cricket bag and to have said that he was going to use it to shoot Javed. When asked about this incident, Botham jocularly replied that he could not recall having brought a gun, before adding: 'If I was going to kill Javed, I wouldn't have needed a weapon.'

Trouble was also brewing at Somerset. Five days before the start of the Pakistan series, the county retained the Benson and Hedges Cup, their fourth trophy in as many years, but the season was otherwise a disappointment for a team fancied to compete on all fronts. Viv Richards, fighting the distractions of a persistent finger injury and a testimonial, had a mixed year while Joel Garner, rarely fully fit, took only thirty-three championship wickets. Hallam Moseley, Colin Dredge and Peter Denning were all less effective than they had been. Brian Rose's batting average fell from 46.9 to 28.7 as six seasons of captaincy took their toll. 'It was pretty stressful because of the strong personalities we had in the side,' Rose recalled. 'It was starting to affect my game and my health, and I was contemplating giving up.'

One of the major problems was the change in attitude of the big-name players. Botham and Richards were two of cricket's greatest stars and to an extent had outgrown the culture of a small rural county club. With more sponsorship opportunities starting to emerge, they were understandably eager to exploit their status within the game. Largely on the back of Botham and Richards, membership subscriptions were raising an astonishing £100,000 by 1980 and after lobbying from some of the senior players, who had threatened to set up their own marketing company, the club had agreed to an amalgamation of the promotional interests of the club and players through a separate limited company, Wyvern Sports Marketing. This was to be the cause of some friction. 'They rather forced it on us,' said Ray Wright, Somerset's treasurer. 'They weren't particularly well paid even though stars like Viv, Ian and Joel got £500 added to their wages for the season because they were international players.' David Seward left the club as chief executive at the end of the 1982 season.

While Botham was away at the first Pakistan Test, Somerset travelled to Bournemouth for a championship match against Hampshire. For some reason Richards was missing. Even so, Somerset dominated a low-scoring game until they were left the apparent formality of scoring eighty-three to win. Inexplicably they collapsed to lose by ten runs. It was a stunning implosion. Peter Roebuck dated the troubles that were to consume Somerset in the mid-1980s from this point. 'The Benson and Hedges Cup final [of 1982] was the last great moment of that side,' he said. 'We turned up at Hampshire and there was something going on. I don't really know what it was but Viv wouldn't play and there was a sense that the first move had been made. Roy Kerslake [the club's chairman] was there and Rose was talking a lot to him. I said to Alan Gibson of *The Times* at the end of the game, "There's something wrong with us." And he said: "It's hubris." At the top, it was fractured. And you could never put it back together again.'

Botham and Richards returned for the next championship game but Somerset performed even more poorly than they had at Hampshire as they were outplayed by Middlesex from start to finish on one of Weston's spiciest surfaces. Somerset lost all ten second-innings wickets in the space of forty-six balls as they were all out for fifty-seven. Simon Hughes, a young fast bowler with Middlesex, was surprised at how carelessly Botham and Richards played. 'Somerset were totally spineless,' he said.

Two weeks later, shortly after England's heavy defeat to Pakistan at Lord's and with the deciding Test at Leeds looming, Botham took the unusual step of sitting out a championship game, although he was present at Taunton for the first day of the game against Leicestershire. It was a Saturday and after he had, in David Gower's words, 'lunched well' at the ground he went out in the evening with Gower and Leicestershire's other star batsman Brian Davison. It was not an early night for any of them and Nick Cook, Leicestershire's left-arm spinner, remembered the fallout the next morning when the teams reassembled for a Sunday league match in which Botham did play. 'Tolly [Roger Tolchard] went ballistic at Gower,' Cook recalled. 'Davo was completely hung over. Davo had a birthmark on his cheek that came up after a lot of alcohol and that morning it was like a Belisha beacon. It was a bit of a giveaway.' Gower remembers spotting Botham in the bath that morning, 'armed with a cigar and the *News of the World*, bright as a daisy as usual'. Somerset duly won the game, although Gower and Davison could not be blamed as they scored fifty-eight and twenty-eight respectively.

Rose was unavailable for the last championship match of the season, which presented Botham – fresh from a 56-ball century that had sped Somerset to victory over Warwickshire and an equally speedy 98 against Worcestershire – with a chance to take over as leader. Rose's thinking had been that when he gave up as captain Vic Marks would be the best man to succeed him, Marks having led the side capably enough in 1980 when Rose and Botham had been away playing with England. However, Botham's status as a former England captain appeared to have established his seniority in the pecking order behind Rose.

Unfortunately for Botham, he failed to enhance his captaincy credentials as a glorious position was squandered against Lancashire, who were led by West Indies captain Clive Lloyd. Lancashire were five down before they cleared their first-innings arrears but after Botham raised eyebrows by not bowling Garner and himself more Somerset found themselves chasing 134 to win. With three hours left, this should still have been a formality. Lancashire's slim hopes rested with spinners David Hughes and David Lloyd and Botham's plan was that Somerset would sweep their way to victory. 'We won't be hitting you in front of square,' he had told them. But Botham fell to Hughes, Lloyd picked up four wickets and Somerset ended up falling fifteen runs short.

Brian Rose decided to stay on for another year as captain.

The Ashes tour of 1982–83 must rank as the biggest disappointment of Botham's career outside his time as England captain. After his heroics against Australia in England, and some of the things he had done since, expectations were high. When people predicted great things for him after 1981, this was what they had in mind: routing the Aussies again.

Yet for the first time as a player unburdened by leadership, he was consistently unable to deliver. In five Tests he made just one half-century and never managed a five-wicket haul, a feat he had made routine. Nor was his form any better in thirteen one-day internationals, averaging less than twenty with the bat and proving alarmingly expensive with the ball; in some of the later games his bowling was caned. He caught some blinders at slip but

England's great match-winner failed to win a match with a significant performance.

But whereas his failures during his time as captain – which were admittedly more profound than now – had caused him a great deal of anguish, he seemed to take these latest disappointments in his stride, as though they were just another turn in fortune's wheel and the good times would soon return. It was probably easy to think like this when so many people were ready to tell him how good he was. 'Everyone patted him on the back,' said one teammate. 'They treated him as a hero and encouraged him to think that he could do nothing wrong. When that happens, it is easy to lose perspective and fall prey to arrogance.' Perhaps he was content to not live up to his great deeds of the past. Perhaps he accepted it just was not possible.

There were extenuating circumstances. Players visiting Australia when Australia were at full strength rarely delivered and Botham's record on previous trips there was only good rather than great. The schedule was brutal and could only have been designed by administrators eager to ensure players did not have time to join another rebel tour. Four weeks and one day after his last match of the English season, Botham was boarding a plane for a trip that lasted more than 140 days, for much of which he was playing against the same two sides, Australia and New Zealand. For an all-rounder who had played cricket winter and summer for six years, this was a mind-numbing undertaking even for someone of his relentlessly upbeat nature.

With the side shorn of its banned players, others in the team struggled too. Graham Gooch was badly missed at the top of the order and Bob Willis was, like Botham, less effective with the ball than he had been. Willis predictably found the captaincy difficult and relied on senior players such as Botham for guidance – it was partly on Botham's advice that he mistakenly opted to bowl first in Adelaide – and by the fourth Test was physically ill with worry. If Botham had spent too little time as captain thinking about his players, Willis thought too much. But the plain fact was that the

Australians were the better side and deserved to regain the Ashes. Even without Lillee for all but the first Test they had the three most dangerous bowlers in Geoff Lawson, Jeff Thomson and Rodney Hogg, while Kim Hughes, back under Greg Chappell's captaincy, made amends for his errors in England in 1981 by finishing as the highest run-scorer in the series.

But as Willis concluded in his tour diary, Botham was the biggest let-down. Botham attributed his struggle to a recurrence of his back problem brought on by bowling so much in the Pakistan series but this hardly explained why his batting fell so far from its heights of the previous twelve months. Remembering the lessons of the previous series, the Australian bowlers took a leaf out of the West Indies' book and cramped him for room.

In truth his body was suffering from years of heroic endeavour and a lifestyle that allowed little time for rest and recuperation. It was obvious to most that he was overweight and although he denied it at the time Botham later admitted that was 'carrying too many potatoes'. Botham's size did not escape the notice of Australian supporters, who smuggled a pig into a one-day international at Brisbane and released it onto the outfield. It had the words 'Eddie' (a reference to Eddie Hemmings) painted on one flank and 'Botham' on the other. Harold Larwood, the mild-mannered former England fast bowler now living in Sydney, was withering in his assessment: 'This fellow is the most overrated player I have ever seen. He looks too heavy, and the way he's been bowling out here, he wouldn't burst a paper bag.'

Conscious of the workload Botham had been subjected to over the years, Willis had intended to use him as more of a strike bowler than a stock one but, Botham's powers of persuasion being what they were, this idea came to nothing. Even though his bulk made it hard for him to rotate in delivery and swing the ball as he once had, Botham bowled more overs than any other fast bowler in the series bar Lawson. He also conceded more runs in a series than he ever had before. With one-third of his eighteen wickets being due to swing, he began his obsessive use of the bouncer.

Botham was now a freer, more independent spirit – as Geoff Cook had noted. Willis found it hard to rein in someone who was a close friend and who always believed he knew what was best for him. 'Ian has been so used to success that he gets very sensitive when things are not going right for him,' Willis observed shortly before the second Test. Willis, who had noted in his diary two weeks into the tour that Botham was 'burning the midnight oil', did not think Botham was doing anything different from other tours; the difference now was that at twenty-seven he needed to work harder on his game than he had at twenty-two.

Botham played in all three warm-up games, even standing in as captain against South Australia, but he may still have found the demand of bowling forty overs in the first innings of the first Test in Perth unusually wearing. According to one team-mate, he was asleep on the physio's bench when England's third wicket fell on the fourth evening and he was required to bat. 'He got up, splashed his face with water, strapped up his pads and went out,' Derek Pringle recalled. 'He was bowled second ball, came back, said, "Sorry, lads, I didn't see it," and went back to sleep.' Willis's view was that Botham had made an 'absolute mess' of a full-length ball. Mind you, Botham was always a big sleeper in the dressing-room. 'He'll sleep for ages in dressing-rooms if he can,' said Mike Gatting, who played forty-four Tests with Botham.

Willis was sufficiently concerned to get Doug Insole, the tour manager, to sit down with Botham and discuss his form and preparation. Insole was a hugely experienced figure. He had been a player and administrator for thirty-five years but was cleverer and shrewder than the average Lord's appointee. He knew more of the outside world for a start: he had gone to grammar school, not public school, and had worked at Bletchley Park, the codebreaking HQ, in the Second World War. He had been chairman of selectors during the d'Oliveira affair, and TCCB chairman at the time of Kerry Packer, and must share some of the blame for the way England's tours were scheduled. But he was nobody's poodle. He had turned down offers to be MCC president because he was set on turning unfashionable

Essex into a force, which he had done, and had upset traditionalists by overseeing the introduction in 1981 of covered pitches, which hurt spinners but ensured more play for the public.

Botham would have tolerated a pep-talk from Insole, but was he really listening? Whatever Willis thought, Botham would have looked back on his great all-round performances against Pakistan at Lord's in 1978 and India at Bombay in 1980 and remembered that his preparation had involved late drinking, as had also been the case ahead of the rest day at Leeds in 1981. Why should he do anything different now? Even if he did moderate his behaviour, things were never going to be turned round overnight.

Botham's form continued to run hot and cold for the rest of the series, although he earned Willis's lasting gratitude by claiming the final wicket to seal a dramatic three-run win in Melbourne, where he had urged a more aggressive approach on the team. It could not hide the fact that Botham's bowling was seldom dangerous and by the time the team left Australia to play three one-dayers in New Zealand he was barely worth his place in a five-man attack. 'His career is now at a crossroads,' Willis observed. 'It is time he stood back and looked at the manner in which he is preparing himself.'

This was to be Botham's tragedy: he never did accept that if he was to be as good as he once was he needed to train more. It was as though he feared above all the internal defeat of knowing he had set out totally prepared – only to still fail.

Botham was under inordinate pressure. England's games attracted huge audiences – more than 550,000 watched the Tests and another 380,000 saw their one-dayers in Australia and New Zealand. Everyone wanted a slice of him and before the Tests began he felt the need to escape the fuss for a day by driving north of Perth to see the Pinnacles, listening to cassettes of Dire Straits and Dexys Midnight Runners all the way. In the dressing-room, he played endless games of cribbage with Geoff Miller, an old mucker with whom he was on his fifth tour; they were known as Higgs and Hill, after the building contractors, as they were so often together. 'By the fifth Test he was claiming Miller owed him something like $1,700,' said Vic Marks, who was making his first England tour. 'The reason he played so much cribbage wasn't for the money but as an escape from the closest possible scrutiny. It was a defensive mechanism against everything that was going on. He was as big as it gets on that tour.' Marks also remembered Botham taking Geoff Cook and himself to visit a sportsman in hospital who had been crippled in an accident. 'He was so nervous he smoked furiously all the way there but he was just brilliant for half an hour, flirting with nurses and talking cheerily to this bloke. He couldn't have been better,' Marks said. 'When he came out he was absolutely shattered. It took its toll, but he did it.'

After the tedium of India, it was inevitable that the players were going to enjoy themselves in countries where there was more to do and much more to drink. The team socialised with many celebrities including Elton John, whom Botham met for the first time. Willis had hoped before the tour that Bernard Thomas, the team's physio, would stop the players on days off sitting around the pool with a bottle of wine, but this was exactly what happened on the rest day of the Adelaide Test, when some of the players went off to the Yalumba winery. It was while there, sitting by the pool with Dennis Lillee, that Botham – who had arrived by helicopter with Rod Marsh and Greg Chappell, with whom Botham got on rather better than his brother Ian – was photographed in only his swimming trunks, providing newspapers back home with the ammunition to argue that he was indeed carrying a few too many potatoes.

Willis, who was thirty-three and had been touring with England since 1970, was struck by how much money the young players in the team now had at their disposal and how much time they were willing to spend in the bar. When Insole tried to impose a curfew in the later stages of the tour, the players immediately rebelled – Derek Randall surprisingly being among the first to speak out – and the idea was promptly dropped. Willis also felt the players ought to show more obviously that they cared about losing. But the fact was that life as an England cricketer was changing. Commercialism was on the rise: JVC, the electrical goods company, had been signed as a team sponsor and this required the players to attend numerous functions. And Willis's leadership itself was questioned. One of the younger players observed: 'Bob didn't show much guidance off the field ... We kind of went under Beefy's wing.'

It was natural that on such an arduous tour the players would need an occasional blowout. After the defeat in Adelaide, which left England 2–0 down, Botham organised a night on Eskimo Pies – jugs of whisky and ice-cream – to improve morale. Much of the cost of the drinks ended up on Botham's room bill, to the anguish of Marks, his room-mate, who ended up paying half. During the evening Derek Randall won a bet with Botham by swapping clothes with a young woman who had entered the bar. Back in Adelaide for the one-dayers, Botham, after a gruelling day in the heat during which England had failed to defend 297 against New Zealand, took part in a trotting race at a local track against Dennis Lillee. 'Botham won purely because he was madder and more prepared to risk life and limb than Lillee,' Marks said.

Botham's willingness to socialise with the opposition, and his encouragement that others should do the same, did not go down well with all team-mates. Randall was one of those who did not like it. 'These people have been trying to decapitate me all day,' he would say. 'I'm not going to have a drink with them.' Chris Tavare was pretty much teetotal so Botham did not give him any pressure, although Botham was not enamoured with Tavare's habit of 'walking' when he had nicked the ball, a policy the Australians themselves never pursued. Botham announced at one team meeting that anyone who 'walked' in Australia would do so over his dead body, but Tavare refused to be intimidated and carried on as he was.

England's failure to reach the finals of the one-day tournament in Australia gave the players some extra days to enjoy themselves in New Zealand. Botham was given permission to take a group of players away on a fishing and golfing trip that included Ian Gould, an old mate from Lord's groundstaff days who was the reserve wicketkeeper, and Allan Lamb, almost as big a party animal as

Botham himself. Botham's only rule as self-appointed tour manager was that no one could go to bed before he did, which in the event meant everyone retiring as dawn broke.

The pressure on Botham was not eased by the conduct of the tabloid press. While his problems with form and weight gave the *Sun*'s rivals plenty to get their teeth into, it was actually the behaviour of the *Sun* itself that proved most alarming as it showed it was now willing to run stories critical of its star columnist. After the second Test the paper claimed there had been a rift between Botham and Willis, both of whom denied any such thing. Later, it repeated a report carried in an Australian newspaper that Botham had been involved in a fight with Rodney Hogg on New Year's Eve; the story was without foundation and the *Sun* ended up running an apology. The *Sun*'s new tactic was a distressing development, and Willis advised Botham to give up his column, but Botham declined, arguing that the 'money is good'. He may also have calculated that all publicity was good publicity and that his status was now such that there was a degree of criticism beyond which no newspaper would go; as one journalist said, 'Publicity was the making of him.' When Botham told the *Sun* that the Test series had been afflicted with poor umpiring he earned himself a £200 fine from his tour manager – even though Insole, like Willis, privately shared his views.

While in Australia, England were invited to play an additional fixture – for extra money – against Pakistan in Dubai on the way home. Dubai, a haven for Asian expatriate workers, was not then an established venue for international cricket, although it was soon to become one. Most of the players, including Botham, chose to accept. The match was lost and to make matters worse Botham found himself getting wound up again by Javed Miandad. 'We were in a horrible hotel in Sharjah, where it was "dry",' Derek Pringle recalled. 'There was a bit of a scuffle in the bar and he [Botham] wanted to punch Javed's lights out. But one of the Pakistan players dissuaded him. He said, "No, no, Ian . . . No one gets more annoyed with him than we do."'

# 9

## His Own Man

'The jamboree that surrounded him was unbelievable. He was the biggest thing in the game and unfortunately he courted all the publicity, good, bad and indifferent, that went with that. We were going through a phase of playing a lot of new people and it certainly rubbed off on some in a negative way. I was quite an outgoing chap but still found it difficult. It certainly got distracting at times. The dressing room should be a sacrosanct place and it wasn't. It was Tom, Dick and Harry as far as I could see. It disappointed me.'

NICK COOK ON PLAYING FOR ENGLAND
ALONGSIDE BOTHAM

Botham's energy may have been superhuman but by 1983 he was wearying in body and mind. Cricket had brought him a lot, including the kind of earnings and celebrity unimaginable to the young man who had walked out of school without a backward glance all those years ago, but his enthusiasm for the game was being sorely tested now. Increasingly, it was giving him problems he was unsure how to solve.

Part of the difficulty was his reluctance to admit, even to his closest friends, precisely what the problems were. He was more likely to grumble about bad luck, or media harassment, than admit he was not fit enough or playing well enough. But the tell-tale signs were there, from the waning faith shown by Bob Willis, the England captain, to Botham's own interest in pursuing commercial opportunities. It was natural that Botham should keep an eye out on the future: he wasn't going to be earning money from playing cricket forever. He was bound to listen to any offers that came in.

It was obvious that Botham was not quite as effective a cricketer as he had been. The fear was that he might never be again. As Willis had suggested, Botham needed to review how he was preparing for matches. And to an extent he did. On returning from the 1982–83 Ashes tour, he started playing more football in an effort to improve his fitness, and there was some improvement in his shape by the time he next toured. But the improvement was never going to be massive. He once played for Scunthorpe reserves on a Friday evening, scoring a hat-trick in the process, and then boarded a plane for Dublin for a boozy weekend of rugby watching. He may have been outrageously talented at many things, but changing his ways was not one of them.

A year earlier, he had batted for England at number five with responsibility and authority. Now his game seemed less patient and more mercurial: some days it was rancid, other days regal. In mid-May, with the World Cup in England looming, he showed both sides of his game in the space of twenty-four hours. At Chelmsford for an important Benson and Hedges Cup zonal game, he tossed his wicket away by attempting to reverse-sweep his second ball from Ray East, Essex's left-arm spinner, and lost his leg stump. 'It was very surprising. I was bowling to short boundaries and he could have practically pushed it for six,' East said. 'He must have been on a dare or something.' Somerset lost the match and failed to qualify for the cup's knockout stage. Next afternoon, again batting with Viv Richards, he pulverised a strong Nottinghamshire attack at Trent Bridge that included Richard Hadlee, he and Richards putting on 138 together.

Despite getting the better of Hadlee on that occasion, Botham's hold on the unofficial title of world's best all-rounder was slipping. At the World Cup, Botham had less to brag about than his rivals. The tournament was unexpectedly won by India, whose star all-rounder Kapil Dev not only captained the side but did some exceptional things as a player. India drew the sting of England's batsmen in the semi-finals with an array of innocuous-looking medium-pacers before stunning West Indies in the final, the turning point of which was Kapil's fine running boundary catch to dismiss Richards. Hadlee had a fine tournament with the ball while Imran Khan, unable to bowl because of shin splints, was among the leading run-scorers. Botham lacked penetration with the ball and opportunity with the bat, facing only fifty-two balls all told.

Hadlee also outshone Botham in the four Tests that followed, his 301 runs and 21 wickets representing one of the finest all-round series by any player. Botham started the series so quietly that after New Zealand had levelled the series at 1–1 with their first win in England on a ropey surface at Headingley, his place in the side was widely questioned in the media.

Unfortunately, at this very time he and Kath went through a personal tragedy when her third pregnancy ended in her losing the child. She had told him during the Headingley Test that a routine check-up had detected no heartbeat in the womb; the day after the game finished he accompanied her to hospital for a scan that confirmed the baby was dead. To make matters worse, the news that they had hoped to keep private leaked out and was given prominent media coverage. Botham was always upset when members of his family were dragged into the news and this incident only further hardened his attitude towards the media.

It would have been a hard captain who abandoned Botham at this moment and Willis loyally defended him now, saying that there was no better all-rounder in the country. This was not the most ringing endorsement as England did not have to pick an all-rounder at all if they did not deem there to be one good enough.

In the end, Botham kept his place but surrendered his position at number five in the order (as it transpired, never to return).

Instead, the England selectors brought in three uncapped players for the third Test at Lord's, taking the number of new players tried in fourteen Tests since the rebel tour to ten. Left-arm spinner Nick Cook received an eleventh-hour call and arrived at the ground late after hitching a lift from the team hotel with Botham. Cook, who played nine Tests with Botham between 1983 and 1989, was both dazzled and disconcerted at the circus that attached to the team's biggest star, with Botham's friends and acquaintances seemingly coming and going as they liked. 'The jamboree that surrounded him was unbelievable,' Cook said. 'He was the biggest thing in the game and unfortunately he courted all the publicity, good, bad and indifferent, that went with that. We were going through a phase of playing a lot of new people and it certainly rubbed off on some in a negative way. I was quite an out-going chap but I still found it difficult. It certainly got distracting at times. The dressing-room should be a sacrosanct place and it wasn't. It was Tom, Dick and Harry as far as I could see. It disappointed me.'

But Cook and Botham were good for each other. Cook took eight wickets, including Hadlee caught at slip by Botham, while Botham himself claimed four wickets and scored an important half-century in the second innings of a game England won by 127 runs. It was Botham's first important contribution to an England win for almost a year – a fact that reflected not only the wane in Botham's power but the decline of the England team. In the final match Botham followed up with a century – his first in twelve Tests and achieved in just ninety-nine balls – as he and Derek Randall tore into all the bowlers as England won again to take the series 3–1.

The impression given by Cook that Botham had become a law unto himself was reinforced by other incidents that year. Botham blocked an attempt by the TCCB to call a halt to his column in the *Sun* and he further upset the board by ignoring its appeals to him to stop playing football, turning out for Scunthorpe United in league fixtures against Hull and Preston only days before going on tour. He accused the board of being dictatorial but more often than not the TCCB caved in to him. He had perhaps become less inclined to be conciliatory since losing the England captaincy.

A gulf in any case was developing between star players such as Botham and the well-meaning amateurs like Donald Carr, secretary of the TCCB, who continued to run the game. These were men who had acquired their positions largely because they had gone to public school and university and played the game to a good standard. Carr had walked the corridors of power during a number of administrative debacles, including the d'Oliveira affair, the Packer defeat, and the rebel tour of South Africa. It was hardly surprising that Botham managed to keep his *Sun* column and played football when he liked. When it came to managing Botham, the mild-mannered Carr was not quite Mike Brearley or Ken Barrington.

Botham, of course, was a special case. Since 1981, he had become an immensely popular and powerful figure. Perhaps only Boycott, who was also inclined to set his own rules, was in a position to be as fiercely independent. But the TCCB hierarchy was afraid not only of Botham but other stars such as Willis, Gower and Lamb, whom Gower said had as good an eye for business as anyone in the team. The players had begun to realise they were worth something; sponsors were as keen as the South African regime to secure their signatures. Moreover, after two years Britain was finally out of economic recession. Botham – whose attitude of 'If you want it, go out and get it' chimed perfectly with that of prime minister Margaret Thatcher – was estimated to be earning around £40,000 from kit endorsements alone by 1984, in itself five times the minimum wage for a county cricketer. To a large degree, big sponsorships from the likes of Cornhill Insurance, who in 1983 raised their annual support for Tests in England from £220,000 to £631,000, were predicated on the presence of the big-name players in the side. It would not have been wise for the TCCB to upset the talent.

Somerset was where Botham could really flex his muscles. Brian Rose's health remained fragile and it was clear he was approaching the end as leader. He played only occasionally after early June. If a successor was needed, Botham, by now established as deputy, was eager to be that man. For a start, it might give him the chance to show that he was right when he said he could have made a good England captain had he had a longer run at the job. Although it was possible that he might not lead his country again – Gower, Willis's heir apparent, was going from strength to strength as a player – he had not yet given up hope and a successful stint in charge of Somerset might yet cause a rethink. Other England players captained their counties, including Willis at Warwickshire and Mike Gatting at Middlesex. Why should Botham not do the job at Somerset? He had been awarded a benefit with them in 1984; most players expected to wait ten years for such a lucrative earner but the Somerset committee had agreed to grant Botham one only eight years after his county cap. He wanted to be captain when it happened.

The problem for the Somerset team, as Rose realised, was that a group of players that had started out together was now reaching maturity together – and had acquired strong opinions about how things should be done. Inevitably, these views did not always coincide. The politics of the situation were starting to get complicated.

During the 1983 World Cup, with Botham and Vic Marks away with England, Peter Roebuck stood in for Rose and under him the team gave some spirited performances. Tony Brown, the new chief executive, had asked Roebuck during the Bath festival whether he would carry on leading the side after Botham and Marks returned. He declined. 'I said to them, "You've got a captain and vice-captain." Doing the job on a full-time basis hadn't occurred to me and I didn't believe I was ready to think about other people,' Roebuck recalled. 'I felt I was about seventh in line. They [the club] were scared of Botham being captain and of sacking him [as vice-captain]. I knocked the idea on the head even though I didn't think Botham as Somerset captain was ever going to work.' Like Roebuck, Rose had his doubts about Botham and thought that Marks, a natural conciliator, would have been the best choice to take over from him. 'Ian was going to be playing for England and not much for Somerset,' Rose said. 'I had some reservations about "Both" because we'd seen the effect of the England job [on him]. It was a different beat but the effect was the same.'

Things came to a head during a championship match at Leicester in early July. Botham had an outstanding game, giving his best performance of the season with the ball – 5–38 on a first-day green-top – before going in at number nine because of an upset stomach and scoring 152. It was the only time he ever scored a century and took five wickets in an innings in a county match, and the only time he and Viv Richards, who hit 216, scored centuries together as Somerset team-mates. Believing the time had come for him to take official charge of the side, Botham called a team meeting to corral support, but the putsch fizzled out when the key figures of Marks and Roebuck opted not to attend.

In the event, no long-term decision was made about Rose's successor that season. For a start, it had not yet been ruled out that Rose might carry on, although in the event he was not to play again that year; nor indeed would he ever captain the side again. But in any case the Somerset committee was large and a lot of opinions were aired that were not easily reconciled. The short-term solution was that Botham would captain the side when available and when he was not Roebuck rather than Marks would stand in.

Already out of the Benson and Hedges Cup, Somerset turned to the NatWest Trophy for hopes of a prize. Leading this campaign was to inspire Botham for the rest of the season. He led the side in a quarter-final tie at Hove only 24 hours after Kath had lost her baby and only 48 hours after his place in the England side had been questioned following New Zealand's victory in the second Test. Bowling at the sort of express pace not seen from him for a long time, he and Joel Garner blasted out Sussex for 65 and the match was easily won. Considering what he had just been through himself, Botham did another remarkable thing while in Hove. Ian Gould, who had moved from Middlesex to Sussex in 1981, had asked him if he would go along after the game to a local pub where they were raising money for the son of a friend who had cancer. 'There were things happening in his private life but Ian still turned up, stayed a long time and helped raise loads of money,' Gould recalled. 'The great thing about him was that he would never let you down.'

Botham produced more heroics in the semifinal against Middlesex in front of 20,000 at Lord's. Chasing 223, Somerset slipped to 52–5, by which time Botham was their only hope of salvation. After an uncertain start, he settled down to play a beautifully measured innings, sharing stands of 104 with Nigel Popplewell and 62 with Marks, although he did then run out Garner. When the final over arrived the scores were level and Botham, on strike, knew that if no wicket was lost Somerset would win by virtue of losing eight wickets to Middlesex's nine. He duly opted to survive the last six balls from John Emburey rather than take risks seeking the winning run – or the four he needed for his own hundred. Survive he did, although he escaped a close lbw shout off the last ball, much to the fury of Emburey, who was bowling only his third over because Gatting had feared Botham would hit him into the Mound Stand – further evidence perhaps of the awe Botham inspired in Gatting. At the finish, Botham threw his arms in the air, before grabbing a souvenir stump and turning for the pavilion. As they ran from the field, umpire Jack Birkenshaw shouted to Emburey: 'Sorry, mate, he might have been out there.'

Botham ranked this as one of the three finest innings he ever played; others said they had rarely seen him play so responsibly.

'He was determined to win the game rather than go for glory,' said Emburey, before adding: 'Which was very bloody unusual for him.'

Matthew Engel, covering the match for the *Guardian*, immediately detected the political implications of the performance. In his report, he wrote: 'Botham blocked all six balls from Emburey knowing Somerset would thus win the game, he would win the man of the match award, of course, and very likely the Somerset captaincy . . . He sublimated the normal Botham beneath a Boycott-like canniness and a Brearley-like sense of stage management.' He also referred to a 'Unilateral Declaration of Independence in the dressing-room'.

Reflecting on the occasion now, Engel added: 'The ninety-six not out was highly significant. It was a most calculated I'm-your-captain moment and a most un-Bothamesque thing. How could he resist going for that boundary to give himself a hundred?! It was the most political act I ever saw by someone with a bat in his hand. He said afterwards: "Hundreds don't worry me." It was a very interesting indication of his character. It showed very clear self-awareness and manipulation of a situation. This was his captaincy bid.' Engel remembers that when Botham spoke to the press afterwards, he was asked where Rose might bat if he was fit to return for the final. 'Where I fucking say,' was his reply.

Straight after this game Botham led Somerset to another victory over Middlesex in the championship – his first-ever win as captain in a competitive first-class match. After that he scored a hundred in the final Test against New Zealand, meaning that he had played large parts in five successive matches being won by county and country.

Botham duly led Somerset to triumph in the NatWest Trophy final over Kent. He played a relatively minor part in a comfortable victory although he did hold the catch that clinched the match. Roebuck said that despite winning this trophy, 1983 remained 'a very unhappy year' for Somerset, adding: 'If things were OK before then, why did my little period as captain make such a difference?'

England's tour of New Zealand and Pakistan in 1983–84 turned into one of the most notorious episodes in Botham's career. It marked the point at which he became as well known for excess as success. This was not wholly his fault. The general behaviour of the team was shoddy. That the team lost Test series in two countries where they had never lost before could hardly be blamed on one player. And he was not the only reason that the patience of the British media finally snapped. Under the weight of evidence of indiscipline off the field and mediocrity on it, the dam of goodwill finally burst.

While the players cannot escape censure for the way they behaved, the TCCB courted trouble by asking them how they would like the tour structured. After two long winter tours, the board felt it owed the players something and proceeded to consult them on the itinerary. While it was understandable, given the health problems encountered by some of team in 1977–78, that the players would want to keep the visit to Pakistan short, the agreed programme was utterly foolhardy: three Tests and two one-day internationals were to be shoehorned into twenty-five days. The New Zealand tour by contrast was to last exactly twice as long even though it incorporated only one extra one-day international. A stopover in Fiji was even arranged, supposedly as a missionary exercise, although a second visit to see how the natives were developing their game never materialised. Apart from anything else, the schedule was an insult to Pakistan, already smarting over the David Constant row the previous year. All in all, it sent a clear signal to the players that they held the power.

Keeping the time the team spent in Pakistan to a minimum not only invited defeat; it also encouraged the players to demonise the place in their own minds and to make sure they enjoyed themselves in New Zealand beforehand. In fact, when they got to Pakistan they found it much improved compared to their previous visit six years earlier, even if Willis did fall ill and miss the last two Tests and the hotels they stayed in still had only one bar between them. But by the time they got there too much damage had already been done.

Despite the concessions over the itinerary, a firmer management team might still have maintained order. The role of manager had passed from Doug Insole to A.C. Smith, another Warwickshire ally of Willis's who had led the county to the championship in 1972, Willis's first season with the club. Educated at Oxford and fond of wearing silk scarves, Smith's inexperience – he had not been to New Zealand for twenty-one years – betrayed itself in the cautious way he dealt with the press, to whom he divulged little. He gave the players little trouble; Botham once described him as a 'long-time ally behind enemy lines'. Norman Gifford, by then a Warwickshire player, was again assistant manager.

It might have helped had TV crews been covering the tour or had the senior players been more experienced. But here again the loss of the rebel players was felt. Had Geoff Boycott, Derek Underwood, John Emburey or Graham Gooch been around, a greater degree of self-policing might have gone on. As it was, only Willis, Derek Randall and Bob Taylor were in their thirties. Willis and Taylor both decried the apparent disinterest with which the team met its defeats but it seemed that no one was strong enough to bring things under control, although Mike Gatting, who played in five of the six Tests, said there were 'a lot of internal squabbles'. Botham spent much of his time with Allan Lamb, who as Gower once observed, shared his energy and vitality. 'Lamb and Botham are similar characters,' Gower said. 'I can't keep up with either after dark.'

The catalysts for the media hostility were the Test defeats in Christchurch and Karachi. That England were in control for much of the first Test in New Zealand, fought hard in later stages of the series in Pakistan, and lost some crucial players to injury, was largely forgotten, as was them winning three of the five one-day internationals. But that was the fault of the players: the tour did not become known as the 'Sex and Drugs and Rock'n'Roll' tour for nothing.

It was not only that the second Test at Christchurch was lost; it was the way it was lost that prompted newspaper editors at home to pose questions that demanded thorough answers. Dismissed for eighty-two and ninety-three, their lowest combined total since the nineteenth century, England were beaten in just twelve hours of play. Despite the wholesale failure of the batting, Willis blamed the bowlers for not making more of helpful conditions. Botham, bowling 'unbelievably badly' as well as dropping a catch, was widely held to be the chief culprit, particularly for the way he bowled at Hadlee, who top-scored with ninety-nine. With the bat, Botham was out for eighteen and nought, swinging a short ball into the hands of fine leg in one innings and being brilliantly caught by Martin Crowe at short leg off Stephen Boock in the other. While Botham did not have a significantly worse game than many team-mates, more was expected of him, especially as he had started the tour strongly, pulverising the bowling in the warm-ups and giving England a chance of winning the first Test by swinging the ball enough to take 5–59 and scoring 138 after being dropped twice before reaching 20.

The result was bad enough but the response of the players caused just as much anger. Don Mosey, who said that some players were involved in alcohol-induced high jinks on the night the match was lost, believed camp followers who had previously shown discretion could no longer resist telling their offices in London how the players had been conducting themselves. It seems that Botham himself did not come under suspicion as he and Willis ended the evening at their hotel watching a spectacularly bad film starring Oliver Reed, but there had been incidents earlier in the tour that were now used against him.

One had taken place on the team's fourth night in New Zealand. An Englishman staying in the same hotel as the players had complained to the *Daily Express* via telex about the 'drunken and surly behaviour' of Botham, Lamb and Willis in the hotel bar.

The *Express*'s Pat Gibson, who was there, said the claim was a wild exaggeration that arose out of the Englishman in question trying unsuccessfully to muscle in on the conversation of players and journalists. But the *Express* had put the story on its front page nonetheless.

About a week later, police were called to the team's motel in Hamilton after a window was broken in the room Botham and Lamb were sharing. The damage had been paid for and the incident not reported in the newspapers at the time.

The locals, too, had been naturally keen to host private parties for their English guests and some of these parties had taken place during the team's stay in Wellington for the first Test. David Gower described one occasion at which the team was presented with a 'birthday cake' containing ingredients that led to a fairly high 'revolving eyeball count'. A.C. Smith managed to avoid having a piece but 'one or two' players indulged. 'It was a fairly harmless evening ... with the press failing to get wind of it,' Gower said.

What raised scrutiny to a new level was a New Zealand reporter inquiring about whether the England players had smoked pot in the dressing-room during the Christchurch Test. This extraordinary claim was never substantiated but the very suggestion sent Fleet Street into high alert. Following the Christchurch defeat, a number of papers sent out news reporters to New Zealand and Pakistan, including a relatively new player in the tabloid market, the *Mail on Sunday*, which had started publication in 1982 and was eager to make its mark. As far as it was concerned there were few bigger fish to fry than Botham. In the past, Reg Hayter might have dissuaded a newspaper editor from pursuing a critical piece about his most famous client, but there was little he could have done now. The mood had changed utterly.

Nor was the scent of blood dissipated by some of the team during their last ten days in New Zealand. After the third Test in Auckland had finished in a tame draw – Botham hitting a sparkling seventy – the team by chance found themselves visiting the same three cities for some one-day games as Elton John was playing during a concert tour. The team had attended a concert in Christchurch and been invited to join John in his suite at the Sheraton hotel in Auckland. Botham and Willis attended three concerts, going backstage once, and socialised with John on other occasions.

John, who had married Renate Blauel a few days earlier in Sydney, was a long-standing football fan and his interest in cricket appeared to date from his meeting with the England team in Australia the previous year. Botham and he had immediately got on, with Botham greatly impressed at how John had managed to cope with intense public scrutiny for fifteen years. In fact, John had not always coped and during the late 1970s had turned reclusive. Over dinner with Willis and Botham one night in Wellington, John had offered an interesting assessment of Botham which Willis recorded in his diary: 'Having studied him on two overseas tours now, he [Elton John] feels we gave Ian too long a lead in Australia last winter and ought to have kept him more under the thumb.' Willis added rather laconically, 'Perhaps he is right.'

It was about a week after the team reached Pakistan that the newspapers started running their sensational stories.

England's preparations for the first Test in Karachi were utterly inadequate. The team arrived in the country sixty hours before the game began, barely time to deal with a six and a half hour time difference from New Zealand, and for one of their two practice sessions they were given only one net in which to work. They had no serious practice on turning pitches or against leg-spin bowling of the type Abdul Qadir would be directing at them. Unsurprisingly, England lost with a day to spare, their batting being only slightly less feeble than it had been in Christchurch. Botham was out to Qadir in the first innings and to Tauseef Ahmed, an off-spinner, in the second. Pakistan made hard work of knocking off the sixty-six they needed but no one was fooled; England had again been outclassed.

A day later, the *Daily Express* ran a story about the broken window in Botham and Lamb's room in Hamilton, alleging that the incident had occurred while they were entertaining women in their room. The report quoted Botham as saying that the players had paid the hotel the cost of the damage. In the team room the following evening, Botham and Lamb discussed the story with Willis, their captain trying to reassure them that they had no need to worry. Now aware of the mobilisation of news reporters, Willis warned his players to be wary. While the team prepared for a one-day international in Lahore, the possible source for the allegations was high in many people's thoughts. Almost certainly rightly, the players could not believe that one of the regular cricket correspondents would have spoken against them and suspicion fell on others. Graham Morris, the photographer, said the finger was wrongly pointed at him. Even Richard Hadlee wrote to Botham denying he was the source, because he had heard that Botham thought it might be him.

With the *Mail on Sunday* news reporters staying in the team hotel, the old camaraderie between players and cricket writers – groups who had begun the tour playing charades together – froze as the weekend approached. 'It was a tense and miserable time for everyone,' Mosey wrote. 'The whole atmosphere was quite awful.' Matthew Engel rejected the suggestion that most cricket writers were ever in a position to protect the players: 'We weren't in each other's pockets. I would say that only two or three journalists would have actually known what Botham got up to.' But Michael Carey, cricket correspondent of the *Daily Telegraph*, wrote a scathing piece about the extent to which the players now socialised on tour, alleging that the TCCB was not getting value for money from its players. 'Every night seems like Saturday night,' he said.

As it happened, Botham broke down with a knee injury during a one-day international and the day after the game Bernard Thomas, the physio, decided that he should return home. There were suspicions that his departure was connected to the scandals engulfing the team but the problem was a long-standing one which had resurfaced early in the tour and he underwent surgery in England a few days later. Botham had been presented with some of the allegations that were to be levelled at him before he left but he was flying when three Sunday newspapers landed on the nation's doormats carrying lurid stories about the team's behaviour. The *Mail on Sunday* ran their story across its first three pages with headlines reading, 'Cricket star "smoked pot" on tour', 'Botham named in drugs sensation' and 'There's coke in the bag, said Botham'. Emerging at Heathrow airport, Botham was engulfed by reporters and in answer to a barrage of questions blurted out a denial, 'I've never smoked dope in my life.'

Eventually reunited with Kath and his children, he discovered that they had escaped reporters themselves only by going to stay with Kath's sister Lindsay and brother-in-law Paul. Back at home and having studied the newspaper reports, Botham and his solicitor Alan Herd – but, much to her annoyance, not Kath – reviewed the situation and decided on a plan of action. Botham instructed Herd to go to Pakistan and collect affidavits from teammates testifying to his good character; a writ for libel was issued against the *Mail on Sunday*.

The following day, Ian Jarrett arrived at the house to write the story for the *Sun*. 'Basically I was interviewing Kathy to support the headline "My Wonderful Guy", as in Guy the Gorilla,' Jarrett recalled. 'The brief was that in spite of the allegations, Kathy still loved her guy. I filed a lot of words only to be told that they wanted it for the front page and centre spread and needed more words. So I lay on Botham's double bed upstairs, talking into a Mickey Mouse phone, ad-libbing garbage.'

A few days later, while he was recovering in hospital and England were involved in the first day of the third Test in Lahore, Botham gave an interview to BBC radio during which he jokingly referred to Pakistan as 'the kind of place to send your mother-in-law for a month, all expenses paid'. It was a crack that backfired on several fronts. Pakistanis, perhaps already affronted at England's star cricketer having managed to stay only eleven nights in their country, were understandably aggrieved. Staff at the Lahore Hilton refused to serve food to the England team. Sarfraz Nawaz branded him 'a drug-crazed opium pusher'. Even the TCCB was moved to fine him £1,000.

Relations between players and press were never the same again. The players gradually retreated from the customary practice of drinking at the same hotel bar as the cricket writers, preferring to spend more time in designated team rooms where confidences could not be overheard. Eventually the team stopped staying in the same hotel as the journalists as a matter of course. Willis noted in his diary that some players had shown a naive faith in the press and that Botham had erred in believing that because he would never let down a mate, everyone else was made the same way. Botham and Lamb made a pact that they would not speak to the press throughout the whole of the 1984 season.

But the TCCB found no player guilty of indiscipline in New Zealand and Pakistan. Less than three weeks after the end of the tour, the board said it had investigated various serious newspaper allegations – some of which then still remained the subject of legal action – and found nothing to substantiate them. It also said that there was no evidence of any off-field behaviour adversely affecting the team's performance on the field. The lopsided itinerary was not mentioned.

Without the events being in any way linked, Bob Willis was however replaced as captain by David Gower.

Things were out of control. Even by his own frantic standards Botham was taking on a lot, and it took its toll, to the point where he pulled out of England's next tour. He needed time with his family, and time to himself, but before getting to that stage he continued to live and play fast. Botham's knee had not long been well enough for him to drive again when he was again picked up for speeding. At one point during the summer he collapsed in a pub car park. He said his drink had been spiked.

While he was recuperating from his knee operation, Botham's

appointment as Somerset captain for 1984 was confirmed. Given the controversies of the winter, this marked something of an act of faith by the club committee, although it would have been dangerously late in the day to switch horses. The county campaign promised to be a challenge as not only was Botham going to miss half the season with England but Viv Richards and Joel Garner were touring with West Indies. Martin Crowe, a promising young New Zealand batsman, was signed instead. This was a gamble but one that was to pay off.

Contacted by two South African 'businessmen' (who were almost certainly messengers of the apartheid government) about whether he would be willing to captain a rebel tour of the republic, Botham agreed to meet them in Taunton but talks broke down when they said that Viv Richards, whom they also wanted to recruit, would be given 'honorary white' status to allow him to move freely around the country.

Shortly before the season started, Jock McCombe, who worked on the Somerset staff and had done so much facilitating for Botham and Richards, died suddenly of a heart attack. He was replaced by Andy Withers, a gentle buffalo of a man who was a former drayman, barman and rugby player from Wiveliscombe, who would become a loyal companion for Botham over the next few years. Withers made sure that Botham was kept in clean laundry and fresh pizza at his bungalow in Pikes Avenue, Taunton; he also acted as his minder, Botham seemingly feeling increasingly in need of protection. Withers also helped Botham keep to the fundraising events that made up his benefit season – village cricket matches, golf days, dinners and suchlike. Inevitably given the difficulty of shoehorning these occasions into the regular schedule, benefit seasons were often chaotic and Botham's was no exception.

Some of Botham's events were held jointly with Geoff Boycott, who was having a testimonial (effectively a second benefit) with Yorkshire. One of these involved them captaining opposing sides in a match at Birtles Hall in Cheshire. This Georgian mansion was owned by Tim Hudson, whom Botham had briefly met during his trip to the United States in 1981. Born into a cotton family at Prestbury, a few miles from Birtles, Hudson was a keen cricket fan who in his youth had made a few second XI appearances for Lancashire. He had gone to the States to try his luck after meeting someone at a cocktail party who had told him he looked like a disc jockey. He had duly become one for KFWB radio station in Los Angeles, where he managed a couple of local bands, and claimed to have discovered the Moody Blues. He had also worked as a voice-over artist in some Disney films including *The Jungle Book* and *The Aristocats*. Whatever wealth Hudson accumulated was dwarfed by that of his wife Maxi Bilber, a divorcee whose family owned LA's Yellow Cab Company.

If his wife had the money, Hudson liked to imagine he had the pedigree and he portrayed himself as English gentry, even calling himself Lord Tim. He parked a Rolls-Royce on the Birtles Hall driveway and staged matches on the adjoining cricket ground.

Botham was impressed by Hudson, as he was inclined to be by people who were rich, clever or talented. He liked his transatlantic hedonism and his ability to make sure there was always a good time to be had. He was intrigued by how Hudson had gone to America and made good. It struck again a chord that had already sounded. The States had offered up riches to Elton John and provided sanctuary to George Best, another friend, when the greatest British footballer of his generation could no longer cope with his celebrity. With Hudson's help, Botham was to increasingly look on the States as a place to which he could escape to make a fresh start. Christopher Bazalgette, who worked as Hudson's assistant at Birtles Hall, said that the friendship between Hudson and Botham developed over the course of this summer. By the autumn of 1984, Somerset had agreed to release Botham between matches to play for Hudson's teams.

In the early weeks of the season, Botham led Somerset with enterprise. He was reluctant to address the team and his plans didn't always work out but he made positive declarations and took bursts of wickets, playing a part in Gloucestershire being rolled over for seventy-two in front of the Taunton faithful, always a good move for a beneficiary. But things got more complicated when he started coming and going between England engagements. In the first one-dayer, Viv Richards tore England apart with an unbeaten 189, and when Botham returned to his county they were knocked out of the Benson and Hedges Cup by Warwickshire, the run-outs of Crowe and Botham in short order sealing their fate. The following weekend at the Bath festival, Botham suffered a freak injury that might have put him out of the first Test. He was getting changed after play when David English came into the dressing-room with a pint of beer in his hand, ahead of a planned night out. 'He [Botham] started throwing water at me,' English recalled. 'I made as though I was going to throw my beer over him, and accidentally cut his hand deeply. I'm not sure if it was his bowling hand but the finger looked to me like it was almost hanging off. I said: "Jesus Christ!" And he said: "No, no. Don't worry. Get in the car." We went to hospital and he had five stitches put in it. He never said a word about it and played in the Test. It was remarkable.' The injury was kept from the press and the following year's *Wisden* recorded Botham as 'absent ill' from the festival match against Middlesex.

Botham not only played in the first Test at Edgbaston but did well with the bat, scoring 64 and 38, but England were crushed beneath the West Indian juggernaut, losing by an innings and 180 runs. Since the teams had last met during Botham's tour as captain, Clive Lloyd's team had continued to carry almost all before them. They had not lost in their eighteen previous Tests. Few gave England much chance and the match (and series) followed a grimly predictable path. With Botham and Willis fit again, England made six changes to the team that had ended the shambolic winter tour, but while several of those who were brought in justified their inclusion the team plainly lacked confidence. 'I believe we knew we were going to lose that series and that Ian thought we were going to lose,' said one England player. 'I never saw anything that said to me that we were going to win. How confident a person was Ian really? I think he was like anybody else. He had an insecurity which the bravado hid.'

After failing so totally with the bat in the Caribbean, Botham had reviewed his strategy for tackling Lloyd's bowlers. He took advice from the India batsman Sunil Gavaskar, who had recently faced West Indies home and away. Gavaskar had often failed but scored three centuries, converting one into a double. On a couple of occasions, he had gone for all-out attack and it had worked. Botham decided to try something similar and in his two innings at Edgbaston he had stood still and hit fourteen fours and a six. He had, of course, tried this approach before but in this series the West Indies attack was not quite as formidable as it had been; it contained three rather than four world-class fast bowlers, plus a moderate off-spinner in Roger Harper. His 64 at Edgbaston, which occupied only 82 balls, was then his best score against West Indies, but he immediately improved on it in the next game at Lord's, where he scored 81 from 111 balls in the second innings and might have made a century but for a poor lbw decision.

The Lord's Test turned out as almost a microcosm of Botham's career. For much of the time he was outstanding, batting well and swinging the ball to great effect in the first innings, in which he took eight wickets, before the promise (and in Botham's mind the certain belief) of more heroics led the team to disaster. England were in a strong position by the fourth evening but there was some hesitancy about a push for victory. Allan Lamb went off for bad light when he would probably have done better to chase more runs. Gower was uncertain when to declare or even if he should, although Peter May, who had appointed Gower captain in the hope of a fresh start, was keen for him to act positively. Gower eventually set West Indies 342, which would have been tough had Botham swung the ball the way he did in the first innings, but he could not. Convinced that a wicket was just around the corner, he railroaded Gower into keeping him on for far longer than was wise. By the time West Indies cantered home by nine wickets, Botham was in his twenty-first over and had conceded almost a run per ball. Blame for the defeat was laid firmly at his door, Gower saying later that he had bowled 'total crap'.

During this game Botham took several of the team along to Elton John's mansion for what turned out to be a party purely for their benefit. Derek Pringle, who had not been on the winter tour and had missed meeting John in New Zealand, recalled: 'I was fielding at slip, and Bob Willis was bowling, when Beefy turned to me and said, "What are you up to tonight?" I said I was meeting some friends. He said: "Do you want to go to a party?" Where? "Old Windsor." Whose? "Elton's." You serious? "Yeah." It was bizarre. It was a beautiful old place with fine paintings on the walls, Lowrys and Magrittes and what have you. There was food for about 150 but it was basically us, Elton and his band, and his wife Renate. As I recall, only Elton John records were played. They'd obviously got to know each other . . . Beefy was a powerful force. People were attracted to that.'

Pringle saw more evidence of Botham's generosity during the next Test in Leeds, where West Indies predictably clinched the series with another win, England being able to compete for only the first half of the game on another poor Headingley pitch. As the England players often did in Leeds, the two of them went to drink at the Junction pub in Otley, where they met a couple of Pringle's mates who had been at the game. 'I introduced them to Beefy and he was really pleasant and open with them,' he said. 'His attitude was always, "Your mates are my mates." One of these guys, Steve, had a fast car with him, a Toyota MR3 or something, and Beefy more or less commandeered it, driving us back to the hotel like a maniac, tyres smoking. We all then had a drink at the hotel. These guys had got nowhere to stay so I said that one of them could take my spare bed and the other could kip on the floor. But perhaps because he'd just caned his car, Beefy insisted that Steve should take the spare bed in his room. Apparently the next morning there was a knock on Beefy's door at around eight o'clock, so my mate put a towel round himself and went to answer it. There was a chambermaid holding a tray containing two pints of milk and copies of the *Sun* and *Sporting Life*. Beefy lay in bed drinking the milk, farting a few times and studying the form guide before getting up and leaving for the ground.'

That night out caused Botham trouble because someone at the pub contacted the newspapers about how England players – but specifically Botham – had been seen drinking during a Test match. A report subsequently appeared in the *News of the World*. In the past such a thing would almost certainly have never attracted attention but after the sensational stories of the winter there was now no such thing as a minor incident involving Botham. His paranoia about the press was no longer misplaced: they really were out to get him. About three weeks after this, Botham was in a Somerset team meeting in a tent at the Weston festival when a *Daily Mail* reporter burst in. He had been sent to write a Botham drinking story of his own. He was given short shrift.

By then, Botham's season was unravelling. His form had tailed away in the Test series, England were heading for a whitewash, and Somerset's defence of the NatWest Trophy had ended in failure after defeat to Kent in the quarter-finals, effectively ensuring that the county would win nothing for the first time in four years. Botham's handling of the game had raised some eyebrows. With the team hit by injuries, he had decided to recall his old mate Dennis Breakwell, who had barely played in three years and was now the club's assistant coach. The move had not worked, Breakwell's seven overs proving costly. Botham himself had been out to Derek Underwood for nought.

It was now that he announced that he was unavailable for the India tour, a decision that summed up his disenchantment with touring and the media circus it created. He felt he owed Kath and his two young children a winter at home. There were few recent precedents for such a move – Geoff Boycott had dropped out of international cricket for three years in the mid-70s and Ray Illingworth had as England captain once opted out of a tour of India and Pakistan – and there were calls for him to miss the fifth Test against West Indies and a one-off match against Sri Lanka to give others a chance. But the selectors wanted him for both and he delivered seventeen wickets – as well as a few choice words to the Sri Lankan batsmen that earned him a ticking-off from the umpires.

The West Indies series ended on an unusually pacy pitch at the Oval. Jonathan Agnew, the Leicestershire fast bowler and future BBC radio commentator, had been brought into the side for his debut and was struck by Botham's fierce determination in the face of what seemed the inevitability of another defeat. 'It was pretty clear what was going to happen, and most people were putting a brave face on an utterly hopeless situation, but with "Both", the loud figure in the middle of the dressing room, it just never came across that that was what he felt,' Agnew said. 'He was an incredible presence. He just dominated the place very positively. It was a glimpse of what he must have been like in '81, when things were going his way, he was on a roll and the team were on a roll. It must have been exhausting.

'The team meeting beforehand was basically "Both" saying how he was going to get everyone out. A few people chortled a bit, because they'd heard it before, but "Both" had plans and he couldn't conceive that they wouldn't work. I stood at mid-on and watched him bowl at the speed of light. I had never seen him bowl like that before. At the start of the second innings, we were still in the game. I got Gordon Greenidge, caught by "Both", for my first Test wicket. When Viv Richards walked out, "Both" came to me and said, "You will not pitch up a single ball at Viv Richards. Let's get two men back." Gower agreed and with "Both" bowling at the other end we bombed him for about half an hour until finally I pitched one up and Viv played all round it and was lbw. Really, "Both" got me both my wickets in that game.'

England lost again but Botham finished as England's second-highest run-scorer in the series behind Allan Lamb and their leading wicket-taker, passing 300 career Test wickets in the process. It wasn't quite true that he did nothing against West Indies in their pomp.

Somerset's two-month drought without a championship win

ended with victories over Gloucestershire and Nottinghamshire, who went into the final round needing to win to take the title. In one of the most memorable of all championship games, Botham led Somerset to a nerve-jangling three-run win, although on a personal level the game produced no runs, wickets or catches.

Botham intended the winter to be a quiet one. He worked on a semi-autobiographical book with Peter Roebuck which was published in 1986. 'It irritates him that, despite his incredible career, he is still often regarded as a muddied oaf,' Roebuck explained. 'He didn't want to be regarded always as a villain ... This book is a part of Ian's campaign to rebuild his reputation.' Roebuck also noted how lonely he felt Botham was. 'His situation forces him into a contemplative world to which he is unsuited,' he wrote, adding: 'He surrounds himself with loyal friends and will not go anywhere without them ... He is deeply grateful to any colleague who invites him out to the pub for a drink, to anyone who accompanies him on a night out somewhere.'

Botham trained with and played football for Scunthorpe United, and finished his benefit season. It yielded £90,000, perhaps the equivalent of a year's earnings. He believed that but for the recent scandals it might have brought in a lot more.

Unfortunately, more trouble was on its way and in curious circumstances that only heightened his sense of persecution. On New Year's Eve, as he and his wife prepared for a party, officers from Humberside Police – the force that had handled his charge for assault in Scunthorpe four years earlier – visited and searched his home in Epworth. They said a drug had been found in a pair of trousers that had been sent for dry-cleaning. The search revealed a small quantity of dope in a bedroom drawer, which Botham said he had been given by a fan at the Oval a few years earlier (subsequent evidence suggested this incident took place in 1982). The following day, a newspaper reporter arrived at Botham's front door, asking questions about the police raid.

Six weeks later, Botham pleaded guilty to possessing 2.19 grammes of cannabis and was fined £100. There were to be other costs. His car deal with Saab was cancelled and a proposed endorsement with a stationery firm fell through. But the cricket authorities were lenient. Almost exactly a year to the day since Botham's denial at Heathrow airport about having ever taken drugs, the TCCB's executive board decided that it would take no specific action against him, although it did later ask all professional cricketers to formally agree to random dope tests and warn them that anyone found to be involved in drug offences would be subject to harsh penalties. It was a disastrous show of weakness.

After a two and half hour meeting, Somerset issued Botham with a severe reprimand but retained him as captain – which in fact they might well have not done had it not been for the conviction. According to Brian Langford, the cricket committee chairman, the club were ready to remove him as captain but decided to keep faith with him after the bad publicity of this case. 'We didn't want to see Ian being kicked when he was down,' Langford said. Colin Atkinson, the club's president, made a statement to the effect that if Botham's 'unwise and brief experiment with cannabis some three years ago . . . had taken place during his term as captain he would not have been reappointed.'

One of the most furious responses to his drugs conviction came from Kath, angry at being obliged to undergo police questioning herself and at the jibes their daughter received at school over their 'drug-addict dad'. In one spectacular outburst, she threw a coffee table at him, which proved to be the beginning of what he described as 'a very rough patch' lasting several weeks. All the hopes for a happy winter at home had dissolved as Kath perhaps realised that, hard though it was to be without her husband for long periods, living with him was not necessarily easier. 'Kath has always said that I was not designed for living with,' Botham once said. After the police raid, Kath wanted to move home and later in the year the Bothams moved from Lincolnshire to an old coach house at Asenby, North Yorkshire.

Botham's conviction came at an unfortunate time because nine days earlier the England team had finally returned to winning ways with a 2–1 win in India which ended a sequence of six successive series defeats overseas (discounting the one-off match in Bombay in 1980). One of the star performers was Mike Gatting, who had so often lived in Botham's shadow. Some were tempted to conclude that England might be better off without Botham and it was claimed that two senior England players were glad he had not been in India. Relatively minor though Botham's offence was, cricket had not been associated with drugs before and many traditionalists were shocked at the development, which only made the TCCB's handling of the case all the more surprising, although in a broad sense Botham's conviction proved a good career move, confirming as it did his anti-Establishment credentials. It was not long before fans were sporting T-shirts bearing the words: 'Ashes to Hashish'.

Tim Hudson phoned Botham from the States to commiserate over his conviction and they agreed to meet when Hudson returned to England. Hudson had heard some reports (far from accurate as it happened) about how little Botham earned from cricket; but even the true figures were dwarfed by the sums earned by the top sports stars in the United States. Hudson told Botham that he could earn much more. This may have been true but the proposals he came up with were probably too radical for the conservative tastes of most people in cricket. Hudson's general belief that cricket could be given wider appeal with more imaginative marketing was fine but his specific ideas that teams could have pop stars such as Elton John as figureheads and that matches could incorporate performances from rock bands were unlikely to be given serious consideration by the TCCB.

Botham should have seen the difficulties a mile off but he was, by his own admission, discontent with his lot, and willing to listen to anyone who thought he could improve it. He shared Hudson's view that his earnings could be better and was conscious that the clock was running down on his time at the top. If there were additional ways to make a buck, he wanted to know about them. He found Hudson's talk that he could make a Hollywood star out of

Botham irresistible. Part of him had always wanted to be the next John Wayne.

Meanwhile, Botham's plans to do something significant to raise money in support of leukaemia research finally took shape. It was something he had been thinking about for a long time. He had talked a few years earlier about raising money by flying around the world with Alan Dyer, a businessman who had completed the trip in 1974, but there were simply too many logistical difficulties. But now the culture of celebrities putting their names to charitable causes was established; Children in Need had been recruiting them for television appeals since 1980, they had been raising money through taking part in the hugely popular London Marathon since 1981, and Bob Geldof had organised an all-star single in support of the Ethiopian famine that was on its way to becoming the biggest-selling single in UK chart history. Botham was now aware that he could use his fame not only to his own advantage but to that of other people: he had recently spearheaded a fundraising campaign at Scunthorpe United which had left the club, in the words of a subsequent chief executive, 'eternally grateful' to him.

During a family holiday in the Lake District over Easter 1985, Botham decided that he was going to walk the 874 miles from John O'Groats to Land's End, something that BBC radio DJ Jimmy Savile had once done for charity. The date for the walk was eventually set for later in the year, shortly before England's next tour. His motives were questioned by those who suspected he was trying to restore a tarnished image. Botham dismissed such suggestions as nonsense but the fact was that at the time his plans for the walk were firmed up his standing in the eyes of the public was lower than it had been for years.

By the time the 1985 season began, Botham had appointed Hudson manager of all his cricketing and commercial affairs. He had wanted Reg Hayter to carry on handling press matters but Hayter rejected this division of labour. Hayter was devastated at Botham's decision, not only for what it would cost him but because he feared Hudson could not deliver what he was promising. It was all change. Botham bleached his hair blond and promoted cricket-related clothing such as jumpers and multi-coloured striped jackets. Hudson's idea was that with Botham's help cricket would become the new rock and roll. It was pure escapism, but escapism was just what Botham needed.

# 10

## The Fearful Treadmill

'Isolating Ian was one of the things I wanted to do. I felt
that the more Ian was isolated the more he would be able
to focus on his cricket – or go. It had to be one of the two.
With his group around him, we would never get him
back on track.'

PETER ROEBUCK ON IAN BOTHAM'S FUTURE AT
SOMERSET IN 1986

Tim Hudson may not have been a great businessman but his value
to Botham went beyond optimistic talk about how much money
he could make him. Hudson helped convince Botham – and
others besides – that the England all-rounder had embarked on a
fresh start in life.

The blazers and blond mullet represented more than a new line
in personal fashion; they symbolised a shaking-off of the scandals
and the fatigue that had tarnished his image over the previous two
years. The celebrity culture was taking off and, in the new mood
of mid-80s optimism, Britons appeared willing to look upon
themselves more positively. Hudson displayed a confidence on
Botham's behalf that Botham himself may have felt but could not
articulate. If Botham shocked the Establishment with his behaviour then so be it; he should be seen as lovable rogue rather than

villain, and celebrated as a great sporting champion. This was the start of Botham as preening, swaggering, anti-hero. However he did it, Hudson proved adept at getting lavish picture spreads on his client in the national newspapers.

Botham, in any case, was refreshed after his winter off and ready to approach his cricket with renewed vigour. To an extent he picked up where he left off in 1984, when he had achieved some success going for all-out attack with the bat and bowling as fast as he could. He now used these tactics again with even greater success, the one discipline crucially feeding off the other, although the only way he could maintain this type of bowling in six Tests against Australia was to hardly bowl himself at all for Somerset. He averaged less than twelve overs per game in the championship. Improbably he appeared to be living up to the swashbuckling role of a latter-day Errol Flynn that Hudson had imagined for him. Botham may have later rubbished Hudson's involvement but it was undeniable that he acquired a new lease of life.

Botham's enthusiasm was clear from the amount of time he now spent at Birtles Hall and Hudson spent at Somerset and England matches. Botham persuaded England and Australia players to take part in celebrity matches at Birtles Hall. In fact, he was there so often that Kath issued him with an ultimatum to choose between the Hudsons and her, before walking out on him for a few days. Botham conceded that this incident shook him up but did not lead him to greatly moderate his behaviour. In the end Kath returned, as much for the sake of the children as anything.

'He was there a lot [in 1985],' said Christopher Bazalgette, who lived at Birtles Hall while working for Hudson. 'We'd see each other at breakfast, things like that. Viv Richards was there a lot too and Brian Close, who also worked for Tim, practically lived there. Andy Withers was there; he drove the car and worked very hard for Botham. They [Hudson and Botham] gelled. How close you actually get to "Both" I don't know, but they were very friendly. The Hudsons threw great parties at which the alcohol flowed. Maxi had plenty of money. That was quite an attraction I should think. Everyone was treated well. It was an easy life. To say Tim did nothing for Botham [financially] would be unfair.' Hudson sorted out a publishing deal in which Frank Keating, the *Guardian* journalist, wrote a book on a year in Botham's life. He also fixed up Botham with a Jaguar to replace the lost Saab.

Bazalgette said that he saw no evidence of Botham smoking dope at Birtles. 'I'm sure he was not,' he said. 'There were people there who did smoke dope. There were sometimes Rastafarians there who naturally did. In fact, what I remember is him regularly going out for runs. I also remember attending a lunch in Mayfair, at which Peter Smith of the *Daily Mail* was present. At one point he called across to me, "Is it right that Botham is smoking cannabis?" I said that it was not right and he should withdraw his remark.'

Unfortunately, after all the Hudson-inspired optimism, there were to be similar allegations of serious indiscipline levelled against Botham and three younger members of the Somerset squad during the very first match of the season. Somerset were playing Oxford at the Parks and one evening during the game, which was badly affected by rain, Botham went with the three to a pub in Wheatley, south of Oxford. One of them was 23-year-old Mark Davis, who was starting his fourth season at the club, another was Stephen Booth, twenty-one, a left-arm spinner who was in his third season; the other player's identity remains a closely guarded secret. Botham's choice of drinking companions was in part a reflection of Viv Richards and Joel Garner still being away on West Indies duty and the changing nature of the Somerset team; few of Botham's old mates remained.

As it happened, Brian Rose, who did not play in the match but had travelled with the squad, was also at the time in the same pub with Trevor Gard, the team's wicketkeeper, but they were not involved in the alleged activities. The matter came to the attention of the Somerset committee, whose chairman John Gardiner, a mild-mannered solicitor from Cheddar, interviewed Rose shortly afterwards. Rose was in favour of some sort of action being taken but nothing more came of the matter for the moment, although the incident may have contributed to Davis and Booth both having poor seasons.

As England captain, Botham was often inhibited and cautious; now, he was determined to be faithful to his attacking instincts. Armed with a heavier bat weighing a mighty 3lb 4oz he wreaked destruction in the championship, hitting ten sixes in his innings of 90 and 50 against Nottinghamshire (who were missing Richard Hadlee) and another eight as he took a 76-ball century off Glamorgan. He was only slightly more subdued in scoring 65 from 40 balls for Somerset against the Australians. Then in late May, in the first match for which Richards and Garner were available, he struck an imperious 149 from 106 balls against a Hampshire attack containing Malcolm Marshall, then widely regarded as the world's fastest bowler. He again reached his hundred from 76 balls.

Given Marshall's presence and the score when he went in (58–4), this must rank as one of the finest innings Botham ever played. He was given an early let-off and played himself in against lesser bowlers, but when Marshall was brought on, he protected his partners and took the attack to him. Putting on his white helmet at the start of every over against him, he pulled and hooked with ferocity; Botham was not reckoned the safest of hookers, but he put Marshall away in style and forced him into the rare indignity of posting five men on the rope. Sam Cook, one of the umpires, said: 'I've never seen anyone play Marshall so well.'

But Somerset lost every one of these games, just as they had all their one-dayers against serious opposition. They failed to qualify for the knockout stage of the Benson and Hedges Cup, while a bizarre selection decision by Botham cost the team a John Player League match against Glamorgan. Amid a minor injury crisis, he called up a friend, Roy Sully, who was thirty-four and had never played for the county. 'He [Sully] was on the physio's table before the game began,' Peter Roebuck recalled. 'He was a handy club cricketer, but a drinking partner. Botham was unlucky. Somerset lost by two wickets. Sully bowled no-balls and his two overs went for goodness knows what and when he batted with me for a while John Derrick was too quick for him. It was one of the few times where he [Botham] asked us what we thought [about Sully playing]. Vic Marks and Brian Rose were sceptical. I commented that the lunatics had taken over the asylum, which put my cards on the table. I never thought he was a bad tactical captain but he would take decisions out of the blue. The problem was where he was taking people. His leadership was going nowhere.'

Vic Marks said that for all the runs Botham was scoring, there was by now an air of 'decadence' at the club. Ray Wright, the club's treasurer, said: 'It wasn't a very happy team. They had been a great team but just fell apart towards the end ... The players became too powerful.' Viv Richards, who had been appointed West Indies captain, was reassessing his priorities. Joel Garner was thirty-two and fighting injury.

Botham left Vic Marks in charge of Somerset and joined England for the Texaco Trophy series with Australia. Despite one Test series win in five, England had good reason to think they would do well. Greg Chappell, Dennis Lillee and Rod Marsh had all retired and Australia were suffering the fallout of a recent announcement that a rebel team was to tour South Africa. Three players, including Terry Alderman, had been forced to pull out of the England tour because of their involvement, and another three had stayed after changing their minds about signing up. For the third time in a row there were serious tensions within an Australian team visiting England. England meanwhile had their own rebels available again and two of them, Graham Gooch and John Emburey, played the entire series.

Botham took his blunderbuss batting form into his first match for England for nine months, striking a rapid seventy-two from eighty-two balls in the opening one-dayer against Australia at Old Trafford. Amazingly, it was his first half-century on home soil in a one-day international. However, the way he was out overshadowed the way he had played because he was bowled attempting a reverse sweep, the shot that had cost him his wicket against Ray East two years earlier. After Botham was out, Mike Gatting ran out of partners and Australia won both game and – ultimately – series. To make his chastisement complete Botham was publicly criticised by Peter May for trying such an unorthodox shot on such an important stage.

Undeterred, he put great effort into his return to the Test side at Headingley, bowling more than sixty overs and hitting an aggressive sixty from fifty-one balls. If England were supposed to be better off without him it was hard to see how. England won by five wickets and although Australia levelled the series at Lord's even Peter May could not have held Botham primarily responsible. He took seven wickets in the game – overtaking Bob Willis as England's leading bowler in Tests in the process – and scored a fighting eighty-five in the second innings as England tried to set Australia a testing target.

Had England been able to set in excess of 200 they might have had a genuine chance but Gower's decision to use two night-watchmen made life unnecessarily difficult. Botham and Gatting found themselves batting together for the seventh wicket and although they put on 131 it was always likely that one of them would run out of partners (Gatting again, as it turned out).

Botham had hit half-centuries in each of the first two Tests but Australia were devising strategies for cutting off the boundaries on which Botham the Showman thrived. They would post men on the cover boundary and at third man from the moment Botham came in: he was caught at deep cover early on in the first innings at Lord's and was frustrated in the second by leg-spinner Bob Holland bowling into his pads. In the end, Botham had gone for a mighty heave and skied a catch to backward point. Returning to the dressing-room, he had, in typical Brian Close fashion, an excuse to hand: his bat had got caught up in his pad. 'Well, your pads must be on your bloody head then,' said John Emburey.

During the Lord's Test, David English introduced Botham to Eric Clapton, Botham lending Clapton a tie so that he could gain entry to the pavilion. Like Elton John, Clapton was a rock and roll superstar who on the face of it had little in common with Botham but, like Elton John, seemed as drawn to Botham's fame as Botham was to his. Clapton was hardly a die-hard cricket fan; his interest would owe something to charity work and a lot to his fondness for drink, but with English's help he started his own celebrity cricket team called the EC XI, which later evolved into the Bunburys. 'Eric would go through fads,' English recalled. 'He was involved with West Bromwich Albion at one point, and went through a horse racing phase. It was partly through fishing that he and Ian developed their friendship.' But drinking appeared to be the most common denominator. Clapton had overcome heroin use in the 1970s but was still fighting an addiction to alcohol and he would say that hanging out with Botham and English did little to curb his excesses. Clapton, who introduced Botham to Mick Jagger, thought that the attraction to Botham was rock and roll's anti-Establishment tradition: 'He's a buccaneer, a risk-taker . . . he's come through and beaten the system.'

Not that Botham was forever falling out with cricketing officialdom. On the field of play, he was rarely the rebel and generally respected the spirit and letter of the law. The drawn third Test at Trent Bridge did, however, provide a rare instance of him clashing with an umpire in an incident in which both he and umpire Alan Whitehead – whose officiousness had never endeared him to Botham – were at fault. After Whitehead had turned down an lbw appeal against Greg Ritchie, Botham's response had been to try to bounce out his opponent; when Ritchie was then caught in the deep off a delivery which Whitehead called a no-ball Botham – who rarely bowled no-balls – lost his temper. After the game Whitehead reported Botham, which resulted in him several weeks later being reprimanded by the TCCB for public dissent. David Gower thought Whitehead's handling of the affair heavy-handed. 'He got it wrong,' he said. Gower attended the board hearing and said there was a distinct air of the board cracking down on Botham 'for the sake of it'.

Botham did not help his case by reacting badly to criticism of his behaviour by Denis Compton in the *Sunday Express* and Fred Trueman in the *Sunday People*. Compton had never been a fan of Botham's – players from the 1950s tended to have a problem with the earnings of the post-Packer generation – and labelled his conduct 'quite disgraceful ... He must not regard himself as bigger than the game.' Trueman had claimed, rather ambitiously, that Botham had been bowling rubbish 'for fully ten years'. Predictably asked to respond in his next column for the *Sun*, Botham said: 'Fred Trueman managed to put down his pint and his pipe for a few minutes to hammer me for wasting the second new ball ... [and] I'd love to know exactly where he [Compton] was watching the action from for most of the day.' The *Sun* headlined the piece: 'Get Lost! You're Talking a Load of Twaddle.' It was another instance of Botham's newspaper column fanning the flames rather than putting them out.

Rejoining Somerset, Botham combined with Viv Richards in a 104-run partnership that decided a rainy NatWest Trophy tie with Yorkshire at Headingley, where some barracking of the West Indian spurred them both on and prompted Botham to afterwards publicly condemn 'racist idiots', comments that led to a long-running row with Yorkshire officials. Then, in two more extraordinary displays of hitting he struck successive championship centuries against Warwickshire and Essex – off fifty and sixty-eight balls respectively – but was again unable to help Somerset secure a championship victory; he had been on Test duty when they had achieved their only win (over Lancashire) in early June.

During the drawn Test at Old Trafford, where England were thwarted by a slow pitch, a staunch Allan Border rearguard and more rain, Botham gave a classic example of how he devised means of buying a wicket. Bowling at Wayne Phillips, he deliberately fed Phillips's love of the cut shot, bowling short outside off stump but with six men in catching positions. Phillips piled in to the tune of five boundaries before being caught in the gully.

Botham returned to Taunton for a NatWest Trophy quarterfinal tie against Hampshire – and Somerset's last chance of a prize. The atmosphere was febrile. When overnight rain delayed the start, Mark Nicholas, the Hampshire captain (whom Botham regarded, in Nicholas's words, as a 'public school toff'), insisted on having the pitch rolled again; Botham challenged the request, demanding clarification from Lord's. Much to Botham's annoyance, Nicholas was proved right. Play eventually began half an hour late. Hampshire scored an imposing 299–5 and Somerset collapsed to 43–5, with Richards among the departed. The game was all but lost when Botham suddenly marched off the field protesting that sunshine reflecting off an adjacent building made batting impossible. His actions did not go down well with a local crowd of 8,500 – who had not seen Somerset win a match of significance all season – and he had to ask Nicholas, despite their earlier argument, if he would go onto the balcony and placate some angry spectators in front of the pavilion. This Nicholas did. Botham struck a belligerent sixty-four from fifty-five balls the next morning, but Hampshire won easily.

Back in the championship, Botham plundered 134 against Northamptonshire at Weston-super-Mare, during which he passed Arthur Wellard's record of 66 sixes in a season.

It was during Weston week that the incident in Oxford at the start of the season resurfaced. Prompted by newspaper enquiries, Somerset proceeded to conduct its own inquiry. 'There was an investigation at Weston conducted by the committee,' Peter Roebuck said. 'In essence some of us were called in by three or four senior members of the committee and asked what we knew. We [the club] had been sent a printout of the proposed article. It caused great consternation. Some of us were completely unaware ... I hadn't been out with the older or younger players in Oxford and was totally unaware of anything untoward occurring.' In the end, the club decided against taking any public disciplinary action. Botham himself was not around for most of the Weston festival; he missed the last two days of the Northants match through illness and then left for the fifth Test at Edgbaston.

Edgbaston was the game in which England's superiority over Australia, evident for much of a series in which the score was still tied at 1–1, finally manifested itself in decisive fashion. Botham's part in the innings victory was small compared to the double-century from David Gower, centuries from Tim Robinson and Mike Gatting and ten wickets for Richard Ellison, but a seven-ball cameo with the bat provided perhaps the lasting impression of the match. To his first ball Botham stepped out and struck Craig McDermott, Australia's fastest bowler, back over his head for six. The next ball went for four and two balls after that he hit another six. It was a moment that encapsulated England's dominance, and Botham's role as playground bully.

Botham's self-confidence would have gained something from a round of golf he had played with some of the Australians at the Belfry on the rest day of the Test the previous afternoon. Partnering Allan Border against McDermott and Ritchie in light rain, Botham had driven the tenth green, a feat that only two professionals – Greg Norman and Seve Ballesteros – had at that time achieved. The 301-yard hole was protected by a lake just off the front apron. Border had urged caution, to which Botham had replied: 'Bollocks, AB, let's have a go.'

Before the decisive Test at the Oval, Botham turned out in what transpired to be an embarrassing final match as Somerset captain. With rain washing out the first day against Lancashire at Manchester, Somerset spent most of the second batting and Botham himself rampaged his way to an unbeaten seventy-six from forty-seven balls. But he and Jack Simmons, the veteran Lancashire spinner, had planned to watch Burnley play at home that evening and with time running short Botham had declared Somerset's innings closed at 329–4 with ten minutes remaining so they could get away early. Joe Neenan, Botham's old mucker at Scunthorpe, was now playing for Burnley. Lancashire's Graeme Fowler said Simmons had told Botham at just past 6.20pm, 'If you go on any longer we'll never get to Burnley.' He had promptly declared. The next day, following an innings forfeiture by each side, Lancashire had knocked off the 330 they needed with something to spare. 'Once it was clear they weren't going to bowl us out, "Both" seemed to lose interest,' Fowler recorded in his diary. 'He came off about three o'clock with some strain or other – the final Test starts on Thursday. When Somerset came off, "Rupert" Roebuck said: "Burnley 1, Somerset 0".'

England duly won the Ashes at the Oval, trouncing a demoralised Australian team, who took only three wickets on the first day, by an innings for a second time. Botham took three catches, including a stunner to dismiss McDermott, and six wickets to finish with thirty-one for the series. He had repeatedly given England early breakthroughs, dismissing the openers Graeme Wood and Andrew Hilditch nine times in the series, eight times for scores under twenty-five. It was an amazing effort – only in the 1981 Ashes did he ever take more wickets in a series – and one that said a lot about the quality of the Australian batting. It was something of a last hurrah for Botham as a champion bowler. He would never be as effective with the ball in Test matches again.

He did not in fact play again that season as an old knee injury flared up again in protest at all the work he had done in the Tests.

The 1985 Ashes restored Botham as a national hero, a status recognised by the National Portrait Gallery commissioning his portrait, only the second cricketer after W.G. Grace to be so honoured. The artist, John Bellany, explained his decision to portray Botham with a large body as an attempt to capture 'an essence of the chivalrous young knight of mediaeval times, the Arthurian paragon and champion'. With time, the summer acquired even greater lustre as England proved incapable of beating Australia again on home soil until 2005. As one heavy Ashes series defeat followed another, the images of Gower lifting a replica urn on the Oval balcony, and Botham pouring beer over his head, took on a golden hue in English eyes. Nor would Botham – not yet thirty years old – ever do much more at Test level in front of home audiences.

England's glorious summer was not shared by Somerset, who finished bottom of the championship for the first time since 1969. Of the twenty-eight matches Botham played for them, they won just six one-dayers.

As the dust settled on the club's very disappointing season, Botham appeared to try to distance himself from what had happened. Interviewed on West Country television, he said that Somerset needed to spend money if they were to be a force again, before adding: 'Who knows if I am going to be playing cricket in a year's time? I'm planning for the future. I've got business interests, a lot of things I've got to think about now.'

Four days later, Botham attended a Somerset committee meeting. Despite the unarguable turbulence of his two seasons as captain, he seemed oblivious to the possibility that the club might want a new leader. Asked about whether the captaincy might change hands, he responded: 'Who are they going to give it to?' He suggested that Vic Marks, his deputy, was not strong enough.

But by the end of the meeting, everything had changed. Botham released a short statement in which he said that he had asked not to be considered as captain because he could not give the job 'the time it requires and deserves'. He claimed that it was not so much the on-field demands of the job that had prompted his departure as the committee meetings he had to attend when he would rather be with his young family. But he issued a note of defiance: 'I'd dearly love to captain England again one day – even just for one game.'

The same question that had hung over his exit as England captain now hovered over his departure from the post at Somerset: had he resigned, or was he pushed? Senior figures had no doubt that the former followed a threat of the latter. Botham's captaincy, it was obvious, wasn't working, and there was too the matter of indiscipline. In *It Sort of Clicks*, the book he was writing with Botham and to which he was now putting the finishing touches, Roebuck wrote: 'He'd expected to survive as captain notwithstanding the club's poor position because he could see no other candidate ready to replace him ... To his surprise he had been relieved of the captaincy and been replaced by myself.' Another player said: '"Both" pulled the same stunt he had with England – he resigned before he was sacked.'

Roebuck's promotion to the captaincy was a surprise. Vic Marks had been Botham's deputy for two seasons and during that time Roebuck had only ever led Somerset when both Botham and Marks had been absent. But Marks, who admitted that he was 'stunned' at being passed over, said he had paid the price for his association with the team's decline. Roebuck, by contrast, represented a fresh start, a new broom.

Roebuck had been unimpressed with Botham's captaincy and believed others shared his view. He thought Botham exhausted and reckless, and not prepared to show how much he wanted his team to do well. At one point in the summer, Botham had asked Roebuck to his house in Taunton. 'Somerset were struggling and he was struggling, and he knew it wasn't working,' Roebuck said. 'I didn't think he should be captain, which is a hard thing to tell anyone. I didn't say it as directly as that.' Nigel Popplewell, who left at the end of this season to pursue a career in law, said that Botham did not always know how to lift his players – he could rant one minute and forget he had done so the next.

The challenge for Roebuck was whether he could captain the side with Botham in it. Brian Rose thought that Roebuck realised this could be a problem even before he had accepted the job and it might have even dissuaded him from taking on the role. 'They got on OK,' Rose said. 'But Peter might not have wanted it [the captaincy] with Botham in the side because it might have been difficult.' But Roebuck had agreed to the appointment and he now had to find ways to make things work. It should have been clear to all involved that rebuilding the side was going to take years. The good times were over.

Botham's reluctance to be captained by someone else was perhaps revealed in his decision to turn down the offer of a new two-year deal with the county and opt instead for a one-year extension.

Botham told the club to sort out the financial details directly with Tim Hudson, but the move backfired when Brian Langford, Somerset's chairman, Tony Brown, the secretary, and treasurer Ray Wright travelled to Birtles Hall. 'We got in touch with Tim Hudson and said, "You'd better come and see us,"' Wright recalled. 'He said: "No, you come and see me." So we went up there. There was a sign on the gate saying, "Please Use Tradesman's Entrance". We were shown into a big room with just a desk at the other end. Tim Hudson was sitting there and behind him was a poster on the wall showing Ian stripped to the waist looking like Sylvester Stallone. I just burst out laughing. The meeting lasted half an hour after which I said, "I'm sorry, money's tight, you're not having any more." And Hudson virtually begged us to pay ten per cent more to cover his commission. I got up, shook his hand and said, "Nice to see you. Goodbye." And we left. It was very embarrassing. Ian was paid exactly what we had offered him in the first place. I think we were talking £35,000 for an entire season.'

Botham may have been riding high in public estimation after the Ashes but his relationship with the club that had known him as man and boy had never been so precarious.

Botham's renewed popularity as an England cricketer helped make his fundraising walk from John O'Groat's to Land's End a great success. His original aim had been to raise £100,000 but at the last minute he revised his target to £500,000. In the end, in August 1986, he presented the Leukaemia Research Fund with a cheque for £880,000.

But this exhilarating achievement came at a price. Completing the walk in five weeks without a day off, even for the birth of his third child Becky (although Kath sprang a surprise by briefly joining him with their new baby), he suffered from a trapped nerve in his back, severe problems with his feet, and the loss of between one and two stone in weight – and said he was still feeling the effects of the walk when he toured the Caribbean with England two months later. What effect this had on his cricket is hard to say, but he had a very poor tour and came close to being dropped from the side.

Although numerous celebrities and team-mates occasionally joined him to walk and hand over cheques, Botham had three people for company for the entire journey – John Border, Allan Border's brother; Phil Rance, a Mancunian whose father had died of leukaemia; and Chris Lander, who was in the process of moving from the *Mirror* to replace Steve Whiting as the *Sun's* cricket correspondent.

The walkers eased their aches and pains by drinking a mixture of fizzy orange and tequila. 'I've seen him on walks when people have trodden on his foot by mistake or a cyclist has gone over his trainer, and it didn't go down very well,' David English said. 'He can be on a short fuse, although he tries not to be. Beefy had an enormous energy. The "Magic Fanta" as he called it was his anaesthetic. He'd start dancing and waving as he went through towns. Twenty-five miles a day was a hell of a lot.'

There were the occasional spots of bother. A young journalist joined the walk for a few days through the West Country before leaving and writing a story claiming that Botham's group had been smoking dope. Devon and Cornwall Police investigated but found no evidence to support the story. Later, as they left Bodmin, Botham became upset when a police escort rider insisted the walkers stayed together for their own safety; it was hardly a practicable suggestion in any case, but Botham found it important to get into a rhythm and did not want to be told at what speed to walk. Losing his temper, he hit the man on the side of his crash helmet. The incident created headlines but was resolved amicably.

The walk marked a watershed in Botham's life. He was touched by ordinary people handing over small amounts of money as he went, and had been reduced to tears by leukaemia sufferers from the Royal Manchester children's hospital at Pendlebury coming into the street to cheer him on. The walk achieved its first aim of raising a worthwhile sum but it also convinced Botham himself, who declared it one of the most satisfying things he had done, to undertake further fundraising walks – more than a dozen over the next twenty-five years.

The walks allowed Botham to give public expression to the very generous side to his nature, a side that had perhaps been hidden from general view since he became very famous. As his fundraising work developed, so his recent reputation for interspersing great highs with ignominious lows was leavened by a halo of charitable saintliness.

Shortly after the walk, Botham left for Palm Springs with Tim Hudson and Viv Richards. The trip would be remembered as Botham's attempt to crack Hollywood but on the eve of departure he described it to Frank Keating as primarily a holiday. Keating recalled: 'He said there was a thought about acting and that if something came up he'd be interested, but he had no illusions. The plan was to take a rest in Tim's beach-house, meet a few of his film friends, and see what happened.'

Hudson was convinced that Botham could make it in Hollywood. He told Botham this and Botham wanted to believe him. He told the newspapers this and they wanted to believe him too. The *Sun* had already run a story that Botham had been guaranteed $1m for a part in an Australian film called *The Perpetrator*, starring Oliver Reed, but this was nonsense. While it was true that the producer of the proposed film, Gary Rhodes, had spoken to Christopher Bazalgette requesting some publicity stills and some proof that Botham was taking acting lessons, there had been no firm offer. Indeed, Rhodes's interest had faded the moment Hudson demanded $40,000 as a down payment. 'How can you do business with a man like that?' Rhodes had asked. Even before they boarded the plane it must have been clear that anyone wanting to get into films – even someone already famous in another field – was going to have to show some sort of commitment if they were to be offered a contract. It was like Botham's flirtation with baseball; nothing was going to come of it unless he himself was serious about it.

Despite the opprobrium later heaped on him, Hudson did

manage to introduce Botham to an influential Hollywood mogul, the Israeli producer and director Menachem Golan. Nor did Golan dismiss Botham out of hand. He looked him up and down and said, 'Well, he's better looking than Tom Selleck.' But Golan too needed convincing that Botham could act and said that if Botham stayed for six months and had acting lessons there was a possibility that he could make it. It was a reasonable request but one Botham could not meet. Whatever he said in interviews back home, cricket was still his priority.

Botham's failed assault on Hollywood might have died a quieter death had it not been for the *Sun*, which had, with typical chutzpah, sent out a reporter and photographer to cover their star columnist's bid for celluloid fame. Without a screen test to write about, they took a tour of Universal Studios where Botham was able to pose – as any member of the public might – as a cowboy. It was a desperate piece of Fleet Street contrivance.

Hudson rejected Botham's later claims ridiculing the trip. 'I'm not sure it was as disappointing as he made out. He got to hang out with John McEnroe and Rod Stewart and said it was one of the happiest times of his life because he could put on a pair of shades, look at any girl in town and nobody knew who he was.' He even turned out in a local cricket match between English and Australian patrons of the Old King's Head in Santa Monica. He arrived at the ground in a black Cadillac limousine with smoked windows, a television in the back and a crate of wine in the boot. 'Botham accepted a late offer of breakfast,' remembered one player. 'Budweiser.' Sadly, he was out third ball to Carl McGinn from Sydney, an importer of car parts. 'I'm disappointed,' McGinn said. 'I was looking forward to watching him bat.'

The Caribbean tour was one of the most poorly run and unsuccessful missions ever undertaken by a modern England team, every bit as bad as that to New Zealand and Pakistan two winters earlier. West Indies remained formidably strong, which meant that a heavy defeat was always on the cards, but England's efforts were feeble nonetheless. Their batting in particular was spineless: in ten attempts they topped 200 only twice, while the timidity of their defence was evident from nearly half of all their wickets falling bowled or lbw.

A lack of leadership directly contributed to a second successive 5–0 'blackwash' and to the subsequent decision to attach a permanent assistant manager, or coach, to the team. The outdated notion of the captain and senior players managing themselves, under the benign eye of a quasi-ambassadorial tour manager, was finally laid to rest.

The make-up of the management team was flawed, particularly as a means of extracting the best from Botham. David Gower, the captain, was not strong enough to control him on the field or inclined to order him into the nets when they were off it; generally he seemed reluctant to contradict his all-rounder. Gower, who personally saw little merit in practice, had started the tour amid personal difficulties – his mother had recently died – but he chose to miss the first warm-up, as did Botham, and while the game was going on they not only went sailing but took a photographer with them. When the match was unexpectedly lost, photographs of the two of them enjoying beers on deck did not look good. Gower admitted he had been naïve. With Botham back in the ranks, the assured handling of the team Gower had displayed in India seemed less apparent. When England lost in four days in Barbados to go 3–0 down, his response was to make net practice optional and neither he nor Botham turned up.

The most surprising decision was to appoint Bob Willis as assistant manager. Willis had been retired from Test cricket for less than a year and was naturally still close to many players. With Botham making his first tour since the controversies of New Zealand and Pakistan, the press were out in force and Willis was in no mood to humour them. Reporters were excluded from official functions in a way they had not been in India. Nor was Tony Brown an ideal choice as manager. As Somerset secretary he had hardly kept the big-name players in check; as manager he tried to be firm but struggled to carry the players with him.

If Mike Brearley got the best of Botham, Gower appeared to get the worst and at times he struggled to hide his disappointment. He said that the team were guilty of overrating themselves and being physically underprepared, 'but this applied more to Ian than anyone else.' Some said they had never seen Botham train less on a tour. The lack of practice might have been a means of retaining a built-in excuse for failure: I could have done better had I tried. This was a defence mechanism Botham was to increasingly employ. 'I thought he was quite cynical in his later years,' Brearley said. 'He got less good and had to prove himself in other ways. Against West Indies he got a bit "knocky", as though he said to himself, "You might as well have a go because you're going to get out anyway." I don't think that was a good influence on the team.'

Botham's apparent lack of commitment aroused the ire of correspondents and resentment of team-mates. They felt he set a poor example with his theatrical complaints about pitches and thought his place in the team should not be guaranteed. His contribution to the first three Tests was minimal, not passing thirty in any innings and falling four times in succession to Malcolm Marshall, and being profligate with the ball. His opening spell in the second Test in Trinidad was perhaps the worst he ever bowled for England. 'Botham in this form has become an acute embarrassment to England,' Henry Blofeld wrote in the *Sunday Express*, while also asking whether Gower had any control at all over Botham's 'massive ego'.

By the eve of the fourth Test, also in Trinidad, some of the team had had enough and in the selection meeting with Tony Brown (who always took a back seat in these discussions), Bob Willis and Mike Gatting, Gower had to defend Botham from being dropped on merit for the first time in eight years. It was the most open revolt against Botham since the late days of his captaincy in 1981.

'He was determined just to run in and bowl as quickly as he could, as he had against Australia the previous summer,' Gower recalled. 'Between us we got that wrong because I gave him his head and it took me three Tests watching the ball whistle past me at cover, while five slips were going, "What the hell?" to do something about it. It was the one time I know of that anyone threatened to drop him . . . It was mooted that he was doing nothing for us. I said we were not going to do ourselves many favours by dropping him. After the meeting, I went and found him and said, "Look, we nearly dropped you." I sort of looked at him and went, "OK?" And that was that.'

Botham clearly took the message on board. He took more part in practice sessions and in the first innings of the Test itself batted nearly three hours for thirty-eight and took five wickets for seventy-one runs. But equally the criticism hurt; Viv Richards said that he never saw Botham looking as gaunt as he did during this game. The improvement did not last: in the final Test, and now needing only four wickets to overtake Dennis Lillee as the leading wicket-taker in Test cricket, he bowled more overs than anyone in the game but took only two wickets for 225.

A big problem was that he found the return to touring life almost impossible. The media attention on him personally was intense. Phil Edmonds's wife Frances, who had been commissioned to write a book on the tour, observed Botham's dilemma with pity. 'The press create the myth and the press undermine the myth,' she wrote. 'The harm they do to the subjects of their oscillating favour and furore is of little concern to them. Poor Botham! Publicity is such a double-edged sword. Initially it was gratuitously foisted upon him. Latterly it has been consciously sought. Presently it is destroying him.'

He was in emotional turmoil and took to his room, where he phoned Kath every day – not something he had always been in a position to do before – and dwelled on what the newspapers might next have in store for him.

Interestingly, he did permit access to one unknown journalist – Mike Weiss, an American, who was planning a feature on Botham for *Esquire* magazine. That Botham was willing to cooperate suggests that his 'Hollywood phase' had not yet run its course; he either still hoped the United States could deliver him riches, or at least give him a fairer hearing than he could get at home. Weiss was drawn to Botham precisely because of the scandals he had brought to cricket, which to American eyes seemed the last bastion of decency and fair play, but if he set out intending to dissect Botham's failings, that is not how his piece ended up. He did indeed give Botham a very fair hearing.

Weiss joined Botham at a crucial time, in the days leading up to and during the fourth Test in Trinidad. During this period, two significant stories broke. The first was that Tim Hudson, interviewed in Los Angeles, had been quoted as saying of Botham: 'I'm aware he smokes dope but doesn't everyone?' Given that Botham still had an ongoing legal case against the *Mail on Sunday* on precisely this issue, this was not a helpful intervention by his manager. Hudson was sacked two days later, much to the relief of those who felt that Hudson was the worst thing that had ever happened to Botham. Soon after, Hudson denied making the comment; subsequently he has claimed he did make the comment but was 'half-joking'.

The second story emerged in the *News of the World* the day after the Test had been lost in three days. Lindy Field, a former Miss Barbados, who had met Botham at a party at Mick Jagger's villa in Barbados during the previous Test, claimed to have had sex with Botham, and shared cocaine with him, at the team hotel. Although one element of her story stole the headlines – she claimed they had broken the bed while having sex – the allegation that Botham had taken cocaine was by far the more serious. But even Hudson had said in his interview that he did not think Botham took cocaine. And there were those, too, who thought Botham had been set up.

On the day of the Lindy Field story, for which she was reportedly paid £25,000, Weiss was with Botham in his room at the Trinidad Hilton. He would describe the scene in his piece:

*Botham's holed up in a room they've been calling the Bat Cave.
It's cluttered with the leavings of a man uncharacteristically in
hiding from the limelight: room-service dishes caked with food,
empty mugs and full ashtrays, a week's strewn clothing, cricket
bats, padded batting gloves, a hard-plastic helmet, and rum
punches sucked dry. He has just been awakened from a three-
hour nap, his first sleep in 30 hours, by a call from his solicitor.*

Weiss, who understood that the most serious allegation related to
cocaine use, which could if proven lead to Botham being banned,
recorded Botham's words to Alan Herd: 'I don't want to say any
more, Alan. Anyone could be listening. I mean, they're capable of
that; they could be tapping my phone . . . No, no, don't fly out . . .
You just do the writ. Have a nice warm glass of milk and do the
writ. We're going to go for their throats, man, that's what we're
going to do.'

It is interesting that while Botham fears being secretly recorded
by British reporters, he trusts Weiss enough to speak frankly in
front of him. After hanging up, Botham searched for an inhaler
and placed it over his nose and mouth. He told Weiss the air con-
ditioning was playing hell with his sinuses, before adding: 'I'm
quite certain they [the press] will say it's cocaine.' He lit a cigarillo.
'Let's face it, I was brought up in the late sixties and early seventies,
so I've seen what a joint looks like, but to accuse me of being a
drug user to get through sports is bullshit.'

As it happened, Kath was due to come to Antigua for the final
leg of the tour. Now, by way of a follow-up to the Lindy Field
story, the *Sun* demanded an interview with her – a wife standing
by her man, plus pictures of them reunited. There really was no
privacy left. Botham later admitted that he and Kath argued about
what had happened, and their relationship became strained to
near breaking point – again. But, staying on in Antigua for a short
holiday after the tour had ended, they tried to patch things up.

The harmony was short-lived. Four days after the Test series had
ended, the *News of the World* ran the most bizarre Botham story

yet. Vivien Kinsella, a confessed drug addict with a hazy memory of places and dates, and the wife of *Sun* journalist Steve Whiting, claimed that she and Botham had shared drugs during the New Zealand tour. Alan Herd originally succeeded in persuading the Attorney General to prevent the newspaper publishing the story on the grounds it might prejudice his client's case against the *Mail on Sunday*, but the decision was overturned on appeal. The torment, it seemed, would never end.

The next four months were among the most emotionally turbulent of Botham's life. Things had come to a head on and off the pitch but, by design or accident, he took some decisions that dealt with the problems well and meant he was able to move forward. He was in need of a fresh start and he made one. Life was never quite so complicated again.

He ended the nightmare of his legal battles with Fleet Street, and cut free of his involvement with Somerset. The separation was messy and got tangled in the club's decision to release Viv Richards and Joel Garner, but there was every chance he would have left anyway. Phil Neale, Worcestershire's captain, said that he knew Botham was unhappy at Somerset even before the Richards–Garner sackings were made known. Botham's failed captaincy was the last straw, not the dismissals of his two friends.

The first step was the hardest. Within a month of the end of the Caribbean tour, Botham agreed to settle his case with the *Mail on Sunday*. He paid the newspaper's costs, estimated at £100,000, and put his name to a front-page story in which he finally admitted that he had after all smoked dope.

Referring to his comments at Heathrow airport two years earlier, he said:

> *I did something that I have regretted ever since ... I denied that I had ever smoked pot at any time in my life and started legal proceedings against the* Mail on Sunday *for what it had said about the New Zealand tour ... The fact is that I have, at*

*various times in the past, smoked pot. I had been with a group of people who had been doing it and I went along with it. On other occasions I have smoked simply in order to relax – to get off the sometimes fearful treadmill of being an international celebrity, trying to forget for a moment the pressures which were on me all the time. I was only a casual user and not an addict . . . I was always in control of myself.'*

He also indicated that he would not be pursuing legal action against the *News of the World*. 'Some of the things I have read about myself have not only been ludicrous but vindictive and vicious as well . . . I have, however, decided that I am not going to bother suing everybody in sight. Life is too short. I need to get on with my life.' Asked in the High Court in 1996 about his decision to drop these two libel actions, Botham said he could not afford to take on a national newspaper with a bottomless supply of money: 'I was not prepared to risk everything I had worked for in my life . . . I am a man of limited means.'

The day after the article appeared the TCCB's executive committee – which included Colin Atkinson, Somerset's president – summoned Botham to appear before a disciplinary hearing. It also suspended him from England's one-day squad to play India. Some sort of punishment was inevitable: he had confessed to using illegal drugs and had lied about doing so. But in his article he indicated only that he had used dope while in his early twenties and that it was a habit that was firmly in the past. This laid claim to some important points: that he had used drugs during a period when he had been playing well for England; and that he had not used them since the TCCB had introduced its anti-drugs regulations in March 1985 (in a direct response to Botham's conviction for possessing cannabis) with its attached threat of harsh penalties for anyone found guilty of drug offences.

After a seven-hour hearing, the TCCB discipline committee banned Botham from all cricket for two months, meaning that for England alone he would miss another two one-day internationals and four Tests. Botham appealed through his legal representative Robert Alexander QC but without success.

The ruling was controversial. The board had effectively passed judgement on 'offences' that were several years old and belonged to a time when its guidelines on drugs were almost nonexistent. In the end, the board's catch-all reason was that Botham had brought the game into disrepute. Specifically, he was being punished for having used cannabis; having denied using cannabis; and having written an article without permission. What the board failed to do was establish whether Botham had used drugs in a way and at a time detrimental to his performance on the field. It appeared to make no effort to substantiate whether other newspaper allegations relating to harder drugs were true, or whether, given what Botham had now admitted, its own investigation into the allegations surrounding the 1984 New Zealand tour (which had exonerated the whole team) had been thorough enough.

There were those, though, who believed that, bearing in mind the unpublished parts of the *Mail on Sunday*'s dossier on Botham, that his punishment could have been a lot worse. David Gower said: 'The *Mail on Sunday* dossier was big ... it wasn't just a couple of wafer-thin allegations, it was obviously quite a meaty piece of kit. It was "a fair cop".' Mike Weiss quoted a good friend of Botham's as saying of the newspaper's investigation: 'They had too much on him ... They had the goods.' In an accompanying piece to Botham's 'confession', the *Mail on Sunday* editor had said that it would have been disastrous for English cricket if the case had gone to court. Botham appeared to agree, saying that had he gone to court, 'a lot of other allegations could be made and that others, apart from myself, would be subject to painful scrutiny'.

David Graveney, who sat on the disciplinary panel as a representative of the Professional Cricketers' Association, recalled: '"Both" probably felt the punishment was draconian but I can assure him that it could have been a lot worse. There were definitely people who wanted a longer ban. That was the time when

"Both" had the striped blazers, and bizarre hairstyle, and he lived life to the full and I'm sure he aggrieved certain members of the TCCB. The guy acting for the TCCB was very sensible. He said that if the board went too far, there would be an appeal and common justice would prevail.'

There was a good deal of public sympathy for Botham, who was cheered when he next went out to bat at Hove. A *Daily Mirror* opinion poll was supportive, as predictably was Chris Lander in the *Sun*. So too was Matthew Engel of the *Guardian*. 'I took his side on the drugs ban,' Engel said. 'It was an outrageous piece of revenge. He wasn't punished for drugs but for being Ian Botham, for being a nuisance and for being too big for his boots.'

Botham had reason to be grateful to Somerset's management committee. Ray Wright, the treasurer, had proposed that Botham should not be paid during his ban but his suggestion was voted down 6–1. 'I had to go on television the following day and say of course we were going to pay him,' Wright said. 'It seemed to me to be all wrong.' The money helped Botham pay for lessons to fly a helicopter.

While England slid to defeat in the first Test of the summer against India – a result that led to Gower being stripped of the captaincy – Botham fished at his old haunt of Loch Lubnaig with a group of mates that included Joe Neenan and Mike Weiss. It was clear from Weiss's article in *Esquire*, published in January 1987, that Botham was devastated at his ban and struggling to keep up his spirits (Botham himself later conceded that he came close to giving up cricket in response to the ban).

One night, during an evening of Guinness, steaks and whisky, Botham's bitterness spilled out. 'Some people at Lord's use this phrase, "You're becoming bigger than the game",' he told Weiss.

*I don't know what it means. I honestly don't. Whatever I do, I try to do it to its fullest . . . I'm a very determined person. And when I go out on the field . . . it's you against them, it's similar to guys being in their Spitfires in the Battle of Britain. I think what*

*scares them is envy. I can captivate an audience. Okay, I like to
wear my hair long. They might not like my coloured shoes, but
who the hell should tell me what to wear? The questions I live
with they're totally unaware of. I'm there to do a job. And I hear
this thing about, "Botham is bigger than the game." This is a
weak, nasty, backstabbing way to get at someone.'*

They ended the evening watching a film of *Breaker Morant*, a story
of three Australian soldiers questionably tried for murder during
the Boer War and, in the case of two of them, executed by firing
squad. Weiss drew a parallel between the fate of Harry 'Breaker'
Morant and Botham as Establishment scapegoats.

While Botham might have had a point about the pettiness of
cricketing officialdom, it was after all he who had taken drugs.
That he might have done something wrong rarely featured in his
thinking. Indeed, before his ban was over he was caught publicly
criticising the powers that be, referring to Peter May and his fellow
selectors as 'gin-swilling dodderers' at a dinner in Manchester. He
was obliged to write letters of apology. He also cocked a snook at
authority by travelling to Ireland – which was beyond the juris-
diction of the TCCB – to play in a match between Lisburn and an
Invitation XI, and scored 101 in 35 minutes. 'I remember he came
back [from Ireland] with a bottle of hooch,' Ian Todd, a *Sun* journalist, said. 'I told him that the last thing he wanted was to get
caught with that. He brushed it off. He thought he was above
normal rules.'

While Botham was away, events were taking a decisive if
unsurprising turn against him at Somerset. There was a general
understanding among senior figures at the club – Roebuck, the
captain, Brian Rose, newly appointed as cricket manager, and the
committee – that Viv Richards and Joel Garner were coming to
the end of their time there. Garner's fitness was not getting any
better and he had already said he did not want to play championship cricket in future, while Richards was unsuited to playing in
what had now become a mediocre team.' He always thought he

could beat anyone and now he could see that he couldn't,' Roebuck said. 'He lost respect for people he was playing with and he was right. The club was a mess. People wouldn't join us. We had a bad reputation. His own mood was variable and dictatorial. At times he was screaming and shouting. There didn't seem any future in it. It was an impossible position for him.'

Brian Rose wanted to sign a new fast bowler but acquiesced to Roebuck's wish, and that of the committee, to go back to Martin Crowe, who had been such an inspiration in 1984 (a change to the rules meant that from 1987 counties could field only one new overseas player). 'The club's recommendation was that Peter Roebuck became captain and Martin Crowe was the overseas player,' Rose said. 'It was not right to point the finger at Peter as the instigator [of Richards and Garner leaving]. The Somerset committee must have been behind the decision to appoint Martin as overseas player.'

Given all that had happened since 1982, the plan to release Richards and Garner was not unreasonable but the club kept it such a well-guarded secret that publicly there was no clue as to what was afoot. This was to cause grave problems.

Roebuck was also keen on bringing in a new wicketkeeper to replace Trevor Gard, partly because he wasn't a batsman and partly because he was one of Botham's few remaining allies. 'Gard was Botham's close friend and looked after him in many ways,' Roebuck said. 'I recognised we needed a wicketkeeper who could bat but I also knew that this would increasingly isolate Ian, which was one of the things I wanted to do. I felt that the more Ian was isolated the more he would be able to focus on his cricket – or go. It had to be one of the two. With his group around him, we would never get him back on track.'

Roebuck also spoke to some players about drugs. 'Drugs were an issue,' he said. 'I sat down with those concerned and said that whatever may have happened before I was captain, nothing was going to happen subsequently. I would protect them from anything before but anything that happened thereafter was going to be a problem. The whole culture of the county had become head-strong, loose and dark, and it showed in the conflicts we had. The side had been there too long and got too old. People were leading very different lives in '86 than they were in '84.'

Roebuck was trying to turn the team around but his methods were somewhat heavy-handed. Rose said he approached the task too much as an intellectual exercise and Roebuck himself admitted that he could not talk to the players as easily as Rose. It did not make a difficult task any easier.

Botham's commitment to the cause was in any case now qualified. He had shown that the previous autumn with his decision to accept only a one-year contract. Although he would say later that he had never intended to leave, that was not the recollection of Phil Neale of Worcestershire. His two-month ban served, Botham returned to first-team cricket against Worcestershire at Weston-super-Mare, where he played in predictably eye-catching fashion, battering a century from sixty-five balls. 'We picked up that he wasn't happy,' Neale said. 'After he'd duly scored a hundred, we chatted and that became clear. He'd said he wasn't happy before, but this was the first time we realised he was serious about leaving. I went back to Worcester and took it straight to Duncan Fearnley and Mike Jones [the Worcestershire chairman] and said, "This guy's serious. We ought to get him." They said, "Are you sure you want to take him? You've got to handle him, you know." I said it wouldn't be a problem. I knew him from football. He'd played at Scunthorpe United, where I'd started, and we'd played against each other, although nowhere near the same part of the field. We weren't bosom buddies but we were friends.' A week later, Botham smashed a Sunday league record of thirteen sixes in an innings of 175 against Northants at Wellingborough School, where about 9,000 packed the grassy banks to see him play.

Somerset's plan to replace Richards and Garner with Crowe was forced into public by Botham's return to the England side for the final Test of the season. Essex had also become interested in signing Crowe but could not do so because Somerset had retained his registration. The club realised that Graham Gooch, who played for Essex, might disclose this to Botham during the game.

Richards and Garner had been great servants of the club and deserved to be forewarned of their fate. With more consideration, Somerset might even have been able to negotiate their departure by mutual consent. As it was though, they were stunned to be called in to the County Ground on Friday, 22 August, the second day of the Oval Test, and told their services were no longer required. Their treatment was insensitive and bound to cause an outcry, not least from Botham. Garner, who in fact quickly accepted the situation, phoned Botham and told him what had happened: 'I can't use the language he used. He was angry. He said: "That so-and-so . . ." And I said: "Don't worry about it, man. There's life after cricket."' Richards also discouraged Botham from getting involved. Botham may have been upset at the way Richards and Garner had been treated but he was surely also angry at the further break-up of the team with which he had enjoyed so much one-day success. He really was one of the last men standing.

Botham returned to Taunton the day after the Test finished for a championship match against Essex. The club may have acted clumsily but it was partly through the intervention Botham now made that the hostility became so firmly focused on Roebuck. On the first night of the game Botham called a meeting of the players – to which Roebuck was not invited – and told them that he was ready to leave Somerset. He referred to Roebuck as Judas – and later hung a placard on Roebuck's peg in the dressing-room with the word 'Judas' written on it – and called for a vote of no confidence in him, but this was defeated. Even Trevor Gard thought his friend should have stayed out of things. 'He was not as popular at Taunton as he thought,' he said. 'Many think he's too big for his boots but they are the people who don't really know him.'

With Richards and Botham to the fore, Somerset took the upper hand against Essex and looked to have the game in the bag when they got to within twenty of their target with five wickets left. But Essex pulled their old trick of playing on Botham's ego by setting the field deep and daring him to trying finishing the job in style. He duly drilled a ball from John Childs straight to long on. Panic set in and Somerset ended up losing by nine runs.

After the game, Botham marched into the Essex dressing-room and announced: 'Right then, me and Viv, a package deal to Essex, what you reckon?' Doug Insole's face was a picture. Essex's chairman had just been party to the TCCB's creation of a new post of England assistant manager responsible for discipline, training and practice – a direct response to the chaos of recent tours of which Botham had been a part.

Botham left, the door closed.

'What you reckon?' said someone, half-intrigued.

Another: '. . . Get lost.'

With neither Richards nor Garner featuring again, Somerset did not win another championship match. Botham helped save a match at Leicester and struck a furious 139 from 79 balls at Old Trafford, but for the second year in a row Jack Simmons had the last laugh by bowling Lancashire to victory as Somerset made a mess of chasing 209. Botham's final innings was a typical, if rather inappropriate, twelve-ball blitz for thirty-six in defeat to Derbyshire, a result that ensured Somerset finished last but one in the table.

In the autumn – with Botham already away on tour – a special meeting was held in Shepton Mallet at which the Somerset committee survived (by a majority of more than two to one) a vote of no confidence. Had the committee lost the vote, Richards and Garner, and possibly Botham, might have stayed on at the club. Crucial to the outcome was Nigel Popplewell speaking eloquently in support of the need for a fresh start. He too felt Botham should have kept out of things. 'I wish he would be a little more discerning at times,' he said.

Botham's return to the England side swept aside a lot of questions that might have otherwise been asked about how much he still had to offer the game. No doubt over a gin and tonic, Peter

May and his fellow selectors studiously declined to pick him at the first available opportunity after his ban ended, but great bowling from Richard Hadlee won New Zealand the second Test and England went to the Oval needing a win to draw the series. They would need their very best team. After Mickey Stewart, who had been appointed to the new role of England assistant manager for the forthcoming Ashes tour, had established that Botham was still willing to tour, Botham was recalled.

Although he was carrying a few extra pounds after his enforced lay-off, Botham's mere presence changed the mood; a dressing-room that had not tasted a Test win for a year was once again abuzz.

The game in fact was ruined by rain but Botham fluked a wicket with a widish first ball that Bruce Edgar chased and nicked to slip; he then removed Jeff Crowe with his twelfth delivery to claim a world record 356th Test wicket. Later, he smashed a fifty from 32 balls against the second new ball, taking 17 off two overs from Hadlee and 24 off one from Derek Stirling, playing only his sixth Test. Botham hit him for three fours and two sixes.

It was a typically rumbustious return from Botham, and the hallmark of a true champion. He had done this sort of thing numerous times before – on his return after losing the England captaincy, and when his place in the team had been questioned. When Gooch caught Edgar off Botham's first ball, he had asked him: 'Blimey, Beefy . . . who writes your scripts?'

Botham knew the answer to that one all right: it was him. And, once again, in his unquenchable optimism, he told himself that whatever the doubters said, he was not finished. In his mind, he never was.

# 11

## Long Journey into Night

'He [Botham] was a product of the way the game was then – a highly talented person, a very competitive person, but if he dropped a catch it would be because he didn't see it in the dark, or somebody had moved. That's how those people are.'

MICKEY STEWART, ENGLAND MANAGER 1986–92

The appointment of Mickey Stewart marked the beginning of the end of Botham's career as an international cricketer. Stewart had been brought in to professionalise what was essentially still a semi-professional system, in which the attitude to practice of its most prominent player said it all.

Botham saw his primary function as playing matches; he felt that what he did outside the hours of play was largely his business. Practice had stopped featuring large in his thinking. If he batted in the nets, he just smashed the ball to assuage boredom and if he bowled . . . well, he tried wherever possible not to bowl, preferring to save his energy. In retirement he justified this carefree approach by saying that this was always the way he had prepared – the soak in the bath with the *Sporting Life*, the pork pie and cigar for breakfast – but in truth he had often practised hard in his early years, his best years. But that was then and this was now, and as his fitness deteriorated and the injuries became more frequent, so it became ever harder to meet the higher standards being demanded by the England management.

Botham was not entirely alone in his laid-back approach. While this attitude might once have been sufficient, it was clearly not by the mid-1980s when England lost seven Test series out of eleven and were beaten by all of their five major opponents. Stewart's arrival signalled the death of the dilettante approach and Botham, at thirty-one, was always going to struggle to adapt to the new ways.

Botham knew which way the wind was blowing and before leaving for Australia he announced that it would be his last tour. On the one hand, this was an understandable decision given the torment created by his two previous winters away; on the other, it was a surprise as players who quit touring risked cutting themselves off from international cricket altogether. Botham might have remembered what had happened to Mike Brearley: once he said he did not want to tour again, his offer to carry on captaining England at home in a transitional role was rejected and he was not chosen again. And Graham Gooch, who opted to miss this Ashes tour, was to find himself unwanted by England for any of the 1987 Tests.

When Botham made an unexpected retreat such as this it was usually because he feared rejection was imminent.

Botham had a plan though that guaranteed him cricket for the next three winters. As a replacement for Tim Hudson he had recruited Tom Byron, an Australian, as his new agent. Byron, who had a penchant for sharp dressing, talked as Hudson had about turning Botham into a millionaire and had appeared to have secured Botham some valuable deals. Here at the outset Byron brokered what promised to be a highly lucrative deal for his client to play state cricket for Queensland. The arrangement seemed ideal: Botham was good friends with Allan Border, the captain, and Queensland were on a mission to win the Sheffield Shield for the first time in sixty years. Reports suggested that he would be paid £200,000 over three years, which was better money than he would have got from three winters on tour, if not perhaps for playing for England all the year round. But there was no certainty that he would continue to play for England all year round. As Botham was aware, it was only a few months earlier that his place in the Test side had been argued over in selection.

Stewart, who had captained Surrey for ten seasons and managed them for eight, barely hid his contempt for English cricket's flawed culture. 'The old environment of the amateurs and pros, when the pros called the amateurs Mister So-and-So, was not the greatest one in which to believe that you're the best,' Stewart said.

Botham, of course, had no more time for the old amateur–professional system than Stewart but what Stewart saw in Botham now was a gifted cricketer who was no longer giving himself the best chance to succeed. In Stewart's eyes, Botham did not keep himself fit enough or practise enough, and was liable to make excuses if things then went wrong. 'I'd always believed that being as fit as you could was going to make you a better cricketer,' he said. 'He [Botham] was a product of the way the game was then – a highly talented person, a very competitive person, but if he dropped a catch it would be because he didn't see it in the dark, or somebody had moved. That's how those people are.'

Even so, Stewart and Mike Gatting, the new captain, believed Botham could play a valuable part on the Australia tour. They told him he would have to take a full part in practice and that he, along with the other senior players, would have to lead the way if the Ashes were to be retained. 'I told them [the seniors] that they were top players but as a team they were rubbish and it showed,' Stewart said. 'If we'd asked "Both" to run around the field ten times he'd never have done it. He was well overweight and had a bad back. But he liked five-a-side football and would not stop until his side had won. So we played five-a-side football. I also challenged him to keepy-uppy. He ended up being one of the last to leave training. Obviously we had our moments [disagreements] but you can't suddenly change the way people go about things.'

Stewart added that Laurie Brown, the team's physiotherapist, believed there was a connection between the quantity of alcohol players consumed and the frequency with which they got injured. 'Laurie said to me, "The amount they consume, you see the amount they get injured." He was right. Allan Lamb was hardly ever injured until the age of thirty and I believe "Both" could have gone on longer but for the injuries he sustained. I used to say to them [the team], "You should have been playing in the 1920s and 1930s, you lot." English [professional] cricket then was an extension of the school and club game.'

It was to take time but Stewart began changing the culture of the England team, first in partnership with Gatting, then Gooch. He demanded that players train for two days ahead of a home Test match rather than one, something that became even more essential as the tradition of a rest day was phased out, and also played a part in the switch from three-day to four-day championship matches. This also demanded higher levels of fitness and was seen as one of the main ways by which English cricket might improve.

The promotion of Gatting to the captaincy after Gower's removal was an intriguing one given his relationship with Botham, who continued to strike an imposing figure in Gatting's mind. 'He was in awe of his fame, his ability to perform even though he'd been out late drinking, and his unbelievable self-belief, which enabled him to win matches in a way that Gatting never seemed able to do,' said Simon Hughes, who played county cricket with both men. 'Beefy often trod all over him. You were definitely better off with Beefy if you fought back a bit. If there is a sign of a contest, a verbal one or whatever, there ends up being a bit of mutual respect. If he can just crush you with his little finger, there's not much of a relationship really.'

Shortly before his appointment as England captain, Gatting had again witnessed Botham's amazing ability to turn a game. With Somerset needing twelve off the last three balls from West Indian fast bowler Wayne Daniel, Middlesex had looked to have a John Player League victory in the bag, but somehow Botham twice swung Daniel over midwicket for sixes. It was an astonishing effort against such a bowler in such a situation. 'After that, Gatting thought Botham basically could walk on water,' Hughes added.

But against the odds, Gatting saw to it in Australia (with Stewart's help) that Botham was servant and not master, at least in terms of strategy if not off-field discipline, the first England captain to pull this off since Brearley. He was given very clear instructions as to his role, and he largely did as he was told.

For all the planning, England's build-up was shaky. Although Botham had a good game in front of his future employers, the first proper fixture was lost to Queensland and the team was ridiculed by Martin Johnson in the *Independent* as one that couldn't bat, bowl or field. With Stewart's blunt assessment that they were 'rubbish' no doubt also fresh in their minds, Gatting's team went into the first Test in Brisbane feeling they had plenty to prove, and for once they delivered.

Botham, who had not played in a winning Test overseas for four years, was particularly hungry for success and he played one of his most important innings – his fourteenth and, as it transpired, last Test century.

It was a properly constructed innings, as he played himself in before cutting loose against indifferent bowling, rather as he had at Old Trafford in 1981. For the Australians, rebuilding with a young team, Botham cast an intimidating shadow. Once he had carved twenty-two off an over from Merv Hughes, a burly Victorian fast bowler playing his second Test, Allan Border set respectful fields and Botham moved serenely to his hundred. Sitting disconsolately outside the dressing-room after play, Hughes reminded Botham of the advice he had given him ten years earlier about golf or tennis being a better career than cricket. 'You should have listened to me,' Botham said, and walked off.

Even without Gooch, England's batsmen scored heavily enough in the next three Tests that the team was in little danger of losing and when a second victory came in the fourth Test at Melbourne the Ashes were duly won. Botham put himself out of the third Test by tearing an intercostal muscle on the final day in Perth but returned surprisingly quickly to play a major part in the win in Melbourne. Still feeling sore, he ran in off an innocuous ten paces and, through a mixture of luck, the Botham 'aura' and incompetent Australian batsmanship, his gentle swingers proved deadly. This, in turn, turned out to be his last five-for in Tests.

After the teams had broken off for a one-day tournament in Perth, which England won, they returned to the east coast for what proved an anticlimactic final Test in Sydney. At one point England, chasing 320, had victory in sight but Gatting's dismissal for 96 triggered a collapse and they narrowly failed to hold out for a draw, six balls remaining when the last wicket fell. Australia's match-winner was Peter Taylor, a little-known off-spinner from North Sydney whose eight victims included Botham in each innings, the second time for a first-ball duck.

At this point of the tour, England could have succumbed to fatigue, but they rallied to win three of their first four matches in a one-day triangular tournament with Australia and West Indies. Qualifying for the best-of-three finals, they then beat Australia at the first two attempts. Until the finals, Botham had had a quiet time but he then sprang into life, winning one match with the bat and another with the ball.

Botham was widely praised for his overall contribution to a highly successful tour but he still found it a tough trip to get through, even though Kath and their three young children were with him for some of the time. The old rule of wives or partners joining a tour for a maximum of three weeks was discreetly waived. Tom Byron ensured that he was provided with a regular supply of cars and drivers, and Botham spent a lot of time with Elton John, who was on hand in Melbourne to share in the celebrations when the Ashes were won.

Gower described how Botham's enthusiasm waned as the tour went on. 'He started full of willing,' Gower said. 'He said, "I'll be fine. Give me one of the young lads to room with. Give me Daffy [Phil DeFreitas, who was making his first tour at the age of twenty].'" At that stage he was as open and sociable as ever. But because he always had opportunities to make personal speaking appearances somewhere or other, he was open to people [journalists] saying, "Well, what's he doing now?" And as the tour progressed, and the prying and needling went on, he got fed up and basically hid away. Forget sharing rooms with young players. He was now phoning ahead to the next hotel and booking a suite, paying the difference, and basically inviting people in. Chris Lander effectively became the doorman to the Bat Cave. You would get a call. "What are you doing tonight? Come and join me in the Bat Cave." For a man who liked being sociable, it was a terrible time.'

Gower said that in a private environment Botham could still let rip, as happened during a warm-up against Western Australia. On the second day, which *Wisden* said was abandoned prematurely because of rain, a group of England players including Gatting, Botham, Lamb and Gower were invited to Fremantle to visit Britain's *White Crusader* yachting crew taking part in the challenger series ahead of the America's Cup. Botham, who arranged for the group to travel in a white limousine, admitted that the evening left him with one of his biggest hangovers. With fellow revellers such as Gower and Lamb getting out without scoring the next day, Botham was obliged to go out and bat with the score at 69–6. 'He normally recovers well but there was just no chance after that sort of night,' Gower recalled. 'He spent much of the morning with his head in a basin full of ice. Then he managed to walk out without his bat. He still got most of the way out there before noticing.' Rather than failing ignominiously though, he bludgeoned a quick forty-eight and finished as the team's top scorer. It was a rare day of embarrassment on this tour.

Early in the New Year and now out of contract with Somerset, Botham formalised his move to Worcestershire. No other county bid for him, although Warwickshire came close. Botham was good friends with David Brown, Warwickshire's cricket manager, with whom he part-owned a horse, and Norman Gifford, the club's captain, but their proposal that Botham be paid £40,000 and given the captaincy was rejected by the committee, who feared unrest from sponsors following his drugs ban and players unhappy at his large salary.

In the end, Botham had to be content with Worcestershire paying him no more than he had finished on at Somerset. In some ways, Worcestershire was a surprising place for him to go; Imran Khan had left the county ten years earlier because he could not bear to live in a city 'so dreary and unappealing' as Worcester, although the club's decision to find their Muslim star a flat above a butcher's shop was hardly the most diplomatic start. Botham, in fact, took a cottage in the countryside near Ombersley, close to where Kath's sister and husband lived. As much as anything, Botham was happy to be among friends. He got on well with Duncan Fearnley, the chairman, Mike Jones, chairman of the cricket committee, and Graham Dilley, who with Botham's persuasion joined the county at the same time.

Once back in England, the Bothams moved house again. Botham may have left behind Tim Hudson and his grandiose schemes, but Hudson's Georgian pile in Cheshire appeared to have made an impression because it was a large Georgian house the Bothams now bought, albeit a dilapidated one in need of repair, near the village of Ravensworth in North Yorkshire. It came with outbuildings and several acres, including a lake and woodland. Renovating it became a long-term project and they have lived there ever since. Botham described it as 'the best money that Kath and I ever spent'.

There was inevitably speculation that Botham had ambitions to captain Worcestershire. Phil Neale said: 'He was very quick to come to me and say, "Look, I've not said anything about that [captaincy] to the press. It's not something I want. I'm happy to just play and you carry on." He was very up front about it. His motivation was to enjoy his cricket and maybe make a statement that he had a lot left in him.'

Worcestershire were a developing side who saw the experience of Botham and Dilley as providing the final ingredient to their mix. Botham's role was not dissimilar to the one he had performed in Australia, playing as an attacking number six and support seamer operating off a short run (his recent rib injury left him unsure if he dared try anything more strenuous). He joked about being 'Mr Economy' but he brought an unquantifiable sprinkling of stardust that helped the team play above themselves. 'Just his presence brought the media and the crowds to Worcester and the rest of the lads thrived on that atmosphere,' Neale recalled. 'Some people questioned whether local lads like Martin Weston and Stuart Lampitt might lose out if Botham and Dilley came but they actually played their best cricket during the time Ian was at the club.'

Neale was not as firm with him as Gatting and Stewart with regard to practice. 'Ian would come to nets but wouldn't have a net,' Neale admitted. 'He might have a rub-down or something like that. But at least he was around and showed willing. Having "Both" around was a different experience for us. We went through a period where the lunch-time food at Worcester wasn't great, so Beefy got his agent to do a deal with McDonald's, and half an hour before lunch Andy Withers would disappear into town and come back with milkshakes and chicken nuggets.' Botham had long been a great 'fixer', always knowing someone among his vast array of contacts who could provide what was needed.

He was an inspirational figure from the start. During his first championship appearance, he hosted a barbecue for his new team-mates and the next day assured them that the match could still be won after Worcestershire slipped to 89–5 in reply to Kent's 378. He began the fightback by hitting Derek Underwood for six. Sure enough, on the last afternoon Worcestershire chased down 322 against the clock. Steve Rhodes, the county's young wicketkeeper who scored a vital seventy-eight, said that Botham taught the team a lot. 'He was always positive. He instilled in a lot of the younger cricketers like myself a knowledge of how to go about winning. He got the best out of Graham Dilley too. That's what I remember about him: he was a winner. He gave us confidence.'

The change of counties may have provided him with a much-needed fresh start but Botham's mood could still sometimes turn dark when he drank, as he seemed to need to. Maybe this reflected an anxiety about whether he could keep performing for England, and about how long he had left in the game. Whatever the cause, it was a worrying development for those who saw him at close quarters on these occasions.

One incident took place early in the 1987 season after a golf day at St Pierre, Chepstow, when he got into a drinking competition with Ian Woosnam and Max Boyce. He abused a waitress and head-butted a waiter who had to be dissuaded by Tom Byron from pursuing legal action. The story appeared in the *Sun* – still the paper for which Botham worked – and Byron reckoned several endorsements were lost in the fallout. Graham Morris was with Botham that evening, although not in the room when the assault took place. 'Beefy should have been dead, he really should, he drank that much,' Morris recalled. 'It was frightening. The first thing I saw early next morning was Beefy standing over my bed telling me to get up. I couldn't believe he was still alive, let alone up at that time. It became clear that he knew nothing about what had happened. Then the phone calls came in.'

Another embarrassment came on the rest day of the Edgbaston Test when Botham returned to New Road to watch Worcestershire play Somerset. He drank steadily even though he was not out overnight in the Test. He did not add many to his score the next morning.

There was even a drinking dimension to his contribution to Worcestershire winning the Sunday league. If the consistency of his opening partnership with Tim Curtis was one major factor behind the county's first trophy in thirteen years, another was him making sure the opposition had plenty to drink on Saturday nights. 'We weren't always allowed at the Saturday night parties,' Neale said. 'It was often just him and the opposition ... He was quite good for us on the social side.'

The most famous case of 'opposition-nobbling' came barely a month into the season when Essex were the visitors. Play in the championship match on the Saturday was curtailed by rain, consigning the teams to hanging around the dressing-rooms waiting for an abandonment. As it happened, Eric Clapton, by now a regular associate of Botham's, had come to watch and he now joined some players in a game of cards.

'The guys lost their shirts to Eric,' said Derek Pringle. 'He won about £400 and there was a bit of disquiet. "As if he needs the money," someone muttered. Then Eric said, "I'll tell you what, lads. Beefy's got one of my guitars. I swapped it for one of his bats. If the local guitar shop sells the right type of amplifier, I'll play for you." So he phoned up the guitar shop. The guy said he'd got the amp and Eric said he'd be along to pick it up. "What if someone else wants it?" Eric told him he certainly wanted it. "What's your name?" It's Eric Clapton. Yeah, yeah, course it is. Anyway, sure enough, he got the amp and took it down to Beefy's local. Eric was a bit of a lost soul at the time and not teetotal then like he is now. It was whisky chasers with his beers. He still played and sang beautifully. It was a great evening.'

The Essex players also put away the drinks and the next day were the worse for wear. Even Botham was a little shaky to start with; having persuaded Clapton to let him drive his Ferrari to the ground, he managed to scrape it on a gate post. By the time he came to bat, though, Botham was seeing the ball well enough to tear Essex's bleary-eyed bowlers apart and easily win the game for his side with a fiercely struck 125 not out. 'Beefy just blitzed us,' Pringle said. 'He hit Hugh Page flat over extra cover so hard that he almost demolished the tea stand. But we had not been on top of our game and we were about to have an inquest in the dressing-room when Eric walked in and said, "Lads, don't worry. The man's the man. There's nothing you can do about it." And Keith Fletcher said, "Excuse me, Ernie, do you mind? We're having a team meeting here." And someone said to Fletch, "Did you just call him Ernie?" Fletch said yes; "Don't you know? That's Ernie

Clapham, the world-class guitar player." Fletch was always hope-less with names.'

Two weeks later Clapton paid another visit to New Road and this time brought with him Elton John, George Harrison and Jeff Lynne.

Interestingly, Clapton, who admitted having a drinking prob-lem at the time, said that he felt at home among cricketers because drinking was such a big part of their social scene, particularly in the case of Botham who 'liked the odd quencher'. Clapton described Botham in his autobiography as a wonderful man, gre-garious and generous, although armed with a 'scaldingly cruel sense of humour'. More often than not, he wrote, David English would be the target: 'David would be the recipient of our scorn-ful attention and would suffer extraordinary abuse at our hands . . . We were pretty merciless.' Soon after this, Clapton began the process of stopping drinking altogether and as a consequence became nervous of meeting Botham again in case it led him to lapse. He claimed to have spent 'half of my last year of drinking' in Botham's company.

Clapton's verdict on Botham was that there was a schizophrenic side to his personality and part of his problem was that he was afraid of failing when he went onto the field. His bravado was just a façade.

England picked Botham for every game that summer. The Test series with Pakistan was spoiled by rain and further bickering between the camps, and won 1–0 by Imran Khan's team. Botham made little impact, save for a battling half-century in partnership with Gatting to ensure that the final match was drawn. Spanning more than four hours, it was as resolute an innings as he ever played and a singular effort against Abdul Qadir bowling to men around the bat. But as an all-rounder he was thoroughly eclipsed by Imran, whose fast swing bowling won the decisive match at Leeds, where Botham himself was unable to bowl because of a bruised foot. During this game, Salim Yousuf, the Pakistan keeper, claimed to have caught Botham even though the ball plainly bounced. It was a disgraceful piece of gamesmanship for which Imran was ready to apologise until he heard Botham swear at Yousuf. Botham conceded: 'I called him a cheating little bastard, warning him that if he ever tried that stunt again I would knock his head off.' The upshot was that Pakistan complained about Botham's language.

Writing after the series, Botham said he regarded Imran as his greatest rival 'in the world all-round stakes', but comparisons were no longer necessary. Three years older but fitter and faster, Imran was clearly the better bowler, as his twenty-one wickets in the series to Botham's seven made plain. Even Gatting accepted that Botham's bowling had gone 'downhill'. Imran averaged forty-eight with the bat to Botham's thirty-three, though Botham did brilliantly run out his rival at the Oval.

Botham's first season with Queensland began a few days after England had lost the World Cup final to Allan Border's Australia in Calcutta. It was a narrow defeat that might have been averted had Botham been playing, a thought that must have occurred to him. Had he done the right thing after all?

His presence gave Queensland the kind of lift Worcestershire had experienced. He contributed fifty-eight runs, three wickets and five slip catches in his first game, and was arguably Border's most valuable all-round player as five of the first six matches were won to virtually guarantee the state their place in the Shield final. One of Botham's best performances came in a defeat to defending champions Western Australia in Perth, where he scored two fifties and bowled more than fifty overs – including twenty-six unchanged – at lively enough pace to break the thumb of Queensland keeper Peter Anderson.

A young Ian Healy, who deputised for Anderson for the rest of the season, described Botham as 'an extraordinary figure who polarised opinions'. He added: 'He lived for the moment, always lavishly, often rude, while being as generous a character as I have met. As a team-mate, I found him inspiring . . . During a match he was remarkable, never believing a match or cause was lost.' This never say die attitude was valuable as the Queensland side was not, in Healy's view, a tight-knit unit.

But long before the Shield final in late March, Botham's season – and Queensland's – had gone off the boil. The old problem of Botham's reluctance to practise had resurfaced, with Greg Chappell, who sat on the Queensland executive, claiming Botham had not attended a training session after January. A poor regime may have played its part in Botham's back problem flaring up again; whatever the reason, his performances tailed away as three of the last four Shield matches were lost. Nor did the team prosper in the one-day competition.

Straight after a one-day loss in Launceston, Border announced that alcohol would be banned during the team's visit to Melbourne, where Queensland needed to win to secure home advantage in the final. While most of the players went straight back to the hotel, Botham stayed behind in the dressing-room to drink with Dennis Lillee, who had come out of retirement after four years to play for Tasmania at the age of thirty-eight. Botham said that the two of them broke 'a few glasses'; Lillee in his autobiography said that Botham had thrown a beer can at a wall and he had attempted to do the same and smashed a fluorescent light instead. Nothing initially came of this minor incident of vandalism, but it would later.

These 'low jinks' complete, Botham returned to the hotel and sought out Border to protest about the drinking ban, claiming that he had never gone a day without a drink in his life. Botham admitted later that this defiance caused a serious falling-out with his captain.

To make matters worse, the match with Victoria was lost and Botham was fined about £300 for swearing at spectators.

Then, during the flight from Melbourne to Perth, where the Shield final was now to be played in Western Australia's back yard, tensions in the camp spilled over. There were arguments between Border and Greg Ritchie, who had lost his Test place and was keen to make his views known to Australia's captain, and between Border and Botham. According to later testimony, Botham played an obscene tape during the flight and swore repeatedly. When asked to tone down his language by another passenger, Allan Winter, Botham responded by allegedly turning Winter's head to the front and shaking him by the hair. He also directed some verbal abuse at a female passenger. After reaching Perth, Botham was arrested on charges of assault and offensive behaviour and on the eve of the final appeared in court and was bailed for a week. Half the bail bond of about £4,000 was provided by Lillee.

Inevitably, amid this unwelcome distraction, Queensland were decisively beaten in the Shield final. Botham did nothing with the ball and a defiant second-innings half-century was too little too late. Healy said that the incidents in Launceston and on the flight to Perth had little impact on his own performance – 'I found them entertaining if anything' – but it was always likely that Botham would take the blame for the collapse in Queensland's season.

After the final, Botham returned to court to plead guilty and be fined about £350 including costs, but there was more punishment to come. Having taken into account what had happened in Tasmania, Queensland fined him about £2,000 and, having read submissions from Border and the team manager Ray Reynolds, unanimously opted to terminate his contract. Some months later, the *Sun* newspaper also decided to dispense with his services, having complained that it had been unable to get hold of him after his arrest in Perth. Thus came to an end one of the most turbulent relationships in Fleet Street history.

When news of his sacking by Queensland reached him, Botham was taken aback. He had not anticipated this and was left to make the best of a humiliating rejection by saying that he had not in any case enjoyed his time at Queensland and was considering breaking his contract. He also complained about preaching from former Australian players, possibly a reference to Ian Chappell having likened him to 'the school bully'. He promised revelations to 'make your hair stand on end', but they never materialised.

The Queensland venture, conceived in part as a means of escaping publicity, had turned into a disaster. Quite apart from the cost of losing his contract, Botham's conduct did not endear him to the TCCB, which now expected the national selectors to take into account behaviour as well as form. This decree followed an acrimonious England tour of Pakistan during which a day's play had been lost as a result of an argument between Mike Gatting and umpire Shakoor Rana.

England did not pick Botham for the early-season one-day internationals against West Indies in 1988 but were willing to consider him for the Tests that followed. However, while playing for Worcestershire against Somerset, he fell awkwardly making a diving stop in the slips. He immediately left the field but did not realise he was suffering anything more serious than familiar back stiffness until he found he could barely stand upright. The next day it was announced that he required surgery to fuse two vertebrae.

Botham maintained with some justification that he had long had a back problem requiring corrective surgery, but had kept putting off the operation. His general lifestyle cannot have helped though. The previous month he had completed another walk in aid of leukaemia research, his third following a week-long fundraiser in Ireland the previous year. This time he had gone for an eye-catching plan to cross the Alps with elephants, retracing Hannibal's march in the third century BC (unfortunately it proved expensive and raised only £300,000). He had walked for three weeks, and finished only shortly before the new season, and it appeared to have taken its toll. He did not bowl in his first championship match and sent down only ten overs in his second.

Not only did Botham miss the rest of the season, he was consigned to six months of tortuous rehab with physiotherapist Dave Roberts not knowing how complete a recovery he might make. His weight ballooned and he conceded that the thought of being on the scrapheap at the age of thirty-two 'scared me to death'. Talk during the Tim Hudson era of giving up cricket to pursue 'business interests' was a distant memory. He was desperate to continue playing and to regain sole ownership of the world Test wicket-taking record. Richard Hadlee was now level with him on 373 and would soon move ahead of him, an achievement that contributed to the New Zealander being knighted in 1990.

Perhaps his one consolation was that England might still have need of him if he did recover. In his absence, they were trounced 4–0 by West Indies and got through four captains after Gatting was sacked following allegations in the *Sun* that he had entertained a barmaid in his hotel room, though he denied any impropriety took place. It seemed that after banning Botham two years earlier the board had got a taste for punishing players for off-field activities.

Determined though he was to get back playing, Botham was on the lookout for fresh challenges, new adventures and no doubt ways of making up for the money he had lost through the termination of his Queensland contract. Nor did he earn anything from England while he was injured. In terms of cricket-related income, he had only his county salary and endorsements to prop him up.

One opportunity that presented itself was a chance to appear regularly on *A Question of Sport*, BBC's long-running quiz show. Botham was asked to take over from footballer Emlyn Hughes as one of the team captains opposite former England rugby captain Billy Beaumont. Botham and Beaumont were to remain rival skippers for the next eight years, filming the shows in blocks of four or five at studios in Manchester.

Perhaps encouraged by his successful foray into television, Botham embarked on another profitable venture, a speaking tour around Britain that spanned several weeks and many venues. It was a splicing together of concepts – the charity walks through towns and cities, and the standard evening talk beloved of cricketers in their benefit seasons. The idea was hatched in partnership with David English, who had compered some of Botham's benefit functions and hosted a question-and-answer evening with

Botham in Berri, South Australia, the previous winter. Botham had afterwards suggested that they try something similar at home. He had done some further speaking engagements around Australia during his time with Queensland. With his winters in England now free, 'An Evening With Ian Botham' duly took to the road, the first stop being Stourbridge, near Botham's Worcestershire home. The first half of the show consisted of a film showing highlights of his career and then after an interval English fed him questions from the audience. In later seasons, Botham teamed up with Viv Richards in a show called 'The King and I', and after that with Allan Lamb in 'Lamb and Beef in a Stew'. Botham and Richards took one roadshow to Australia.

'He really enjoyed it and got quite good,' English recalled. 'Allan Lamb was probably more natural but Ian worked hard and developed some good stories. He enjoyed performing. He was not a natural actor but loved an audience and we got some big ones. We had two thousand in Perth once. Our record low was six Sikhs in Edinburgh – there had been a mix-up over venues – and another time we got twelve in a mining town called Iron Knob in Australia. However small the turnout, he'd always insist on giving a performance. He'd never let anybody down. If his name was on the poster, he did it.' These roadshows ultimately led him into pantomime, Botham first persuading his friend Max Boyce to let him appear in *Jack and the Beanstalk*.

If these theatricals helped fill winters and pockets, the downside was that he was once again on the road and travelling in less comfort than on a cricket tour. For transport they had a Winnebago and a driver. If they arrived at a venue in the afternoon, they would check into their hotel, take a look at the hall where the show was taking place, then English would fetch a bucket of Kentucky Fried Chicken by way of an early supper. After the show they would drive to the next location, Botham insisting they watch endless action movies in the back of the van. 'It was always *Rambo*, *Conan the Barbarian* and *The Professionals*,' English recalled. 'I'd say, "Not again." But that's what we'd watch. If there was time, Beefy would probably like to play golf during the day. Viv didn't play golf so he would have his hat on and walk around town, or sleep in his room.'

English caddied for Botham before he got fed up walking around for four hours holding a bag for someone he jokingly referred to as a 'psychopath'. He remembered Botham once playing golf at Royal Tunbridge Wells at the invitation of Colin Cowdrey, who was as near to a cricketing Establishment figure as you could get. 'Cowdrey had the crisp corduroys and fine shoes, Beefy had the Greg Norman this and the Tom Weiskopf that,' English said. 'Cowdrey kept beating him all the way – and kept apologising for playing so well. Beefy was steaming, biting his lip, hating losing. Cowdrey beat him just like he batted, with great grace and exquisite timing. It was an interesting encounter.'

Botham's claim that he needed to drink to help him sleep was not without foundation. He often found sleep hard to come by, certainly in the later stages of his career. English found this out to his cost during the road-shows. 'Beefy was an insomniac,' he said. 'He could not go to sleep early so he would stay up, then become paranoid. He always needed mates he could trust and was careful with outsiders. I used to sit with him many nights until about 4am, when he'd finally to tell you to get lost and he'd go to sleep. But before that you'd get a lot of hard stuff coming out, extraordinary talk about the old days.'

Even before he returned to playing in 1989, Botham's hopes of an England recall took a blow with the TCCB's decision to overhaul the selection process. Teams were to be picked by an England committee consisting of Mickey Stewart as team manager plus the captain and a chairman – who was named as Ted Dexter, Peter May having stood down as chairman of selectors, a beaten and bewildered figure after the chaos of the previous summer. As an Oxbridge man and former England captain of aristocratic mien, Dexter was essentially more of the same, but he was a more flamboyant figure than May and not shy of publicity. He had once stood as a Conservative parliamentary candidate and was so eager to present himself to the world that he held his first press conference before he had even been confirmed in the job. Dexter's appointment was not necessarily good news for Botham. For a start, he was simply too eccentric: on the eve of his first Test back, Botham along with other players was handed a song sheet by Dexter, a devout Christian, with adapted lyrics to the hymn 'Onward Christian Soldiers'. More to the point, Dexter had been charged with rebuilding the team and his enthusiasm for thirty-somethings was qualified.

Botham did have one stroke of luck. Dexter and Stewart's wish that Gatting be restored to the captaincy was vetoed by the board and David Gower regained the job by default. Gower still believed in Botham's capacity to turn matches.

By the time of the one-dayers against Australia in late May, Botham had played solidly for seven weeks and had acquired a bandwagon of media support. Several journalists had accompanied Worcestershire's pre-season tour of Queensland purely to monitor Botham's return to the state that had sacked him. He clinched his England recall after an absence of almost two years with a season's best score of forty-two in a tight run-chase against the Australians, an effort that was instrumental in Worcestershire getting home by three wickets. It was to be the touring team's only defeat in twenty first-class matches and it was clear why: the game was played on the type of 'sporty' pitch that did much to help Worcestershire retain the championship but was never seen in the Test series, which Australia won 4–0 and but for rain would have taken by an unparalleled 6–0 margin. A team that had endured many struggles had finally turned the corner under Allan Border. England were to be the first of many to suffer at their hands.

Thanks to Gower, Botham would have been involved in the Ashes matches from the start, but three days before the first Test he sustained a fractured cheekbone when he mistimed a pull at Glamorgan's Steve Barwick and top-edged the ball into his face. On a New Road pitch with little pace in it, he had not bothered wearing a helmet. In the end, he had to wait until the third Test at

Edgbaston for his chance, by which time England were 2–0 down and battling injuries. Not everyone supported his recall, Geoff Boycott arguing in a newspaper article that he was finished, but he had probably merited his inclusion with eleven wickets at Northampton, his best match figures in the championship since 1976. The problem was that a bigger-seamed ball was in use in that year's championship and it was making many medium-pace bowlers of Botham's type seem more dangerous than they really were. The ball swung less but generated pronounced movement off the pitch and turned many shire horses into apparent thoroughbreds. Unfortunately, a lower-seamed ball was in use in the Tests and England could dismiss Australia only four times in six matches.

Even from a short run-up, and despite being less mobile than before, Botham could still bowl a 'heavy' ball, which only convinced him he could still lure people into mistakes against short-pitched deliveries. 'We gave up on team meetings because he wanted to bounce them all out,' said Neale, who added that Botham was far better at remembering the men he got out in this fashion than the hundreds of balls that disappeared for four in the attempt.

Like most of the twenty-nine players England called on in the six Tests, Botham made little impact in the three matches he played. England were outclassed on all fronts and in any case had their own internal problems with another rebel tour of South Africa in the offing. With a less helpful ball to work with, Botham's gentle bowling was ineffective but he did help secure a draw at Edgbaston in his first game back by batting two and a half hours for forty-six. At Old Trafford, where the Ashes were surrendered, he was out to leg-spinner Trevor Hohns for nought attempting a reckless swipe that reflected English frustration. And at Trent Bridge, he dislocated a finger misjudging a catch, an injury that meant he batted at number nine in the first innings and not at all in the second. Unfit for the Oval, he had played what proved to be his last Test against Australia.

The fallout from the loss of the Ashes was severe. Gower was replaced by Graham Gooch as captain and when Dexter, Stewart and Gooch met to pick a squad to tour the Caribbean, Gooch was told at the outset that Botham and Gower were to be discounted, even though Botham was now keen to tour again. 'Ted and Mickey wanted a new influence,' Gooch said. 'They wanted to get away from the champagne-set image and go with some new faces.' Gooch said he had not planned to include Botham anyway.

Botham, naturally, maintained that he could still perform well at the highest level. There was some evidence to support this; he had batted well in the championship on an unusually fast pitch at Old Trafford in July; against a Lancashire attack containing Patrick Patterson and Paul Allott, Botham had scored seventy-three, the highest innings of a feisty game, and Neale said he had played the bowling as well as anyone. But the selectors were conscious of Botham's previous struggles in the West Indies. Stewart's view was that Botham simply was not fit enough to tour.

Botham took his exclusion badly. It was the first time he had been left out of a Test match side strictly on merit for almost twelve years. The last Test tour he had missed against his wishes was in the winter of 1976–77, and it had taken him a long time to forgive Tony Greig for that slight. When Dexter phoned Botham the night before the tour party for the Caribbean was announced to tell him of his omission, Botham's response had been to rant – before slamming down the phone. He did not seem to realise that England had got used to his regular absences during two previous years. They had moved on but clearly he had not. Dexter was unmoved. At the next day's press conference, he was withering in his analysis of why Botham had been left out, saying that his form had 'not even nearly approximated to Test standard'.

The hurt this incident caused Botham was not lost on Imran Khan, who during their High Court battle in 1996 said that in his view Botham had not realised his potential as a cricketer and had blamed everyone but himself for being 'shunted out of cricket in an undignified way'.

In one sense, Botham responded positively. If his initial fear was that he would never play for England again, he seemed more sanguine by the time he spoke to Gooch. 'He blustered a little but vowed to come back,' Gooch said. He also promptly signed a new three-year contract with Worcestershire which committed him to playing county cricket into his thirty-seventh year (an arrangement that in the end proved too much for both parties). Any thoughts he might have had of retirement were now shelved: he wanted his England place back.

But at the same time he demonised the selectors for their temerity in dropping him. He claimed, bizarrely, that he felt doubly angry because he had kept himself available for the West Indies tour when he could have pursued other options. With another rebel tour of South Africa being hatched, he argued that he could have gone on it had he known England did not need him. Quite why England's management should have given any player early indication that he would not be required for an official tour so that he could go on an unofficial one is beyond comprehension. He further claimed that not only had he been asked to keep himself available, but Mickey Stewart had 'pleaded' with him to do so.

Others do not remember events in the same way. Stewart strongly denied ever having pleaded with Botham. 'I wouldn't plead with anyone to represent their country,' he said. 'I would have thought any English cricketer would have wanted to do that as a matter of course. Obviously I was keen for everyone to be ready to play for England, but I couldn't give assurances to anyone that they would be picked.'

Botham said that he had demanded from the South African organisers £500,000 for a three-year deal encompassing two tours and a season of provincial cricket, plus compensation for any lost sponsorship deals, and that they had not blinked; 'We'll discuss it and get back to you,' was their reply. Botham had eventually told them he was not interested in mid-August, which was actually two weeks after a sixteen-man squad captained by Mike Gatting had been publicly unveiled without Botham's name in it.

In fact Ali Bacher, the chief executive of the South Africa Cricket Union and one of the tour's principal organisers, confirmed that he did contact Botham, but said that it was quickly clear the idea was unfeasible. 'We came to a mutual agreement that it would not be in the interests of either party for him to come,' Bacher said. 'I spoke to Alan Herd about Ian's commercial arrangements and it was obvious that Ian could have lost a lot in terms of sponsorships and endorsements. It was obvious from our side that it was going to be too expensive. They were not extended negotiations.' Asked if he was aware of Botham's possible involvement in the tour, Mickey Stewart replied: 'That's the first I've heard of it.'

Nor was the prospect of TV appearances, roadshows and pantomimes enough to keep Botham happy. By his own admission, he spent the winter in a 'pretty foul mood'. He blamed it on his treatment by the selectors but Kath said also that he was drinking too much whisky. 'She has always said that if I get on the Scotch then that is the time to run for cover,' he conceded. Another friend confirmed this view: 'He was fine on beer but if he got on the Scotch he didn't always know what he was doing.' On Valentine's Day – the day of England's first international in the Caribbean – Kath gave him a dressing-down that was every bit as withering as Dexter's verdict on him as a cricketer. She told him that he had become impossible to live with and that she would not put up with him taking out his disappointment on her and the children. He had to either change his ways or she and the children would leave. 'It was a numbing experience,' Botham recalled. 'For possibly the first time, I was able to see myself through Kath's eyes.' They had recently bought a second home in Alderney and Kath used it to give herself space from him. Botham was faced with the classic dilemma of every top sportsman nearing the end of his career: how to adjust to the give-and-take of everyday life.

Botham may not have been doing well without England but they coped fine without him. Ten days later, they beat West Indies in a Test match for the first time in sixteen years, and although they eventually lost the series 2–1 they were unlucky not to come away with a draw. At home, they then beat New Zealand and India without losing a game. Botham started the 1990 season brightly in one-day cricket but his body was not up to the workload. A minor knee operation sidelined him in the run-up to the early Texaco Trophy matches and he missed the last six weeks of the season with a hamstring strain.

Worcestershire failed to win a trophy for the first time in four seasons, although they made strong bids in the two knockout competitions. The NatWest Trophy threw up a return for Botham to Taunton, where Worcestershire successfully chased down 284. There was an awkward incident before play when Peter Roebuck made an attempt to bury the hatchet over the acrimony of 1986.

They had barely spoken for eighteen months, largely choosing to keep out of each other's way, but Chris Lander had suggested to Roebuck that Botham was interested in patching things up. 'He [Lander] said, "Look, Ian wants to get talking again, but pride won't allow him. Will you approach him? He'll just say, 'Let's put it behind us.'" I said, "OK. There's nothing on my side that's irreparable." And there he was next morning on the field. I said: "Hello, Ian. Shall we let bygones be bygones?" Well, he told me to get lost, which considering the whole thing had been cooked up by Lander purely to cause mischief, he was entitled to do. I didn't hold it against him but I did feel that after that it was up to Ian to make the next move. That was twenty years ago now. Our paths haven't crossed much and when they have I think we've both behaved courteously. We've not exchanged a cross word but we've not exchanged a friendly one either.'

In the next round at Northampton, Botham narrowly failed to be the hero, taking the man of the match award for an unbeaten eighty-six. With Worcestershire chasing 264, Botham was frustrated by not seeing enough of the strike in the closing stages and the task of scoring ten off the last over with last man Stuart Lampitt for company proved beyond him.

In the Benson and Hedges Cup, Worcestershire finished runners-up to Lancashire. Botham's two wickets and thirty-eight runs in the final was a decent effort but his team were never really in the hunt.

By the winter of 1990–91, Botham's cricket career was going in no clear direction. He appeared to be finished with England. He had two years left on his Worcestershire contract but it was to become clear that a parting was likelier sooner than that; during the following summer the team entered a new era as Phil Neale was replaced as captain and Basil d'Oliveira as coach. Although he had developed some useful financial sidelines, Botham had no firm plans as to what he would do in retirement, whenever that would be. In the absence of anything else, playing on seemed as good an idea as any, even if his body was protesting.

It was at this point that he received an attractive offer to move county for a second time. Durham had long aspired to join the ranks of the first-class counties; since the mid-1970s, they had won the Minor Counties championship four times and in 1990 it was agreed they should enter the county championship in 1992. Geoff Cook, the former Northants and England batsman, was appointed to assemble a squad and Botham was one of those targeted, as much for his marketing potential as anything. Botham's signing would help attract sponsors and provide the enterprise with credibility. He would light the region's imagination.

He was offered a package that he would have been a fool to turn down, reportedly £175,000 for two seasons and some promotional work for a local brewery, and he gave the club his verbal agreement in April 1991. He had friends at the club – Paul Romaines was commercial manager – and an additional appeal was that Durham was near to his North Yorkshire home. He had often stated that he was a Northerner at heart and now he was going to play as one.

Botham said that among the initial inducements had been an offer of the captaincy but when he met Cook to finalise details he was told that the captaincy had already been offered to David Graveney, who had been sacked as Gloucestershire captain in 1988 and had since moved to Somerset as a player. 'I was not happy but there was nothing I could do,' Botham said. At least he was in the situation he often found himself in of being captained by an old friend who was not going to make life too awkward for him. Graveney said: 'I don't know whether that [the captaincy] was promised to him but there was certainly no drama between us.' Worcestershire agreed to not hold Botham to the last year of his contract. 'We were sad to see him go because he was a popular guy but it was a fantastic opportunity for him,' Neale said. 'It was the right time for both of us. He'd got some cricket left in him but we'd had his best years since leaving Somerset.'

Botham would later describe the move to Durham as one of the worst mistakes he ever made but initially the plan energised him as he began his final season with Worcestershire. Perhaps sensing he could yet be recalled by England, who had spent the winter losing badly in Australia and New Zealand, he announced himself fed up with people writing him off and promptly took 5–125 against Gloucestershire, his first five-wicket haul for two years, and scored a century against Lancashire.

This was indeed enough for England to include him in their one-day squad against West Indies and on the day he learned he was back in favour he happened to be playing against the touring team for Worcestershire. His response was typical: he hammered a century off 83 balls and went on to score 161 with one six and 32 fours. It was his first hundred against a West Indies team and although only two of the four fast bowlers he faced played in the first Test, it was a striking declaration of intent.

Frustratingly, his return turned into a damp squib. In the first one-day international, he tore a hamstring and put himself out of action for a month. By the time he was fit again, England were 1–0 up after two matches in the Test series and when they made a change to their squad for the third Test they brought in Warwickshire all-rounder Dermot Reeve, who in the event did not play. Reeve's inclusion at least indicated that England were thinking about all-rounders again. After several players including Derek Pringle, David Capel, Chris Cowdrey and Phil DeFreitas had been tried with little success, Mickey Stewart and Graham Gooch had largely called off the search for a new Botham. *In extremis* in Australia, they had twice used Alec Stewart, Mickey's son and a batsman who kept wicket, as a pseudo all-rounder but that idea had also been dropped. Botham's response to these pretenders varied. Sometimes he barely acknowledged them as rivals; on other occasions he appeared to recognise they might constitute a threat. Reeve recalled a match in which Botham was overtly hostile towards him, which Reeve took as a great compliment.

It was now that his luck changed. England decisively lost the third and fourth Tests, which meant they faced the final match at the Oval needing to win to tie the series at 2–2 – if they could avoid a series defeat by West Indies it would be the first time in seventeen years. Emboldened by the crisis, Gooch, Stewart and Dexter attempted to strengthen both batting and bowling by bringing in Stewart for Russell as keeper and Botham in place of a specialist batsman. Botham, they accepted, remained the best all-rounder at their disposal and would not be overawed by such a big occasion. He had recently helped Worcestershire win the Benson and Hedges Cup, his exemplary bowling killing off Essex in the semifinals before revenge was taken on Lancashire for their victory the previous year. Over the weekend of his selection, Botham gave an eye-catching performance by scoring 81 runs and taking 7–54 as Reeve's Warwickshire were trounced by an innings. He was up for it, all right.

Expectations were far in excess of what they should have been for a player who had appeared in only three Tests in four years and whose role was to bat seven and act as fourth seamer. But Botham's luck – or was it his inspirational presence? – held good as England won in style, outplaying West Indies from the moment Gooch won the toss and put on a century stand for the first wicket with Hugh Morris. All of the four players brought in for the game came off, Botham included. Without doing anything astonishing he contributed thirty-five runs, three wickets and three catches, and – as though he was again writing his own script – it fell to him to hit the winning runs. He swung his first delivery to the boundary to seal England's win and his first Test victory over West Indies or his old friend Viv Richards, playing his last Test match.

What started as a one-off pick turned into something more. Ten of the side that had played at the Oval, including Botham, were retained for the last Test of the summer against Sri Lanka and Mickey Stewart argued, against the wishes of his masters, that Botham should be taken to that winter's World Cup.

While Stewart had had his doubts about whether Botham was fit enough for regular Test cricket, he thought he could play a part in the one-day game, though work would still need to be done on his stamina. Stewart and Gooch were intent on raising fitness levels and in the two previous winters the team had undergone intensive training before touring. Botham was naturally delighted at the idea of going away with England for the first time in five years, and agreed to join the team partway through their Test tour of New Zealand that preceded the World Cup in order to get in shape. He also accepted Stewart's suggestion that while he was appearing in pantomime in Bournemouth he should train with the town's football team. But he baulked at taking instruction from Colin Tomlin, an athletics coach and motivator whom Stewart was using to help players get fitter.

Despite Stewart's efforts, Botham arrived in New Zealand overweight. This would not have been in itself a big issue – he had time to work off the extra pounds – but it became one after some of the tabloids got stuck into him for lack of preparation. Geoff Boycott, in his column in the *Sun*, labelled Botham's attitude towards training as 'totally unprofessional and unacceptable'; this might have mattered less was Boycott not being used by England as their batting coach.

As it happened, an injury crisis led to Botham being pressed into service for the final Test in Wellington, where he became the fourth England player – after Cowdrey, Boycott and Gower – to win one hundred caps. The game was drawn and personally uneventful for Botham. It was to be the only Test Botham played outside England that was shown live on television in the UK, Rupert Murdoch's British Sky Broadcasting – a satellite subscription channel – having secured the live rights to all England's cricket overseas, including the World Cup, three years earlier. This contract was ultimately to transform the coverage and financing of the sport.

One incident encapsulated how outmoded Botham had become. England were practising in Sydney ahead of the World Cup when he produced a giant water pistol and started indiscriminately soaking fellow players and the occasional newspaper reporter. Afterwards it was made clear to him that his behaviour had not been appreciated. He still wanted touring to be fun but had failed to grasp that for others it had become a grimly professional business. This was why the likes of Ted Dexter had wanted to leave him at home in the first place.

Botham's role at the World Cup was to open the batting and act as fifth seamer, but this changed as the tournament went on. Bowling well, he was brought into the attack earlier and earlier, so that he ended up opening the bowling in the semi-final and coming on first change in the final. Unfortunately, these proved to be his most expensive games with the ball and Gooch did not entrust him with his full allocation of ten overs in the final.

He did, however, open the batting throughout. He was sent in first because Gooch thought it the best way to fit him into a strong batting line-up. In the early stages the move worked well as he scored fifty-three against Australia (having earlier taken four wickets in seven balls) and forty-seven against Sri Lanka, and England won five of their first six games. 'We didn't think he was best suited to number six,' Gooch said. 'We had loads of batters and thought he had a bit of presence and could make an impact up front.' But as with his bowling, his batting fell away in the second half of the tournament. He scored 69 runs in his last five innings – including 21 in the semi-final against South Africa, and falling for a duck, caught behind off Wasim Akram, in the final against Pakistan. Botham was desperately disappointed at being given out and smashed his bat in frustration in the dressing-room, but Wasim was adamant that Botham had gloved the ball and TV replays supported his case. At the business end of the competition, Botham was a big disappointment.

The tailing-off of his game may have been connected to his level of fitness. He later criticised the management for their enthusiasm for training, complaining that long before the end of the tournament the players were 'knackered' and had they been given more time off they might have had the energy to win the final in Melbourne. Wasim confirmed that after fielding first England looked weary and all but beaten. 'They were shattered towards the end of our innings,' he said. 'Their fielding flagged on a big playing arena. They were gone before we bowled a ball.' Gooch conceded that Botham may have had a point: 'He said we didn't quite get it right and were tired. He may have been right. But it was difficult to say at the time.' But Gooch insisted that he and Mickey Stewart never compelled older players to practise. 'We didn't force them to do anything as long as they were seen to be doing something. I would take issue with him [Botham] if he were to say he was forced to train.'

Botham was not alone in feeling hard done by at England losing another World Cup final (their third and Botham's second). They had made the early running in the tournament and had it not rained in Adelaide, Pakistan would have been eliminated during the group stage. Despite the appetite of the locals to see them beaten – Gooch and Botham had walked out of an eve-of-final dinner at which an Australian 'entertainer' had mocked the Queen – England had started the final well, only for Pakistan to rally through a stand of 139 between Imran Khan and Javed Miandad, who was lucky not to be given out early on. The fact was that England had not had a good final and nor had Botham. Pakistan had deserved to win, leaving Imran the enviable pleasure of retiring from international cricket on an absolute high.

Botham would have been wise to have announced that this was his last match for England too.

# 12

## National Treasure

'I met him for dinner one night in London. He'd had a meeting beforehand, something to do with leukaemia. It turned out he had met this chap – a wonderful man, a good-looking bloke, forty years old, attractive wife, young family, real go-getter, making something of his life. He had been diagnosed with leukaemia and had very little time, and all he wanted to do was meet Ian Botham. Beefy was visibly distressed, emotionally drained. He needed that first drink to cope. I'd not seen him like that. He finds those things quite tough.'

ROD BRANSGROVE, HAMPSHIRE CHAIRMAN

Knowing when to retire is one of the hardest decisions for any top sportsman. Everyone wants to go out on a high, at a major event in front of a big audience. It rarely works out like that. Finding the right opportunity is one challenge, another is recognising the opportunity for what it is. The 1992 World Cup final was Botham's chance but he passed up on it. Whether England won or lost, he could have taken a last bow in front of 90,000 spectators and hundreds of millions watching on TV. Having given so much pleasure to so many people, it would have been the grand send-off he deserved.

In a sense, it was a surprising error by a man with a gift for great timing. But Botham's judgement was never foolproof. This was one of the reasons why he commanded such loyalty among friends and team-mates; they knew he needed protecting from himself because he could get things horribly wrong. They had seen that in the use of drugs, the failed terms as captain, the appointment of Tim Hudson and other agents, and his decision to quit touring with England. By opting to play on, he faced the strong possibility of being dropped by an England management that had never been enamoured of him.

When eventually he did retire, sixteen months after the World Cup, his enthusiasm for playing the game was all but extinguished. His final championship appearance came in a massive defeat at the Oval, a game that was an embarrassment both for him and the Durham team.

The problem with retiring as an England player after the World Cup was that Botham had already signed a two-year deal with Durham, and they would have been two long seasons without the hope of international cricket to keep him going. He played on because of money, because of an uncertainty about what he would do when he stopped and because, initially at any rate, he was certainly still good enough for county cricket.

Botham's mere presence did everything Durham had hoped for in the early weeks of their inaugural season. His performances at the World Cup had helped hoist membership above 4,000 and the early one-day matches were sold out; a dressing-room that might otherwise have subsided under a weight of self-doubt was boosted by his unquenchable self-belief. He himself was galvanised into bursts of brilliance. He scored a century off eighty-six balls in the first championship match against Leicestershire. Pouncing at short midwicket, he executed the run-out that won Durham's first home fixture in the Sunday league, a match against Lancashire that was watched by 6,000 at the county's temporary headquarters at Durham University. Mobbed by team-mates, Botham told them it was all part of having a good scriptwriter.

His sixty-seven runs and two wickets ensured Durham won the following Sunday league game as well. Two group matches in the Benson and Hedges Cup were also won and in mid-May came the first success in the championship – a three-day victory over Glamorgan at Colwyn Bay. 'At times it was like watching Peter Pan,' said David Graveney.

Simon Hughes, who had joined Durham from Middlesex, was able to observe Botham's impregnable ego at close quarters. He remembered an incident in an Italian restaurant in Canterbury, where Durham were playing their first championship match away from home. Botham wanted to order some cheese and had asked the waiter for some 'dolecetti'. Hughes corrected him: 'It's Dolcelatte.' Hughes recalled: 'There was a pause while he absorbed the information. Then he snapped: "Well . . . How many bloody Test wickets did you get?"'

Determined to keep his England place, Botham had targets beyond lifting Durham and his sparkling early efforts duly earned him selection for the first two Texaco Trophy matches against Pakistan. Both were won but Botham's demotion in England's thinking was plain: he was asked neither to open the batting nor take the new ball. He was selected for the first, rain-blighted Test of the season in Birmingham and – despite struggling with a groin strain – the second at Lord's.

This Test, which proved to be his last, was an epic contest which Pakistan won by two wickets after England fought heroically to try to prevent them scoring 137. Wasim Akram and Waqar Younis took Pakistan home after their side had slumped to 95–8. Botham played only a minor part. He was twice cleaned up cheaply by Waqar and his toe was broken by a ball from Wasim; that, combined with his groin problem, restricted him to bowling just five overs. Although fit again in time for the third Test, England decided they could do without him.

He must have immediately feared that he would not play Test cricket again, and his form for Durham now deteriorated as the club's results nosedived. In nineteen matches, he scored four fifties and averaged little more than a wicket a game; indeed, he took his last wicket of the season for Durham on 6 August. A week after England had played the third Test without him, Botham – sleepless as usual – summoned Hughes to his hotel room at 2am during a championship match in Nottingham, insisting that he share a bottle of burgundy. 'We sat talking for an hour about cricket politics and the ineptness of the TCCB while a Guns'n'Roses concert blared out on TV,' Hughes said. Botham suggested a second bottle but Hughes managed to make an escape. Botham missed the next match at Leicester in order to receive his OBE, recently announced in the Queen's Birthday Honours.

Botham was perhaps never as solitary in his fame as he was at Durham, although he was always a generous and sociable companion who threw regular parties for team-mates and opponents at his nearby home. One night he invited Hughes to come to dinner with Kath and the children. 'They seemed happy and content and at ease with each other,' Hughes wrote in *A Lot of Hard Yakka*. 'Liam, then fifteen, and Ian behaved more like brothers than father and son ... Did he have any real friends, I wondered? His wife, certainly. She stood up to him and his chequered past probably gave her a psychological authority. But it is hard for anyone else to really relate to him.'

As the Worcestershire dressing room found, having Botham in the team made for a very different life for the Durham players. 'Our side was a cross section of very young and very old but we all had one thing in common, which was being in awe of him,' Graveney said. 'Fortunately we didn't have ice-baths in those days, so we would sit after play and just talk – well, just listen to him, really.'

Maintaining motivation was only one of Botham's problems. His relationship with Geoff Cook, Durham's director of cricket, was strained. They had got on well as team-mates on two England tours, when Cook had kept up with Botham's drinking better than most, but things were different now. Botham suspected that Cook had never actually wanted him at the club; he had heard rumours that Cook had threatened to quit if Botham was recruited. What was unarguable was that politically they were polar opposites. Botham said that Cook did not want a 'star system' at the club but a 'socialist cricket republic', adding that if Cook had had his way the team would have sung 'the Red Flag', the old Labour Party anthem, before every match.

'Beefy was further right [politically] than Genghis Khan while Geoff was very big on social equality,' Hughes said. 'Beefy couldn't stand that. But another problem was that Geoff wasn't in awe of him. Geoff stood up to him and was quite belligerent.' Cook was conciliatory when asked about Botham's contribution to the Durham project. 'As an England team-mate he had been fun, unpredictable and brilliant; as an employer ten years later, you wanted some of those qualities but perhaps not all. He gave credibility to an enterprise that needed it, but his impact on the field was not that big.' Cook would not have been pleased with Botham turning up more or less when he liked and rarely practising seriously.

Botham was perhaps fortunate to be recalled by England for the last three one-dayers, which took place in late August after Pakistan had taken the Test series 2–1. During Botham's absence, the bad feeling between the sides had resurfaced. Both sides harboured grievances. Pakistan, now led by the combative Javed Miandad, bridled at how they were treated by English umpires; England suspected foul play as Wasim and Waqar swung the ball devastatingly late to reap forty-three wickets, Mickey Stewart hinting that they had been tampering with the ball. When England now took an unbeatable 3–0 lead in the one-dayers, trouble flared in the fourth game at Lord's, where the umpires decided to replace the ball being used by Pakistan. Although neither umpires nor match referee would publicly comment, the implication of ball-tampering was clear, and after the game – won by Pakistan despite the ball change – Botham told Chris Lander, with whom he now wrote a column for the *Daily Mirror*, of England's suspicions. With this act, he was pouring petrol on some already mighty flames. Wasim Akram and Waqar Younis vehemently denied any wrongdoing.

While the press played the story for all it was worth, officialdom buried its head in the sand. The ICC (International Cricket Conference) ruled the matter closed without convicting or clearing Pakistan and the TCCB told the England players to keep quiet. Botham's friend Allan Lamb, who had already been told that he would not be chosen for that winter's tour and who (also in the *Mirror*) alleged that the Pakistanis had cheated and that former Pakistan fast bowler Sarfraz Nawaz had shown him how to tamper with the ball when they had played together at Northamptonshire, was punished by the TCCB as well as his county and never played for England again.

The final one-dayer in Manchester was not only Lamb's last England game but Botham's too – he did not bat and took no catches or wickets. While neither could have known this for sure, they treated it with an end-of-term mischievousness. On arriving to bat, Lamb handed umpire Dickie Bird a mobile phone, then still regarded as a new-fangled instrument. Moments later the phone rang in Bird's pocket. He answered it and found Botham on the other end, calling from the dressing-room and asking if he could speak to Lamb. It was all done as a joke at the expense of Bird, who was easy to tease and would never have thrown the book at them.

At the start of the 1993 season, Botham announced that it would be his last. It was a tacit admission of the obvious, that he no longer had the ability or desire to carry on. But even so, he had not given up hoping for the grand farewell he had missed out on in Melbourne. With the Australians touring, what better way would there have been for him to go out than in an Ashes Test, hopefully helping England to win in the process?

Botham rapidly convinced himself that this scenario was possible. It helped that during the winter – while he had been making a lucrative speaking tour around Australia with Viv Richards – England had lost badly on the subcontinent, so there was every chance of team changes when the summer began. No sensible judge, though, would have advocated Botham for an England recall at this late stage; he was plainly yesterday's man. But when had logic ever stopped anyone writing a story about Botham? When he was then invited to face the Australians at Arundel for the Duchess of Norfolk's XI, Botham and some sections of the press interpreted it as his opportunity to impress the selectors – conveniently ignoring the fact that this was essentially a social fixture and the make-up of the Duchess's team was determined by which counties were not otherwise engaged. Hence the Duchess's XI contained four players from Kent and four from Durham. The three remaining members of the side were retired from professional cricket.

In no way was the match a Test trial but when Botham bowled ten tidy overs for two wickets, including that of Australia captain Allan Border, some newspapers felt they had a story and Botham believed he had made a case. Ted Dexter, reasonably but in a typically heavy-handed fashion, brushed aside in a BBC radio interview the idea that Botham remained a credible pick. 'Perhaps the Aussies want us to pick him,' was his gist. Botham, furious, demanded an apology, and eventually received one during a contrite telephone call from Dexter. It was a ridiculous episode that served as a reminder not only of Dexter's poor man-management skills but of Botham's capacity for self-delusion. Botham even devoted a lengthy passage to this apparent snub in a chapter of his autobiography.

Needless to say, he heard nothing from the selectors about playing against Australia, even after three one-day internationals and the first two Tests had been lost. England opted instead for youth when wholesale changes were made for the third Test, giving debuts to four players. Botham in fact had just had a very good match against his former county Worcestershire, scoring 101 in a backs-to-the-wall situation, as well as showing sustained commitment by bowling 51 overs during a taut game. But he had done nothing before that to suggest Dexter's disinterest had been a mistake. Durham, who had won only one game against serious opposition all season, were not even giving him the new ball.

When Dexter, perhaps seeking a conciliatory gesture, then called and asked if he would lead an England A team on a short tour of Holland, Botham gave him short shrift. A 'clog-dancing mission' was a very long way from his idea of a big send-off.

While the third Test was going on, Botham endured probably the most miserable championship match of his life, Durham being bowled out twice by Surrey on the second day after conceding 473 runs on the first. Botham went wicketless and lasted a total of eight balls in two innings. A few days later, Durham's last hope of silverware disappeared with defeat in the NatWest Trophy to Glamorgan, a contest given added spice by the presence in the opposition of Viv Richards. In this last meeting Richards once more came out on top, taking the catch that removed Botham and scoring an unbeaten forty-five.

With nothing left to play for, Botham arrived at the Durham University ground for the county's match against the Australians and told Cook and Graveney that he was ready to make it his last first-class appearance, although he was ready to carry on playing in the Sunday league. Unsurprisingly, Cook thought it best that he should stop playing altogether with immediate effect. This decision was to be vindicated when Durham without him went on to win their last six Sunday league matches, their first sustained success.

The suddenness of Botham's decision to quit did not go down well with either club or sponsors. Don Robson, the chairman who had been instrumental in Durham achieving first-class status and in signing Botham, was upset that he had not been informed in person and this probably had something to do with the club's hard-line attitude, Botham being told that he would not receive his final pay cheque until he had returned his sponsored car. Botham also became embroiled in a contractual dispute with Scottish and Newcastle Breweries, who claimed he had not appeared in sufficient speaking engagements on their premises; Botham counter-claimed by saying that the brewery had halted the agreement.

His final appearance, albeit it against his favourite enemy, was a shabby, unsatisfactory affair – the fiercest of competitors finishing his career in a fixture on which nothing rode. Although he had little to do with it, Durham made the Australians follow on, but the touring team held out for a draw easily enough.

Botham would not publicly confirm his retirement until he had 'revealed' the news in the *Daily Mirror* on the final morning, after which a drove of reporters and camera crews descended for the last rites. Having given a lengthy farewell press conference during a rain break, Botham took the field for a final, fruitless spell with the ball. For his very last over at David Boon he pulled faces and mimicked Jeff Thomson's action, before unzipping his trousers and letting his 'old man' dangle free while he sent down the final delivery. Boon managed to control his astonishment sufficiently to not get out.

This prank appeared to go undetected by those beyond the boundary and the crowd gave Botham a warm salute as he took his sweater from the umpire. 'Even the old grumps who usually moaned about his lost commitment got to their feet,' said Kim Hughes, who was watching from the players' area. Botham then kept wicket in batting gloves and no pads. But word of his antics got out and *Wisden* expressed its displeasure, describing his performance as 'unbecoming and flippant'. He had been determined to do something memorable, even if it meant a Harvey Smith-style gesture. A World Cup final in Melbourne it was not.

Among many tributes to his playing career was one by Jonathan Margolis in the *Sunday Times*, which hailed Botham as a symbol of Thatcherite Britain. There were some striking similarities in the personal histories of Botham and the former prime minister – from the long years of service (Thatcher led her party from 1975 to 1990, Botham represented England from 1976 to 1992) to the inability to sleep more than a few hours a night; from the raw energy in the face of opposition (Thatcher hand-bagging Michael Foot and Neil Kinnock; Botham savaging vulnerable bowlers) to the proximity of their defining hours (Headingley '81, Falklands '82).

Botham, with his go-getting attitude and rags-to-riches story, was an example of what someone could achieve in Thatcher's Britain. 'More than any other popular hero he does symbolise the era,' Margolis claimed. 'They [the public] love Botham because he is anti-Establishment, outspoken and had a rumbustious social life.' He had created tales that were 'not so much Boy's Own Paper as Yob's Own Paper'.

What was he to do next? This problem was one reason why he had carried on playing for so long. If he had dreaded the day of stopping, he had at least had time to get used to the idea as he had not toured during three of the last four winters. But so much of his life had been structured that retirement was bound to be an upheaval.

He had enough irons in fires that neither his diary nor bank account was in grave danger of falling empty. The speaking tours continued, as did the TV appearances on *A Question of Sport* and his column in the *Daily Mirror*. So too did the mighty charity walks. He fished and played golf, at both of which he was accomplished, and went on safari in southern Africa, which proved the start of another major passion, and eventually inspired an enthusiasm for photography. Two days after Botham's last match, his son Liam, who had already played for England under-15s, made his debut for Hampshire's second XI and in typical Bothamesque fashion walked off at the end of his first day with four wickets to his name.

But it was an uncertain time. It was clear that he needed some sort of day job, both for financial reasons and to satisfy his restless energy. A player of his stature could have gone into coaching – most teams now had head coaches – except that he had always had little time for them. In the years to come he would advise many players informally, but predictably never occupied a full-time post despite his name being linked to several jobs. It just was not his style.

Another option was to take up commentary. The rise of satellite TV had led to the broadcasting of a lot more cricket. The BBC was covering England's home Tests but BSkyB had the rights to tours and some domestic one-day events such as the Sunday league and Benson and Hedges Cup. Retired players were the ideal men to have in the commentary box as they understood (for the most part) what was going on out in the middle. Strong opinions were valued but, almost regardless of what they said, famous ex-players could provide a product with the seal of authenticity. At the 1992 World Cup, BSkyB's commentators included Tony Greig and Geoff Boycott while David Gower worked for Australia's Channel Nine. But Botham was reluctant to explore this route. When David English suggested to him during a charity walk that he should try his hand at commentary, he had replied: 'Oh, stuff that.' He said to others that he didn't want to have anything to do with cricket.

Was he really going to slide into a pipe-and-slippers phase without a murmur of dissent? It looked that way when in August 1994 it was announced that he had buried the hatchet with Somerset and accepted honorary life membership of the club eight years after his acrimonious parting. Viv Richards and Joel Garner had been made life members the previous year. Botham said the bitterness was gone. 'Life must go forward,' he said. 'I would rather remember all the good years than the bad one.' The relationship was to grow closer over the years. A new stand at Taunton was named after him in 1998 and he was to act as a club ambassador.

But even at this point, trouble was brewing. Relations between England and Pakistan cricketers had not recovered from the trouble-strewn series of 1992. In November 1993 Sarfraz Nawaz had taken Allan Lamb to court over his allegations in the *Daily Mirror*. During the fourth day of the libel trial, and just before Botham himself was due to give evidence on Lamb's behalf, Sarfraz dropped his action, but the episode had done nothing to take heat out of the situation. In May 1994 Imran Khan had produced a book in which he had confessed to having tampered with the ball during a county match in 1981. This revelation was pounced upon by the British media and as a result Imran, in the course of a number of interviews, was obliged to explain himself. He only made things worse.

Two articles in particular caused trouble. In the *Sun*, Imran said he had copied ball-tampering methods from English players and said: 'The biggest names in English cricket have all done it. And when I say big names, I mean as big as you can get.' And in *India Today*, Imran implied – Botham would maintain – that racism had played a part in the criticisms Botham and Lamb had made of the Pakistan team during the ball-tampering row. He said (although he was to later maintain he had been misquoted): 'Look at people such as Lamb and Botham making statements like, "Oh, I never thought much of him anyway and now it's been proven he's a cheat." There is a lot of racism in [Western] society. Where is this hatred coming from?' Imran added that 'educated Oxbridge types' like Christopher Martin-Jenkins, Tony Lewis and Derek Pringle, all active journalists, were rational while his critics were not. 'Class and upbringing make a difference,' he said.

Soon after, Imran had written to Botham to assure him that he had 'not once called anyone lower class or under class' since he did not believe in the class system. He added that he had never intended for the issue to get personal and had simply wanted the ICC to define acceptable limits of ball-tampering. Three days later Alan Herd, Botham's solicitor, responded by saying that Imran had grossly libelled his client and a public retraction and apology was in order. Imran offered to write an open letter to *The Times* clearing up the matter but the view of Botham and Herd was that the thrust of Imran's defence – essentially, that he had been mis-quoted in the articles – was unsustainable. Six weeks after Imran's original letter, Botham, through Herd, issued a writ of libel. Allan Lamb followed suit. That was the end of the matter, for the time being.

In the meantime, work was nearly complete on Botham's autobiography. The original plan had been for Reg Hayter's agency to write the book but following Botham's split from Hayter nothing more was done until Alan Herd belatedly contacted Hayter after Botham had retired and asked if his agency would still assist in putting the book together. Hayter agreed but the project was beset by further problems. Botham himself had had it in mind that Vic Marks, a former team-mate who had been cricket correspondent of the *Observer* since 1989, would act as ghostwriter but Marks declined. Instead, two of Hayter's reporters were seconded to do the work: Chris Dighton carried out interviews while Peter Hayter, Reg's son and himself cricket correspondent of the *Mail on Sunday*, put together the narrative. Reg Hayter's intention was that the manuscript would be edited by his old friend Frank Nicklin, the former sports editor of the *Sun*, but fearing leaks Herd insisted that it should be handled by as few people as possible. Then, at the age of eighty, Reg Hayter suddenly died.

It was quite common for the subject of sports memoirs to leave the ghost to inject many of the facts, if not some of the expressions of emotion, and this appeared to be the case with Botham. One of the main themes of the book was Botham's admission that he could have treated Kath better over the years – he confessed to having been too wrapped up in his career to give her the time she deserved. Peter Hayter felt that these were among the most honest passages in the book. What also came across was a reluctance to admit to mistakes and an eagerness to bury enemies.

The book sold very well but the reviews were not universally kind when it came out in September 1994. 'If ever a career deserves celebration, it was this one,' Simon Barnes wrote in *The Times*. 'But in his desire to "set the record straight", Botham does the precise opposite. He comes across as a grudging, resentful, small-minded person. He does himself and his career the most colossal disservice.' Christopher Booker, in *Wisden*, called it a 'maundering, self-justifying, two-dimensional ramble, not particularly aimed at a cricket-loving audience'. Imran Khan said that the real hero of the story was Botham's wife, to whom Imran wished all good luck 'in the remainder of her marriage'. (As it happened, Botham's marriage to Kath would outlast Imran's own to Jemima Goldsmith.)

Peter Roebuck, who like Imran had had his differences with Botham, also gave his verdict. 'The thing that probably aggravated most was the way he portrayed himself as the bluff, modest yeoman of England,' Roebuck recalled. 'It was a load of cobblers. People like him have an ability to rewrite events to fit with their imagination, their self-creation, and that is why in some respects they have achieved greatness. Things don't bring them down. They don't get cornered by facts. They rewrite them. Ian had the capacity to out-stare failure and out-stare the truth.' Some corrections were made for later editions.

At around the time that Botham launched his book at the Café Royal in London, he received a major break. In a new broadcasting deal covering English cricket, Sky Sports' stake was significantly increased. Although live coverage of home Tests remained with BBC, Sky won the rights to one-day internationals in England as well as retaining all England's cricket overseas. Sky would also show highlights of England's home Tests. This was a major investment by Sky – the overall deal was worth £15 million per year, a three-fold increase – and the company decided it wanted a team of commentators exclusively its own. The old practice of sharing commentators with other broadcasters ended.

For the sheer potency of his name, Botham was a natural target. He was approached and duly signed up to a lucrative contract that would have overridden any reservations he might have had about commentary work. Sky heralded their new team as 'the youngest, freshest and most committed cricket team we have ever selected'. Their commentators would have a 'positive and constructive' approach. By contrast, Geoff Boycott and David Gower were to now work solely for the BBC.

Botham relished a return to touring life, which had few of the

pitfalls of his time as a player. No one badgered him to practise
and reporters were not monitoring his every move. As long as he
was there for the Tests and one-dayers, he could come and go as he
pleased – and he did, sometimes going back to Britain for a few
days or flying off for a few rounds of golf at an exotic location. He
enjoyed being part of a team again. His family had grown up with
him rarely being at home so it was hardly a novel experience when
he started going away again.

Botham went through the same learning process as every
other player-turned-commentator. He was as initially reluctant
as they all were to dish out criticism of players he knew, but his
deep-seated loyalty towards old mates made this particularly
difficult in his case. Another problem was that he had never
been keen on watching cricket, even matches in which he was
playing, so his knowledge of what was going on, particularly
around the counties, was not always strong (he often got cricket
questions wrong on *A Question of Sport*). But he was a sharp
observer and often 'called' an incident correctly without recourse
to replays.

Botham was not yet two years into his commentating career
when events took a turn for the worse. In July 1996, his libel case
against Imran Khan reached the High Court. Botham said later
that he had never imagined it would get so far but it did so in part
because of his own determination to defend himself. He was stung
by the allegation that he had no class. He had always met challenges head on and his response to Imran was no different. Indeed,
it appeared that one of the contributory factors in his eventual
defeat was that he and Allan Lamb had during the previous two
years rebuffed Imran's attempts at apologies that might have seen
the case settled out of court. 'In your search for the truth,' George
Carman QC, acting for Imran, asked the jury at one point,
'remember this. Who offered the hand of friendship and who
spurned it?'

The case centred on two claims: that Imran had a) called
Botham and Lamb cheats in the *Sun* with respect to his comments

about English cricketers having ball-tampered; and b) had in an article in *India Today* called them racists and said they lacked education and class.

The case lasted thirteen days and provided drama as captivating as any Test match, with Botham and Lamb on one side and Imran on the other summoning an array of past and present big-name cricketers to testify. The sense of theatre was heightened by some witnesses being involved in a Pakistan–England Test match a few miles away at Lord's, with David Lloyd and Michael Atherton, England's coach and captain respectively, being called by Imran's side on the eve of the game (which England eventually lost). It seemed appropriate that after almost fifteen years of cricketing antagonism between England and Pakistan the biggest stars on the teams in Botham and Imran should do battle in court.

It was a case that aroused fierce passions in both countries but in fact its eventual effect was cathartic. Relations between the teams and their boards improved after this and remained amicable even when a ball-tampering row erupted during the 2006 series although after spot-fixing allegations were made against some Pakistan players in England in 2010, Botham himself called for the Pakistan team to be suspended from international cricket, saying, 'They have got to sort their own back yard out.'

It was always going to be a difficult case for both sides, not to mention the jury, who were presented with a prolonged debate about the intricacies of ball-tampering, an issue which confounded many insiders let alone laymen.

For a start, a defamatory statement is presumed to be false unless the defendant – in this instance Imran – could prove its truth. This proved to be a challenge. The thrust of Imran's argument was that he had been misquoted and never called Botham and Lamb cheats or racists in the first place; he said he knew they were not racist. Carman argued that a hundred bowlers could have sued over the *Sun* article in which Imran had said that the world's greatest bowlers had all doctored the ball – but only Botham had complained. Botham and Lamb had attacked Imran in their newspaper articles; Imran was only defending himself. In fact during the trial Imran's side dropped its attempts to show that Botham and Lamb had ever tampered with the ball.

There was to be a test too for Botham. In an effort to diminish any claim for damages resulting from defamatory statements it was open to the defendant to illustrate that the claimants – Botham and Lamb – had poor reputations in the community. This resulted in Carman focusing on the scandals in which Botham had been implicated. Carman, a showman who specialised in celebrity libel cases, tore into Botham with gusto, demanding to know if he had taken drugs and cheated on his wife (Botham admitted to taking a certain amount of pot but assured the court that he and his wife had a very successful marriage). This process occupied three days of the trial and it must have been a harrowing experience for Botham and his wife, who attended the entire trial. Botham said that he felt it unfair that Kath was required to sit through such an ordeal while the same treatment was not meted out to Imran but this missed the point: it was the characters of Botham and Lamb that were at issue.

Atherton said he had feared for Botham's chances when he stood in the witness box and saw Imran's pregnant wife Jemima looking balefully at the jurors with her big doey eyes.

A jury of seven men and five women found for Imran by 10–2, which constituted a majority verdict. Botham's side were stunned. Charles Gray QC, who acted for Botham, was puzzled by the verdict: 'The result remains a complete mystery to me and to most other people. The jury must have taken the view that sportsmen should not be litigating against one another in court.'

Mr Justice French said the proceedings had been an exercise in futility. Costs to Botham and Lamb were estimated by 1999 (when they finally dropped an appeal) at £260,000 and £140,000 respectively. However, the parties were still squabbling over the costs in 2004. Thanks to his well-paid job with Sky, Botham was better able to afford his bill than Lamb, who had retired from playing in April 1996 in order to publish an autobiography free from TCCB censorship. In a later edition of the book, Lamb said that he and Botham had sought financial compensation as well as an apology from Imran, 'but nothing silly'. Imran continued to insist that the libel suit was unnecessary. 'Botham totally overreacted and took the whole thing too personally,' he said.

Although with time Botham's hostility towards Imran softened as they were brought together through charity work, he had suffered a bitter and expensive defeat. It was perhaps all the more bitter for several fellow England cricketers being brought on to support Imran. Apart from Atherton and Lloyd, these included Tony Lewis, Derek Pringle and Geoff Boycott.

Botham certainly objected strongly to the involvement of Boycott, who had been subpoenaed by Imran's side to repeat what he had said on a TV programme about ball-tampering, that while it might not be strictly within the laws it was not in many instances a heinous offence.

Boycott said that after the court case Botham spoke badly of him, particularly in the updated versions of his autobiography. 'He criticised me as a person and player and did things which he ought to be embarrassed about. It wasn't fair and I found it very sad because I admired him immensely. It was ridiculous. I don't think I uttered a wrong word against him. He wrote outrageous things about me in his book, so I wrote him a letter and explained that I'd been subpoenaed and there was nothing I could have done about it. We have been fine ever since and get on well. It was a shame [because] I don't think deep down he thought those things about me. I hope one day he'll admit they weren't a fair reflection. I know they weren't.'

To Botham's credit, he did tone down his comments on Boycott. In the updated versions of his first autobiography, published after the libel trial, he was critical of Boycott as a team-mate, as a player, and as a witness at the trial, where he accused him of 'childish posturing' and making a 'mockery of a very serious business'. However, in his second autobiography, which drew heavily on the first book and was published in 2007, all reference to

Boycott's appearance at the trial was removed, while coverage of the trial itself was cut from twenty-three pages to three. Elsewhere, Boycott was twice referred to as 'legendary' and once as an 'absolutely brilliant batsman', and even when Boycott was described as 'extremely selfish' Botham conceded that the same could be said of him. Botham did though still claim he had deliberately run out Boycott in Christchurch in 1978. Probably another factor in the moderation of his comments was that Boycott had recently overcome throat cancer.

If taking Imran to court proved to be one of Botham's more serious errors, another was to follow. While commentating in Australia during the Ashes tour of 1998–99, Botham met a waitress in Sydney called Kylie Verrells and began a sexual relationship with her that was to last two years. He not only saw her when he was in Australia but also brought her to Europe. When Kath suspected something was going on and challenged him about it, he denied it.

As was perhaps inevitable – had he learned nothing from past experiences? – details of the affair reached the ears of the tabloid papers. In January 2001, Botham took a phone call from the *News of the World* telling him they were to run a story about it the next day. At that point, he confessed to his wife, telling her that he had been infatuated with Ms Verrells but that the affair was now over. 'I told her I wanted to stay and try to repair the damage to our marriage that I'd caused, but I'd understand if she wanted me to go,' Botham admitted in his second autobiography. 'She was white with anger but she didn't shout or scream, or cry. As she later told me, "I'd done nothing wrong and I wasn't going to show a weakness".'

Kath had warned him once, more than ten years earlier, that she would leave if he did not moderate his behaviour at a time when he was upset at not being selected for England's 1990 tour of the Caribbean. She might have considered herself well within her rights to do so now. Botham said Kath discussed the matter with her mother, who advised her that she should only leave if it was going to make her life better. 'In the end, Kath decided to stick with the marriage for the sake of the children,' Botham added, 'and we've come through those sometimes turbulent years to a time when we are both genuinely content in each other's company.'

Kath insisted that he tell his children before they found out elsewhere. Sarah was so furious that she didn't speak to him again for several months. 'I was so, so hurt by him,' she recalled in a newspaper interview in 2010. 'It was only my mum who eventually got us talking ... I thought he was perfect. I can't to this day get my head around it, and I still think how lucky he is to have my mum because not many people would have put up with it.'

Perhaps against the expectations of many, the Bothams have remained married for more than thirty-four years – and counting. One reason may be their belief that families are at the centre of life and not things to give up on lightly. 'It's a catholic – with a small "c" – thing,' said Rod Bransgrove. 'I'm sure that Kath had a tough time in the early years but they are actually very close. If Ian speaks to her on the phone he'll say, "How are you doing, how are the kids and how is the dog?" Even Pinot, their Jack Russell, who he will sit cuddling, is a member of the family. Liam lives in the extension of the same house and Sarah is there a fair bit. His mum is often there, as are Kath's parents. He is big on family.'

Liam, having retired from playing professional rugby in 2005, ran a pheasant farm on the family's thirty acres, while Sarah eventually took over from Kath as the organiser of her father's charity walks and worked for Leukaemia and Lymphoma Research.

Botham had lived an enviable and affluent life since hanging up his boots. Just as he caught the first wave of money that went to the players through the Packer revolution, so he rode the first one to seriously enrich ex-players in the commentary box. In the late 1980s, some contemporaries had worried what might become of him when he stopped playing, but he eventually found himself in the most assured and stable of positions.

As the most famous of Sky TV's cricket pundits, he travelled in style and was reportedly paid better than any of his colleagues. This work consolidated his already substantial wealth and helped fund a large home in North Yorkshire and a villa in Almeira, Desert Springs, in Spain, where four generations of his family decamped for holidays and where Botham's daughter Sarah ran a restaurant, Los Pepes. He drove a Bentley and owned a third-share in a wine label with Bob Willis and Geoff Merrill, the Australian producer.

He knew how to enjoy himself, as he always had. He once described how he liked to end his day commentating at the Melbourne Cricket Ground. It involved having a Harley-Davidson on standby outside the ground which took him to a helicopter waiting at a helipad a couple of miles away which in turn flew him to Mornington Peninsula, where he rented a house. 'We've got it down to such a fine art,' he said, 'that exactly seventeen minutes after the umpires have removed the bails to signal the end of the day's play ... I'm already sitting down with Kath on the terrace outside the house with a glass of wine in my hand.' Not bad for a lad from Yeovil.

Crucially, his reputation had not suffered with the years; indeed, on the contrary, it had grown enormously. Finding another cricketer of Botham's stature was always going to be difficult, if not impossible, but English cricket went through such dog days in the late 1980s and 1990s that harking back to the glory days of Botham became a natural game to play.

There were a variety of reasons for England's decline. While other countries became stronger and more adventurous – Sri Lanka followed India and Pakistan in winning their first World Cup in 1996 – England appeared to squander whatever talent came their way. Gifted players such as Mark Ramprakash and Graeme Hick inexplicably floundered in the Test arena and the team seemed perennially stuck in a backs-to-the-wall frame of mind. The most successful players were scrappers such as Graham Thorpe and Michael Atherton rather than ones who trusted their instincts as Botham had done. England went twelve years without winning a major Test series and were utterly anonymous in four World Cups after 1992. Whenever they were in a desperate situation in a Test, the spirit of Headingley '81 was invoked without ever summoning a repetition of that great escape.

The problem of finding an all-rounder worth the name stretched into the new century – Chris Lewis, Dominic Cork and Craig White all flattered to deceive and Ben Hollioake tragically died in a car crash – and it was not until Andrew Flintoff blossomed in 2003 that a solution was found. Flintoff produced some major performances with bat and ball over the next two years and was central to England regaining the Ashes in 2005. Briefly, he matched the kind of performances managed by Botham, but his body was unable to stand the strain and he was rarely fit from 2006 onwards.

If all this was frustrating for England, it only ensured that the legend of Botham lived on and the fact that he was regularly on hand to bemoan the deficiencies of the modern generation only highlighted the comparison. One of his main grouses was the physical frailty of so many modern players – but then coping with pain was one of Botham's specialist subjects. 'One thing that makes him spit blood is someone getting a blow on the glove and going off for a scan,' David Gower said. 'You'll see him stomping around at the back of the commentary box, swearing away. "What does he want a scan for? . . . Tape it up and get out there again." When he was playing for England, he would try and ignore pain. He is delightfully grumpy about the way injuries are treated now. It's very old-fashioned and pure Fred Trueman.'

Botham's well-heeled existence at Sky TV effectively ruled him out of any formal administrative involvement with English cricket. Lord MacLaurin, the first chairman of the England and Wales Cricket Board, which replaced the TCCB in 1997, frankly admitted that the board could not afford him. And why would a former England captain have wanted to get his hands dirty trying to sort out what was still a sclerotic system when he could take a job in the commentary box that was unlikely to be cut short when results proved unsatisfactory? Far more England captains from Botham's time onwards ended up working in the media than in coaching or administration, an area that was now dominated by businessmen rather than former players who had enjoyed a good education.

Botham was consulted informally. David Lloyd, the England coach, invited him to speak to the team during the 1996–97 tour of Zimbabwe and New Zealand. Lord MacLaurin said he spoke to him occasionally over a glass of wine and found Botham supportive of some of the innovations brought in during the late 1990s, including the idea of central contracts. David Graveney, who became chairman of selectors in 1996, often sought Botham's advice. 'I used him as a sounding board,' Graveney said. 'He never watched domestic cricket but he was close to the players. His input was about how people [might] cope on the big stage.'

Rod Bransgrove said that as Hampshire chairman he regularly drew on Botham's views. 'He's often the first person I speak to about players and coaches because he is usually very honest and open, although I might make a different decision in the end. He spends a lot of time attending functions and talking to people about cricket. He's very aware of what's going on.' Botham also talked often to Geoff Miller, an old friend, after Miller took over from Graveney as chairman of selectors.

'He's quite compulsive,' Bransgrove said. 'He will come to a rapid conclusion and fight like mad to protect it. But the following week, when he's digested everything, he could end up arguing the exact opposite with somebody else. In some respects he is a bit like Malcolm Marshall. Malcolm was a fantastic font of knowledge but maybe not the best coach because he could never quite understand why the person he was coaching couldn't immediately do what he could do. Sometimes people didn't recognise that Botham and Marshall were slightly different because they were blessed with this bit of genius.'

It was through Botham's auspices that Bransgrove's county Hampshire signed Kevin Pietersen in 2005. Pietersen had been looking to leave Nottinghamshire since 2003 after falling out with team-mates and his agent was Adam Wheatley, managing director of Mission Sports Management, of which Botham was chairman. Botham had initially encouraged Pietersen to join Somerset but subsequently put him in touch with Shane Warne, the Hampshire captain, and after Pietersen and Warne immediately hit it off a deal was soon done. Botham, it was noted, was not big on criticising Pietersen during commentary.

It was not only Pietersen that Botham backed. He was also very loyal towards the England team in general, regularly predicting in his column in the *Mirror* that they would win the big series, including the Ashes. He even got it right in 2005 and 2009. But this was not simply blind faith. He genuinely believed in the abilities of many of the players and his support was appreciated by many.

It was perhaps as well, though, that he was not involved in England cricket in an official capacity because he would have had sections of the media on constant alert. In New Zealand in 1997 he commandeered England coach David Lloyd as his drinking partner during a fishing trip and Lloyd admits that as a result he 'lost' a day of the tour.

There were other times when his behaviour on tour was not appreciated. Botham was initially supportive of Duncan Fletcher, a specialist coach from southern Africa who had never played Test cricket, when Fletcher took over from Lloyd in 1999, but relations between them were to deteriorate during Fletcher's eight years in charge. They were difficult by the start of England's tour of the Caribbean in 2004 when, according to Fletcher, Sky called a meeting with Fletcher and Michael Vaughan, the England captain, aimed at improving the relationship between broadcaster and the national team. 'Most of the conversation centred around him [Botham],' Fletcher wrote in his autobiography, 'as he appeared the one obstacle to improving the relationship.' Fletcher added:

'Some critics said he was inconsistent in his thoughts and did not do enough investigative work before a day's commentary.' He claimed that the England players did not listen to Botham's views and were surprised at some of his opinions.

An incident that cannot have endeared Botham to Fletcher occurred later on the same tour, when Ashley Giles picked up a groin strain that put him out of two one-day internationals. The injury was sustained while Giles was sitting on a two-man inflatable towed by a speedboat driven by Botham; according to Vaughan, Giles was at the time 'holding on for dear life and being flung about at the end of the rope'. During the Ashes tour of 2006–07 there was to be further trouble when Botham and Flintoff got together in Sydney. Vaughan claimed they were out 'until late into the wee hours'. Fletcher said that they [Botham and Flintoff] were up 'the whole night' drinking and did not get to bed until 7am. He claimed that when Flintoff turned up for practice at 10am still under the influence, Fletcher cut short the session and threatened to drop Flintoff from the team, though in the end he pulled back from doing so. His fear – that the media would turn on him if he dropped Flintoff, 'the national hero' – might have been recognisable to those who had handled Botham in earlier times.

When, several weeks later, Flintoff was suspended for a late-night drinking session thirty-six hours before a World Cup match, Botham defended him by saying that Flintoff's only crime had been 'getting caught'. It looked a weak argument alongside the more withering condemnations being offered by his fellow commentators, but Botham was in a difficult position, not least because he belonged to a generation that had often drunk heavily on the night before a game, let alone two nights before.

There was a danger of Botham the commentator suffering the fate that had befallen him as a player, with modernising forces leaving him looking outdated. Sky generally had to review their cricket coverage in response to the innovative approach provided by Channel Four, who took the rights from the BBC to England's home Tests in 1999 before Sky themselves acquired them in 2006. One thing they did was bring in two more ex-England captains as commentators in Nasser Hussain and Michael Atherton. Sharp and more in tune with how the England team operated, they raised the bar for all of those already ensconced behind the microphone, but Botham survived the make-over.

Some who were not keen to be quoted suggested Botham's staying powers might have been on the wane, but David Gower thought it would be unwise to push this point far. 'He might fall asleep earlier but he hasn't quietened down that much,' he said. 'His basic methods are the same. We were on safari in South Africa and ended up sharing a room for three nights. It must have been the first time I'd shared a room with him in thirty years. Each morning there would be a 5am knock at the door and off we'd go in the Land Rover, looking for leopards and the like. Despite the long days, there would be no let-up over dinner. Even when you were supposed to be relaxing, he found competition in trying to out-drink everyone else. He'd stumble into bed at some ungodly hour but come 5am he'd spring up again, have a quick shower and a massive cup of black coffee, and attack the day as though nothing had happened. There may be a few signs of wear and tear, but not many.'

Bransgrove, on whose yacht Botham has often stayed during Caribbean tours, agreed. 'He's so enthusiastic and positive. A glass is always more than half full with Beefy – in more ways than one. There's always a way around every problem and he never gets tired. He's constantly going from one commitment to the other. It's hard to imagine him ever being unwell – he won't acknowledge illness – but he does work on maintaining his fitness. He is starting to take account of the fact he's mortal.'

Botham's drive was never more in evidence than with his charity work. This remained a major feature of his life, if not an obsession. Charity work not only allowed him to give full expression to his selflessness and generosity but also his long-standing desire to be at the head of any mission. As he marched through towns and villages, at a ferocious pace that most followers could only keep up with by breaking into a run, he was captain of a team once again, and once more in a position to show off his indifference to pain. Indeed, conquering pain seemed to be another excuse for a competition, something else he could win at. But what also drove him on were the memories of his meetings with leukaemia patients, some of which were harrowing even for someone exposed to many such encounters.

'I met him for dinner one night in London,' Bransgrove said. 'He'd had a meeting beforehand, something to do with leukaemia. It turned out he had met this chap – a wonderful man, a good-looking bloke, forty years old, attractive wife, young family, real go-getter, making something of his life. He had been diagnosed with leukaemia and had very little time, and all he wanted to do was meet Ian Botham. Beefy was visibly distressed, emotionally drained. He needed that first drink to cope. I'd not seen him like that. He found some of those things quite tough.'

Botham's mantra was that the walks would go on until the disease was beaten. By 2010, when he walked from Manchester to London through ten cities to mark the twenty-fifth anniversary of his original fundraiser from John O'Groats to Land's End, he had generated about £12 million for Leukaemia and Lymphoma Research and the five-year survival rate for acute lymphoblastic leukaemia, the most common form of childhood leukaemia, had improved from 20 per cent in 1985 to 90 per cent. As a benefactor for LLR, Botham stood head and shoulders above all others.

He also worked on behalf of other charitable causes with equal energy. He became involved in the rebuilding work in Sri Lanka following the devastation wrought by the 2004 tsunami and he spoke at HIV fundraising events in South Africa.

It was his fundraising that clinched his knighthood in June 2007, which was officially awarded to him in recognition for services to cricket and charity work. He was the tenth English cricketer to be knighted and, of the previous nine, seven had been as much administrators as players. The exceptions were Jack Hobbs and Len Hutton, both of whom had elevated the status of the professional cricketer at a time when the amateur–professional divide still meant something. When Botham received his award from the Queen a few months later, their conversation had concentrated on his charity work. 'I've had some great moments in sport and other walks of life but nothing matches this,' he said. 'It was mind-blowing, magnificent.' He celebrated afterwards with a reception at Lord's for family and close friends. 'He found it a very moving occasion,' said one who was present. 'It was a momentous event in his life.'

Some detected a change in him after that. 'He's always been a great man of England, the Queen and all that, and being Sir Ian Botham means an enormous amount to him,' said another friend. 'He feels the knighthood has raised his profile. He likes people to call him Sir Ian, although he doesn't mind if you call him Beefy either. Being a knight has changed him. He's different. It has put a spring in his step. He's going to do a lot more walks.'

Of his charity work there could only be good to say. Unequivocally, he made a difference to the lives of many leukaemia patients.

As a cricketer the final verdict was less clear. The good certainly outweighed the bad, but the bad must come into the reckoning. He will be remembered as the great champion and great hero of his younger days, when he made the remarkable a routine occurrence and played with a talent and energy few cricketers have ever matched – in English history perhaps only W.G. Grace himself, and from other countries perhaps only Gary Sobers and Imran Khan. He was obviously highly talented but, as so many of those who knew him when he was young testified, he did not obviously stand out as a future world-beater. His special gifts were an unquenchable self-belief, a belief that bordered on the delusional, and a breathtaking capacity for physical endurance and bravery. Had he been a soldier, he would have won a VC, probably posthumously.

Some of his talents were quite un-English. He had an ability to engage with the ordinary men and women watching him from the terraces, perhaps because he understood he was one of them, and in other circumstances might have been sitting where they were. He wanted to entertain them and knew exactly what was required to do so – such as beating the Aussies and hitting sixes. His willingness to take risks was also a trait rarely found in England cricketers, among whom caution and calculation are more common features, and much of his career was a tribute to what can be achieved by daring and positive thinking. He was unashamedly competitive with everyone.

For the five years from 1978 to 1982 he was the best and most glamorous cricketer in the world, and few cricketers in history have enjoyed periods to match it. He should not be marked down too severely for facing teams depleted by Kerry Packer: others made hay too at the same time and – with the exception of the West Indies – he performed pretty well against these same sides when they were at full strength.

The sheer scale of his Test record – 5,200 runs, 383 wickets, 120 catches – silences most dissent, but not all. There is a curious arc to Botham's career and to his involvement with those sides he played for. If it is undeniable that his presence inspired and enhanced the performances of every team he was involved with – England, Somerset, Worcestershire, Queensland and Durham – it was also unarguable that at the point he left them they were in difficulties, and in the period afterwards they won little. He taught team-mates much about how to win, but perhaps also showed them some things about how to lose. Not only was he not suited to captaincy, he was not much suited to leading by example. The power was somewhat wasted.

He was truly a victim of his own success. He came to believe too much in his own legend. To the end of his career he remained in thrall to the inspiration that had served him so well but forgot the perspiration that had got him to the pinnacle of the game. General standards rose but he refused to recognise this by modifying his approach and when the results tailed off, cynicism set in.

One English trait that he had been loyal to was a fondness for not wanting to look like he was trying too hard – ironically the last legacy of the amateur tradition that the young Botham would have so despised.

# Botham's Record

## How Botham Performed against Each Country in Tests

|  | Matches | Runs | Avge | 100s | Wkts | Avge | 5 wkts | Won | Lost | Drawn |
|---|---|---|---|---|---|---|---|---|---|---|
| v Australia | 36 | 1,673 | 29.4 | 4 | 148 | 27.7 | 9 | 16 | 11 | 9 |
| v West Indies | 20 | 792 | 21.4 | 0 | 61 | 35.2 | 3 | 1 | 13 | 6 |
| v New Zealand | 15 | 846 | 40.3 | 3 | 64 | 23.4 | 6 | 7 | 3 | 5 |
| v India | 14 | 1,201 | 70.6 | 5 | 59 | 26.4 | 6 | 3 | 1 | 10 |
| v Pakistan | 14 | 647 | 32.4 | 2 | 40 | 31.8 | 2 | 4 | 4 | 6 |
| v Sri Lanka | 3 | 41 | 13.7 | 0 | 11 | 28.2 | 1 | 2 | 0 | 1 |
| TOTALS | 102 | 5,200 | 33.5 | 14 | 383 | 28.4 | 27 | 33 | 32 | 37 |

Botham missed 54 Tests during his career. After playing his first two games in 1977, he was injured for the following match and not selected for the next three. He then appeared in 65 consecutive Tests between February 1978 and March 1984.

From March 1984 until his final appearance in June 1992, he appeared in 35 Tests and missed 50. Of those 50, he was injured for 12, unavailable for another 12 during winter tours he chose not to join, missed four through serving a drugs ban and was not selected for another 22.

## How Botham Served His Test Captains

| Captain | Matches | Runs | Avge | Wkts | Avge | Balls bowled per match | W | L | D |
|---|---|---|---|---|---|---|---|---|---|
| Mike Brearley (1977–81) | 26 | 1,489 | 41.4 | 150 | 18.8 | 257.3 | 17 | 4 | 5 |
| Geoff Boycott (1978) | 3 | 212 | 53.0 | 17 | 18.3 | 269.3 | 1 | 1 | 1 |
| Ian Botham (1980–1) | 12 | 276 | 13.1 | 35 | 33.1 | 184.3 | 0 | 4 | 8 |
| Keith Fletcher (1981–2) | 7 | 453 | 50.3 | 20 | 36.3 | 227.4 | 1 | 1 | 5 |
| Bob Willis (1982–4) | 18 | 1,276 | 41.2 | 61 | 35.0 | 219.9 | 7 | 5 | 6 |
| David Gower (1982–9) | 21 | 933 | 26.7 | 74 | 36.2 | 210.5 | 3 | 14 | 4 |
| Mike Gatting (1986–7) | 10 | 480 | 36.9 | 19 | 42.7 | 160.1 | 2 | 2 | 6 |
| Graham Gooch (1991–2) | 5 | 81 | 13.5 | 7 | 35.0 | 106.8 | 2 | 1 | 2 |
| TOTALS | 102 | 5,200 | 33.5 | 383 | 28.4 | 213.9 | 33 | 32 | 37 |

Botham played in fifteen winning Test series – seven under Mike Brearley, three under Bob Willis, two under Graham Gooch and one under each of Keith Fletcher, David Gower and Mike Gatting. He also won two one-day international tournaments under Gatting in Australia in 1986–87. He was a losing finalist in the World Cup under Brearley in 1979 and Gooch in 1992.

## Botham's Place among the Leading All-rounders in Test Cricket

Those scoring 3,000 runs and taking 140 wickets, with a bowling average no more than five runs higher than batting average:

| Player | Matches | Runs | Avge | Wickets | Avge | Catches | Difference in Avges |
|---|---|---|---|---|---|---|---|
| GS Sobers | 93 | 8,032 | 57.8 | 235 | 34.0 | 109 | +23.8 |
| JH Kallis | 140 | 11,126 | 55.1 | 266 | 31.6 | 159 | +23.5 |
| Imran Khan | 88 | 3,807 | 37.7 | 362 | 22.8 | 28 | +14.9 |
| SM Pollock | 108 | 3,781 | 32.3 | 421 | 23.1 | 72 | +9.2 |
| AW Greig | 58 | 3,599 | 40.4 | 141 | 32.2 | 87 | +8.2 |
| IT Botham | 102 | 5,200 | 33.5 | 383 | 28.4 | 120 | +5.1 |
| RJ Hadlee | 86 | 3,124 | 27.2 | 431 | 22.3 | 39 | +4.9 |
| CL Cairns | 62 | 3,320 | 33.5 | 218 | 29.4 | 14 | +4.1 |
| Kapil Dev | 131 | 5,248 | 31.1 | 434 | 29.6 | 64 | +1.5 |
| A Flintoff | 79 | 3,845 | 31.8 | 226 | 32.8 | 52 | -1.0 |
| DL Vettori | 100 | 3,962 | 30.7 | 325 | 33.9 | 55 | -3.2 |

(figures correct up to 6 October 2010)

## The Five Phases of Botham's Career

Botham's career as a professional cricketer, which began in September 1973 and ended in July 1993, can be divided into five roughly equal periods (in the tables below the 'year' begins in September). From the tables it becomes clear how much of his best cricket was played between 1977 and 1985 – he was at his peak as a bowler from 1977 to 1981 and as a batsman from 1981 to 1985.

He was a hugely influential figure between 1977 and 1981, helping England to win 49.3 per cent of Tests and one-day internationals and Somerset to win 78.3 per cent of one-day matches, including the first three trophies in their history.

While his form in Test and first-class cricket fell away after 1985 – England winning only four out of 23 Tests with him in the side – he remained valuable in the one-day arena, helping England to win 65.9 per cent of their one-day games and Worcestershire 65.1 per cent of theirs.

Overall he took part in 99 victories for England – 33 in Tests and 66 in one-day internationals – more than any other England player at the time he retired.

## All first-class cricket

| Period (Sep–Aug) | Matches | Runs | Avge | 100s | Wkts | Avge | 5wkts | Won | Lost | Drawn/Tied |
|---|---|---|---|---|---|---|---|---|---|---|
| 1973–76 | 77 | 2,785 | 24.9 | 2 | 246 | 25.6 | 12 | 22 | 24 | 31 |
| 1977–80 | 98 | 4,629 | 34.8 | 13 | 389 | 22.9 | 26 | 36 | 17 | 45 |
| 1981–84 | 94 | 6,023 | 43.6 | 14 | 261 | 29.6 | 12 | 25 | 27 | 42 |
| 1985–88 | 77 | 3,404 | 30.4 | 4 | 165 | 33.0 | 6 | 22 | 29 | 26 |
| 1989–93 | 56 | 2,558 | 33.7 | 5 | 111 | 31.6 | 3 | 8 | 18 | 30 |
| TOTALS | 402 | 19,399 | 34.0 | 38 | 1,172 | 27.2 | 59 | 113 | 115 | 174 |

## All one-day cricket

| Period (Sep–Aug) | Matches | Runs | Avge | 100s | Wkts | Avge | 5wkts | Won | Lost | Tied/NR |
|---|---|---|---|---|---|---|---|---|---|---|
| 1973–76 | 82 | 1,276 | 20.6 | 0 | 98 | 26.1 | 0 | 38 | 41 | 3 |
| 1977–80 | 110 | 2,064 | 26.8 | 1 | 143 | 22.8 | 0 | 80 | 29 | 1 |
| 1981–84 | 109 | 2,674 | 31.5 | 1 | 157 | 23.3 | 0 | 61 | 46 | 2 |
| 1985–88 | 78 | 2,230 | 34.3 | 4 | 106 | 24.6 | 3 | 44 | 30 | 4 |
| 1989–93 | 91 | 2,230 | 33.8 | 1 | 108 | 29.4 | 0 | 55 | 33 | 3 |
| TOTALS | 470 | 10,474 | 29.5 | 7 | 612 | 24.9 | 3 | 278 | 179 | 13 |

## Test cricket

| Period (Sep–Aug) | Matches | Runs | Avge | 100s | Wkts | Avge | 5wkts | Won | Lost | Drawn |
|---|---|---|---|---|---|---|---|---|---|---|
| 1973–76 | 2 | 25 | 12.5 | 0 | 10 | 20.2 | 2 | 2 | 0 | 0 |
| 1977–80 | 39 | 1,952 | 33.1 | 8 | 192 | 21.3 | 15 | 16 | 9 | 14 |
| 1981–84 | 38 | 2,432 | 39.9 | 5 | 141 | 33.8 | 8 | 11 | 13 | 14 |
| 1985–88 | 18 | 710 | 26.3 | 1 | 33 | 48.1 | 2 | 2 | 8 | 8 |
| 1989–93 | 5 | 81 | 13.5 | 0 | 7 | 35.0 | 0 | 2 | 1 | 2 |
| TOTALS | 102 | 5,200 | 33.5 | 14 | 383 | 28.4 | 27 | 33 | 31 | 38 |

## One-day internationals

| Period (Sep–Aug) | Matches | Runs | Avge | 100s | Wkts | Avge | 5wkts | Won | Lost | Tied/NR |
|---|---|---|---|---|---|---|---|---|---|---|
| 1973–76 | 2 | 21 | 10.5 | 0 | 2 | 28.5 | 0 | 0 | 2 | 0 |
| 1977–80 | 34 | 542 | 20.8 | 0 | 40 | 28.7 | 0 | 20 | 13 | 1 |
| 1981–84 | 39 | 685 | 22.8 | 0 | 58 | 24.7 | 0 | 19 | 20 | 0 |
| 1985–88 | 23 | 482 | 25.4 | 0 | 18 | 48.4 | 0 | 14 | 8 | 1 |
| 1989–93 | 18 | 383 | 27.4 | 0 | 27 | 23.3 | 0 | 13 | 4 | 1 |
| TOTALS | 116 | 2,113 | 23.2 | 0 | 145 | 28.5 | 0 | 66 | 47 | 3 |

## Botham's Best Matches

In his 402 first-class matches, Botham either scored 80 runs in an innings or took five wickets in an innings in a winning cause on 40 occasions. Up to 1983 he averaged one such performance every 6.5 games, after that one every 30 games. None of these instances occurred while he was captain.

He scored a century and took five wickets in an innings of the same Test on five occasions. Only three other players (Gary Sobers, Mushtaq Mohammad and Jacques Kallis) have done so even twice.

| Batting | Bowling | Match |
|---|---|---|
| 39, 4 | 5–59, 2–58 | Somerset v Leicestershire, Weston-super-Mare, 1974 |
| 44, 0 | 6–16, 0–10 | Somerset v Hampshire, Bournemouth, 1976 |
| 80, 167* | 1–59, 1–16 | Somerset v Nottinghamshire, Trent Bridge, 1976 |
| 88, 0 | 1–43 | Somerset v Leicestershire, Taunton, 1976 |
| 62 | 4–111, 6–50 | Somerset v Sussex, Hove, 1977 |
| 0, 59 | 5–76, 1–74 | Somerset v Warwickshire, Edgbaston, 1977 |
| 114, 40 | 4–69, 4–43 | Somerset v Hampshire, Taunton, 1977 |
| 25 | 5–74, 0–60 | England v Australia, Trent Bridge, 1977 |
| 0 | 5–21, 0–47 | England v Australia, Headingley, 1977 |
| 0, 4* | 3–33, 7–58 | England XI v Otago, Dunedin, 1978 |
| 103, 30* | 5–73, 3–38 | England v New Zealand, Christchurch, 1978 |
| 12 | 1–70, 6–66 | Somerset v Glamorgan, Taunton, 1978 |
| 86 | 5–53, 2–101 | Somerset v Gloucestershire, Taunton, 1978 |
| 100 | 1–52, 0–47 | England v Pakistan, Edgbaston, 1978 |
| 108 | 0–17, 8–34 | England v Pakistan, Lord's, 1978 |
| 20 | 6–43, 3–37 | Somerset v Warwickshire, Weston-super-Mare, 1978 |
| 8 | 6–34, 3–59 | England v New Zealand, Trent Bridge, 1978 |
| 21 | 6–101, 5–39 | England v New Zealand, Lord's, 1978 |
| 56 | 0–41, 5–51 | England XI v New South Wales, Sydney, 1978 |
| 6 | 3–66, 5–70 | England XI v Queensland, Brisbane, 1978 |
| 120 | 2–38, 2–54 | Somerset v Glamorgan, Swansea, 1979 |
| 33 | 2–86, 5–70 | England v India, Edgbaston, 1979 |
| 114 | 6–58, 7–48 | England v India, Bombay, 1980 |
| 94 | 0–18, 1–33 | Somerset v Worcestershire, Weston-super-Mare, 1980 |
| 50, 149* | 6–95, 1–14 | England v Australia, Headingley, 1981 |
| 26, 3 | 1–64, 5–11 | England v Australia, Edgbaston, 1981 |
| 0, 118 | 3–28, 2–86 | England v Australia, Old Trafford, 1981 |
| –, 98 | 1–55, 0–26 | England XI v India Under-22s, Pune, 1981 |
| 67 | 5–46, 1–103 | England v India, Lord's, 1982 |
| 57, 4 | 4–70, 5–74 | England v Pakistan, Headingley, 1982 |
| 41, 131* | 2–24, 1–41 | Somerset v Warwickshire, Taunton, 1982 |
| 98 | 3–29, 5–50 | Somerset v Worcestershire, Taunton, 1982 |
| 152 | 5–38, 0–9 | Somerset v Leicestershire, Leicester, 1983 |

| 103, 27 | 1–33, 0–73 | England v New Zealand, Trent Bridge, 1983 |
| 104*, 17 | 1–70, 0–55 | Somerset v Worcestershire, Weston-super-Mare, 1986 |
| 138 | 2–58, 1–34 | England v Australia, Brisbane, 1986 |
| 29 | 5–41, 0–19 | England v Australia, Melbourne, 1986 |
| 0 | 6–99, 5–76 | Worcestershire v Northamptonshire, Northampton, 1989 |
| 81 | 1–43, 7–54 | Worcestershire v Warwickshire, Worcester, 1991 |
| 61, 0 | 5–67, 1–40 | Worcestershire v Surrey, Worcester, 1991 |

\* Not out

# Acknowledgements

I would like to thank David Luxton, who first proposed the idea for this book; John Witherow and Alex Butler at the *Sunday Times* for their support; and Mike Jones, Rory Scarfe and Ian Allen at Simon & Schuster.

Although this is a work about him rather than with him, Sir Ian Botham himself was unfailingly helpful, as were all of the following:

Jonathan Agnew, Michael Atherton, Ali Bacher, Jack Bannister, John Barclay, Christopher Bazalgette, Scyld Berry, Henry Blofeld, Sarah Botham, Geoff Boycott, Rod Bransgrove, Dennis Breakwell, Mike Brearley, Stephen Brenkley, Chris Broad, Graham Burgess, Neil Burns, Roland Butcher, Ian Chappell, Brian Close, Geoff Cook, Nick Cook, Geoff Cope, Ted Corbett, Colin Croft, Chris Dighton, Barry Dudleston, Ray East, John Emburey, Matthew Engel, David English, Duncan Fearnley, Keith Fletcher, Arthur Francis, David Foot, Joel Garner, Mike Gatting, Pat Gibson, Graham Gooch, Ian Gould, David Gower, David Graveney, Tony Greig, Gideon Haigh, Tim Harms, Peter Hayter, Mike Hendrick, John Hendry, Derek Hodgson, Mike Holding, Simon Hughes, Robin Jackman, Ian Jarrett, Bill Jones, Frank Keating, Roy Kerslake, Ken Lawrence, Geoff Lawson, James Lawton, Alan Lee, Vincent Lench, John Lever, Simon Lister, Barry Lloyd, David Lloyd, Lord MacLaurin, Vic Marks, John Miles, Graham Morris, Phil Neale, Mark Nicholas, Rodney Ontong, Graham Otway, Derek Pringle, Mike Procter, Clive Radley, Derek Randall, Steve

Rhodes, Barry Richards, Viv Richards, Peter Robinson, Peter Roebuck, Brian Rose, Mike Selvey, Don Shepherd, Ed Smith, Graham Stevenson, Micky Stewart, Chris Tavare, Bob Taylor, Ivo Tennant, Ian Todd, Chris Twort, Derek Underwood, Andrew Wagner, Mike Walters, Paul Weaver, Steve Whiting, Peter Willey, Dean Wilson, Ray Wright.

# Bibliography

Atherton, Mike, *Opening Up* (Hodder, 2002)

Bedser, Alec, with Alex Bannister, *Twin Ambitions: An Autobiography* (Stanley Paul, 1986)

Berry, Scyld, *Cricket Wallah: With England in India 1981–82* (Hodder, 1982)

Birley, Derek, *A Social History of English Cricket* (Aurum, 1999)

Botham, Ian, with Peter Hayter, *Botham: My Autobiography* (Collins Willow, 1994)

Botham, Ian, *Head On: Botham, the Autobiography* (Ebury, 2007)

Boycott, Geoffrey, with Terry Brindle, *Put to the Test* (Arthur Barker, 1979)

Boycott, Geoffrey, with Terry Brindle, *Opening Up* (Arthur Barker, 1980)

Boycott, Geoffrey, with Terry Brindle, *In the Fast Lane* (Arthur Barker, 1981)

Brearley, Mike, *Phoenix from the Ashes* (Hodder, 1981)

Brearley, Mike, *The Art of Captaincy* (Hodder, 1985)

Carman, Dominic, *No Ordinary Man: A Life of George Carman* (Hodder, 2002)

Chalke, Stephen, *Tom Cartwright: The Flame Still Burns* (Fairfield, 2007)

Chappell, Ian, and Ashley Mallett, *Hitting Out: The Ian Chappell Story* (Orion, 2005)

Chatfield, Ewen, *Chats: The Autobiography* (Moa Publications, 1988)

Clapton, Eric, with Christopher Simon Sykes, *Eric Clapton: The Autobiography* (Century, 2007)

Doust, Dudley, *Ian Botham: The Great Allrounder* (Cassell, 1980)

Edmonds, Frances, *Another Bloody Tour* (Kingswood, 1986)

Emburey, John, with Pat Gibson, *Spinning in a Fast World* (Robson, 1989)

English, David, *Mad Dogs and the Englishman* (Virgin, 2002)

English, David, *Confessions of a Dedicated Englishman* (Macmillan, 2006)

*Fire and Ashes: How Yorkshire's Finest Took on the Australians* (no author, Great Northern, 2009)

Fletcher, Duncan, with Steve James, *Behind the Shades: Duncan Fletcher, the Autobiography* (Simon & Schuster, 2007)

Fowler, Graeme, *Fox on the Run* (Viking, 1988)

Francis, Toby, *The Zen of Cricket* (Stanley Paul, 1992)

Garnett, Mark, *From Anger to Apathy: The Story of Politics, Society and Popular Culture in Britain since 1975* (Vintage, 2008)

Gatting, Mike, with Angela Patmore, *Leading from the Front* (Queen Anne, 1988)

Gooch, Graham, with Alan Lee, *Out of the Wilderness* (Collins Willow, 1985)

Gooch, Graham, with Patrick Murphy, *Captaincy* (Stanley Paul, 1992)

Gower, David, with Martin Johnson, *Gower: The Autobiography* (Collins Willow, 1992)

Healy, Ian, *Hands & Heals: The Autobiography* (Harper, 2000)

Hill, Alan, *Brian Close: Cricket's Lionheart* (Methuen, 2002)

Hughes, Simon, *A Lot of Hard Yakka* (Headline, 1997)

Keating, Frank, *High Wide and Handsome* (Collins Willow, 1986)

Lee, Alan, *Lord Ted: The Dexter Enigma* (Witherby, 1995)

Lillee, Dennis, with Bob Harris, *Menace: Dennis Lillee, The Autobiography* (Headline, 2003)

McKinstry, Leo, *Boycs: The True Story* (Partridge, 2000)

Mosey, Don, *Botham* (Sphere, 1986)

Murphy, Patrick, *Botham: A Biography* (Dent, 1988)

Oborne, Peter, *Basil D'Oliveira – Cricket and Conspiracy: The Untold Story* (Little Brown, 2004)

Reeve, Dermot, with Patrick Murphy, *Winning Ways* (Boxtree, 1996)

Richards, Viv, with David Foot, *Viv Richards* (Windmill, 1979)

Roebuck, Peter, *It Sort of Clicks* (Collins Willow, 1986)

Ryan, Christian, *Golden Boy: Kim Hughes and the Bad Old Days of Australian Cricket* (Allen and Unwin, 2009)

Sandford, Christopher, *Imran Khan: The Biography* (Harper Collins, 2009)

Steen, Rob and Alastair McLellan, *500–1: The Miracle of Headingley '81* (BBC Worldwide, 2001)

Turner, Alwyn W., *Rejoice! Rejoice! Britain in the 1980s* (Aurum, 2010)

Vaughan, Michael, with Mike Dickson, *Time to Declare: My Autobiography* (Hodder, 2009)

Vesey, Wayne, *KP Cricket Genius? The Biography of Kevin Pietersen* (Know the Score, 2009)

Weiss, Mike, 'Black Botham', *Esquire* magazine, January 1987

Willis, Bob, with Alan Lee, *The Captain's Diary: England in Australia and New Zealand 1982–83* (Collins Willow, 1983)

Willis, Bob, with Alan Lee, *The Captain's Diary: England in Fiji, New Zealand and Pakistan 1983–84* (Collins Willow, 1984)

Willis, Bob, with Alan Lee, *Lasting the Pace* (Collins Willow, 1985)

# Index